The Passport as Home

The Passport as Home

Comfort in Rootlessness

Andrei S. Markovits

Central European University Press

Budapest–Vienna–New York

Published in 2021 by

Central European University Press

Nádor utca 9, H-1051 Budapest, Hungary

Tel: +36-1-327-3138 or 327-3000

E-mail: *ceupress@press.ceu.edu*

Website: *www.ceupress.com*

ISBN 978-963-386-421-0 paperback

ISBN 978-963-386-422-7 ebook

LIBRARY OF CONGRESS CATALOGING-IN-PUBLICATION DATA

Names: Markovits, Andrei S., author.
Title: The passport as home : comfort in rootlessness / Andrei S. Markovits.
Description: Budapest : New York : Central European University Press, [2021]
Identifiers: LCCN 2021018351 (print) | LCCN 2021018352 (ebook) | ISBN 9789633864210 (paperback) | ISBN 9789633864227 (ebook)
Subjects: LCSH: Markovits, Andrei S. | Jews--Romania--Timişoara--Biography. | Jews, Romanian--United States--Biography. | Jews--Cultural assimilation--New York (State)--New York. | Universities and colleges--Faculty--United States--Biography. | Timişoara (Romania)--Biography.
Classification: LCC DS135.R73 M376 2021 (print) | LCC DS135.R73 (ebook) | DDC 974.7/10049240092 [B]--dc23
LC record available at https://lccn.loc.gov/2021018351
LC ebook record available at https://lccn.loc.gov/2021018352

Table of Contents

Foreword by Michael Ignatieff vii

Preface and Acknowledgements ix

Chapter One
Origins: The Virtues of Rootlessness 1

Chapter Two
A Paean to Tante Trude (Who Might or Might Not Have Been a Nazi) 47

Chapter Three
Four Friendships: Discovering America in Vienna 61

Chapter Four
**Daphne Scheer, Real Madrid and Internazionale Milano (Inter Milan):
The Personal Meets the Political** 93

Chapter Five
The Rolling Stones Play Vienna (Resulting in Bodily Harm to the City's Jews) ... 103

Chapter Six
Arrival in New York: The Dream Meets the Reality 113

Chapter Seven
Columbia 1968: How the World—and Andy—Changed in a Single Year 151

Chapter Eight
Kiki: Big Politics and Little Andy 167

Chapter Nine
The Grateful Dead: My American Family 199

Chapter Ten
Harvard's Center for European Studies: The Interloper Finds a Home 213

Chapter Eleven
Dogs: The Rescuer Rescues Himself 257

Chapter Twelve
Germany: Admiration for the *Bundesrepublik*, Discomfort with *Deutschland* ... 265

Epilogue 305

Foreword

I do not know Andrei Markovits, though we are nearly the same age and must have overlapped at the Center for European Studies at Harvard in the 1970s, but I wish I did know him, for his memoir is a cheerful, idiosyncratic dissent from the entire tradition of writing about exile, especially Jewish exile. Its subtitle—"comfort in rootlessness"—is a challenge to an entire tradition.

Here is a Jew, born in Timişoara, after the Holocaust which claimed so many members of his family, who emigrated first to Vienna, then to the United States and who does not look back in anger, nostalgia, or longing for his lost roots. On the contrary, rootlessness, he says, was a "source of joy not a source of anguish."

Consider the weight of the tradition, especially in the Jewish faith, which he is resisting in this delightful memoir. Remember, for example, these great verses from Psalm 137:

"By the waters of Babylon, there we sat down, yea we wept, when we remembered Zion."

In the Jewish tradition of exile that begins with this lament in the Psalms, there is no comfort, only hurt and anguish and nostalgia, in recalling a lost home. For the Jewish faithful, it is obligatory to keep your gaze fixed on home. In the words of the Psalm, "if I forget thee O Jerusalem let my right hand forget her cunning" and "let my tongue cleave to the root of my mouth"—let me be rendered speechless—if I do not hold Jerusalem at the center of my life and my loyalties.

Markovits breaks with all of this, throws its weight off his shoulders and embraces a different path away from home, away from roots, away from ancestral claims. While remaining steadfastly and proudly Jewish, he does not accept any idea that he can only be at home in Zion or anywhere else for that matter. On the contrary, he takes delight in being a "rootless cosmopolitan," embracing an antisemitic epithet once used by Stalinists, fascists, and nationalists. He has been a "wandering Jew" all his life and it has allowed him to be free.

Having been uprooted in 1958, months after the death of his mother, leaving Romania forever, first for Vienna and then for New York a decade later, he never sought to belong again. By his own admission, he has cultivated "orthogonality," never fitting in anywhere, all his life. Now in his 70's, happily married and beloved as a professor at the University of Michigan, he tells us cheerfully that he remains "completely marginal and tangential to all three" of the departments he is associated with at the university. Most unusually, this is a memoir that counts only the gains of coming to America. If not for exile, Markovits asks us to remember, would he have discovered how much he loves baseball, the Grateful Dead, and the University of Michigan's stadium on game day?

In this attitude towards loss, Markovits resembles that great artist of exile, Vladimir Nabokov, who always held the view that being forced from Russia by the Russian Revolution was the "syncopal kick" that turned an aristocrat into a writer. Unlike Nabokov, however, he has no interest in nostalgia, no commitment to recreate the lost paradise before exile.

Markovits is not a novelist but the memoir often has the remembered detail, the specificity as to place, time and character that marks good fiction. He remembers the house in Timișoara that his family shared with other families; he can guide you through the rooming house in Vienna where he and his father stayed on their first arrival in the West. It is all vivid yet unclouded by nostalgia or regret.

Markovits is free of the Jewish past in Central and Eastern Europe, yet proudly affiliates with its best traditions. For there was in Habsburg Europe a multiculturalism that was never liberal, but made possible a complex accommodation between Jews and Gentiles, Catholics and

Protestants, languages, nations, and minorities. This Habsburg multiculturalism was able to survive fascism and communism alike, and the proof of its resilience was in the apartment house Markovits grew up in: home to Jewish, Catholic, Protestant, and Romanian Orthodox families, Hungarian and Romanian speakers all living together in rivalrous fraternity under a communist regime.

This Habsburg multiculturalism meant that a Jewish family, who had lost family in the Holocaust, still revered German *Kultur*, adored Beethoven and Mozart and spoke the language of their persecutors, all the while despising the Germans who were responsible for their families' torments. This multiculturalism was anything but liberal or rights-based: Roma were universally despised, and Jewish-Gentile accommodation was tinged with a complex mixture of fear, contempt, and attraction. Hitler and Stalin tried to smash this complex pattern of "live and let live" into pieces and now democratic authoritarians in Central and Eastern Europe seem determined to lock Poland and Hungary into ethno-nationalist states in which Habsburg multiculturalism will only be a nostalgic memory. This memoir is the record of a life lived with good cheer and without regret. But there is poignancy in the fate of Habsburg multiculturalism that produced Andrei Markovits. We can be grateful that he both remembers its strengths and ended up embodying its most attractive qualities: a sense of the comic and absurd, an unfailing curiosity towards others and a sharp grasp of reality, driven by an unblinking awareness that it can suddenly turn dangerous.

MICHAEL IGNATIEFF
President and Rector
Central European University
Budapest and Vienna

Preface and Acknowledgments

The origins of this book go back to the spring of 1998 when Erich Später, Director of the Heinrich-Böll-Foundation in the Saarland, hosted me on a ten-city book tour featuring my work *Grün schlägt Rot: Die deutsche Linke nach 1945* that was published in the late fall of 1997 by Rotbuch Verlag. Co-authored with my former student and now friend, Philip Gorski, this was the German translation of our book *The German Left: Red, Green and Beyond* published in 1993 by Polity Press in the United Kingdom and Oxford University Press in the United States.

Anchored in our research on the relatively recent and conceptually novel party "Bündnis '90/Die Grünen" and its milieu, I was deeply honored that the foundation associated with this party and movement invited me to offer readings and lectures on our book to audiences all across the Federal Republic. Riding from town to town in Germany's wonderful trains, Erich and I spent many an hour talking about different things, including our lives. It was on one of these rides—possibly from Bonn to Hamburg—that Erich asked me whether I had ever entertained the idea of writing a memoir since, so he believed, my life's stories were worthy of such an endeavor. I dismissed this immediately and never thought anything of it until, in saying good-bye to me at the Frankfurt Airport, Erich's last words were something to the effect: Don't forget about your memoir! Write it!

"Yeah, yeah" to invoke legendary Columbia University philosopher Sidney Morgenbesser who, with this remark, emanating from the back of the lecture hall, so memorably refuted J.L. Austin's claim that a double negative often implies a positive in many languages while in no language does a double positive constitute a negative.[1] Nothing happened! Then, in June of 2012, my friend Getta Neumann, daughter of the late Dr. Ernest Neumann, Timişoara's renowned chief rabbi, invited me to deliver lectures at the Universitatea de Vest, Timişoara, as well as to the city's Jewish community. It was the first time in 40 years that I visited Timişoara and only the second time since leaving with my father for good as a young boy in 1958.

In the course of a memorable three days in which I also paid daily visits to my mother's grave, Getta conducted a lengthy interview with me about my life in Timişoara as a youngster. These meetings also included a detailed conversation about my subsequent life as an adult in Europe and the United States. Of course, Getta conducted the interview in English, since my rusty Romanian would never permit my drawing the necessary nuances such an endeavor demanded. Getta published the interview in Romanian in a volume that she edited and entitled *Destine evreieşti la Timişoara: Portretul comunităţii din perioada interbelică până azi* (Jewish Lives in Timişoara: Portrait of the Community from the Interwar Period until Today), published by Bucharest-based Editura Hasefer in 2014.

It was the entirety of this experience—from my conversation with Getta to the reactions I received to both the English and Romanian texts—that first made me ponder aspects of my past in a serious way. I began to take notes that, in the course of the next few years, mutated into what I came to call "vignettes," of which I had six varying in size from approximately 1,000 to 5,000 words. I did not tell anybody about these other than my wife Kiki and my friend Michael Guthrie, whom I had met as a 12-year old in my secondary school days in Vienna's Theresianische Akademie. I had completely lost sight of Michael for many decades,

---

1 Sidney Morgenbesser was a legend on the Columbia campus with faculty and students alike in the eight years that I was there. One of my regrets was never taking a class with him. However, just before leaving Columbia for good in the fall of 1975, I made it a point to visit Morgenbesser in his office hours. When I told him that I had come to see him solely because I did not want to depart from Columbia without having met him, he proceeded to regale me with a string of anecdotes and jokes relating to paying homage to somebody all anchored in the deep well of Jewish humor for which Morgenbesser was so renowned.

only to reconnect with him via the Internet as my Michigan neighbor living only an hour's drive away. We began meeting each other for lunch at an Olive Garden halfway between his home in Okemos and mine in Ann Arbor, and it was during one of these that I mentioned the vignettes to Michael. He insisted that I show him some and, after having read them, he would not stop badgering me to do something more, to produce more of them and compile a meaningful book of some sort. Michael remained relentless over a number of years. I found this intriguing precisely because Michael was not an academic. Still, not much happened.

I sent a few friends in Europe and in the United States some, even all, of my vignettes and received encouraging comments, which I never pursued. Not even Hanna Doron's insightful and supportive exhortations, for which I will remain forever grateful, led me to action. Then, in October 2019, my friend and colleague Mitchell Cohen contacted me with an idea that I found wonderful. Mitchell, whom I have known since the late 1970s via our associations with the Department of Political Science at Columbia, where both of us received our doctorates, and I shared many a passion over the years. With the exception of my love for and preoccupation with sports and dogs, neither of which Mitchell shared, the subjects that concerned Mitchell were always crucial to me as well. They included all things Jewish, featuring the complex issues concerning Israel and Zionism; all matters related to the European and American Left; global politics; and, of course, music, especially our mutual love of opera, which, in my case at least, remained firmly ensconced in woeful dilettantism and, in Mitchell's, led to his writing award-winning books published by Princeton University Press.

Mitchell suggested that I contact *Tablet Magazine,* where I had published previously, and ask them whether they might be interested in my writing a piece for the magazine in connection with the impending 30-year anniversary of the Ceauşescu dictatorship's fall in December 1989. This demise, as Mitchell of course knew, had commenced with demonstrations in Timişoara, my birthplace. That, thought Mitchell, might offer a great hook, a fine occasion, and an ideal location to publish one of the vignettes on growing up Jewish in Timişoara that Mitchell found particularly attractive. I contacted *Tablet Magazine,* who indeed did publish my article on December 19, 2019, literally thirty years to the day of the Timişoara uprising. The reactions were overwhelming and completely unexpected. I received glowingly positive emails from all over the world, many from fellow Timişoarians, most of whom I did not know, but also from others who had no ostensible relations with Timişoara, Romania, or Europe.

And then COVID-19 hit the land! After the end of a hectic semester in late April 2020, a big void confronted me that was truly unsettling, even frightening to me. I had a wonderful four months all planned and ready to go: travel to a conference in Budapest in the middle of May, followed by lectures in Stuttgart and Munich; two talks in Santa Fe in early June; then across the Atlantic once again for lectures in Düsseldorf and Berlin. I was also planning to catch a few matches in person of the ongoing EURO 2020 soccer championship in various European venues. Then come home to see that tournament's final games on television and have them move seamlessly into watching the Olympic Games in Tokyo. I had plans to end the summer by enjoying some fine theater performances in Stratford, Ontario and then begin the new semester by attending the season-opening game of Michigan Football in my beloved Michigan Stadium a.k.a. "The Big House," in hopes of a better season than the last one. None of this was to happen.

With absolutely no sports live or on television, excepting South Korean baseball in the middle of our night and the occasional soccer from Belarus, life seemed bleak and, quite frankly, scary. Then, on the afternoon of May 1—I will never forget the date, in good part because I have somehow always continued to observe May Day since my childhood in Timişoara by, among others, chanting a slogan in Romanian extolling the virtues of the working class[2]—things took an auspicious turn. My wife Kiki and I were walking our darling golden retriever Emma in our leafy neighborhood in Ann Arbor when we happened on my colleague Susan Parrish, eminent professor in the University of Michigan's Department of English, also walking her dog. Scotti, as everybody called her

---

2   Întâi Mai, Întâi Mai; Zi de mare sărbătoare; pentru clasa muncitoare! The first of May, The first of May; great day of celebration for the working class!

on campus, was never primarily a colleague to me, but rather a friendly neighbor and a conscientious dog guardian, whom Kiki and I admired for the warmth she bestowed on her canine partner. Above all, Scotti was the mother of Grace Judge, arguably one of my most talented undergraduates at Michigan, who had graduated with highest honors by writing a senior thesis of publishable quality on her way to attending law school at Yale.

For reasons that were never clear to me, I proceeded to ask Scotti on this particular walk whether she knew anybody in Michigan's very large English department—faculty or graduate student—who might be willing to work with me in editing and improving the six vignettes that I had sitting untouched on my computer. To my surprise, Scotti answered that she, in fact, did: Had I ever heard of Eileen Pollack, longtime director of the Helen Zell MFA Program in Creative Writing and a professor in Michigan's Department of English? Eileen had just left the university and retired to New York City, where, so Scotti believed, she continued to work with authors on their manuscripts. Should she, Scotti, make the connection to Eileen? I agreed enthusiastically, and this changed my life.

Eileen Pollack *is* the reason this memoir exists! Pure and simple! No doubt about it! It will always be impossible for me to express in words what Eileen brought to the table, even with the exquisite pedagogy that improved my writing immeasurably. Eileen would be the first to condone, possibly even welcome, my employing a sports metaphor in this context: Eileen became my transformative coach! For three full months of frenzied writing, without a single day of respite, not even weekends, Eileen put me through the ringer concerning virtually every sentence in this 120,000-word manuscript. She cajoled and chided me, praised and pushed me, challenged me on every level: stylistic, content-related and conceptual. She came to know me so well that I now regard her as an intimate friend, even though I have never met the woman and only saw her once on a FaceTime communication when the book was already completed. I had hired an editor who, I hoped, would make my writing a tad better! I ended up with a dear friend whose soul will forever live in these pages! Thank you, Eileen!

Manuscript finished, the issue of publishing the work appeared. Where to turn? What to do? As with everything in this book as well as most ideas I have had over the past 30 years, this one, too, came to me during one of my wonderful walks with my golden retrievers, in this case the beautiful Emma who, as fate would have it, hails from Timișoara. What about the Central European University Press? My only connection to it was my having published an article on European anti-Americanism and Antisemitism in a periodical called *Jewish Studies at the Central European University* in 2005. I was very pleased with every facet of that experience. Of course, I owned a few books published by CEU Press and had encountered its titles with regularity in book reviews in scholarly journals, on occasion in popular and journalistic publications as well. Above all, I knew the institution by dint of having visited it twice, in October 2004 and May 2018, for a series of lectures on topics as diverse as comparative sport cultures and German politics. I knew two of the university's previous rectors, and I had fine colleagues there as well, two of whom had become close friends over the years.

It was one of them, Michael Miller, whom I decided to contact about having CEU Press as the possible publisher of my memoir. I envisioned this press as *the* ideal publisher of my work: The publishing house of an American university situated in Budapest, and now also in Vienna, publishing the life story of a Romanian-born, Hungarian-speaking, Vienna-schooled Jewish American professor. This seemed to be out of central casting: sort of an Andy Press for Andy's story! Michael Miller and I had developed a wonderful friendship over two decades of seeing each other in places such as Budapest, Jerusalem, and Ann Arbor. When Michael was a visiting professor for an academic year at the University of Michigan, he was a regular at our house and we spent many a meal discussing our mutual interests in Jewish matters, as well as Central European culture and politics.

I turned to Michael with my idea of having CEU Press be my book's home. To my delight, his reaction was warm, confident, even enthusiastic. He told me that he was going to get in touch with the powers that be and that I would hear from the press officially before too long. Then, one day, I received a wonderful email from Linda Kunos, who expressed delight in the project and asked me to send her my manuscript. The rest is history, as they say. Working with Linda almost on a daily basis was a blessing. Even though I never met her physically, quite analogous to Eileen, my coach; Linda, too—again analogous to Eileen—somehow became a close friend. I came to adore her lovely young daughter Emma, who established a bond with our Emma; I could never stop admiring Linda's impeccable English writing style, which exhibits the standard not only of a native speaker's eloquence, but is also graced by a rare elegance of its own. Working with her on this project was a total delight. I cannot wait to meet Linda Kunos in person!

One of her acts of efficiency and generosity was her assigning Michael Blumenthal as copyeditor of this manuscript. Truth be told, I never achieved any rapport beyond the necessary formalities of the publication process with any of the many copy editors I encountered in the nearly fifty years of my professorial existence on either side of the Atlantic. This was not the case with Michael. Michael, you see, is a multiple award-winning poet who is an accomplished author, a teacher of creative writing at Harvard, and a lawyer and law professor as well, who also happens to speak perfect German, and a beautifully-accented Hungarian, in addition to his native English. The overlaps in our lives have been nothing short of stunning. Thank you, Linda, for introducing me to Michael, this truly rare individual.

A propos Michael, I am so grateful and honored to have another Michael, in this case Ignatieff, grace this book with his foreword. Not only by virtue of his voice being precious to me because of his being the Rector and President of the institution that is the publisher of my book, but also by dint of his being a leading public intellectual, whose knowledge of the many worlds that informs this work is profound and nuanced.

At the end of the day, in this case, too, readers will be the sole judges of this book's worth. I have no idea whether they will enjoy what they will read or not. However, I know with certainty that I very much enjoyed writing all of it. As with everything else in my life, I could not have done any of it without the love that my darling wife Kiki bears to me every minute of every day. Supplemented by the love that our golden retrievers have shared with us over our 30-year blissful relationship, I have been the beneficiary of a sweet life that on occasion, perhaps, I have not deserved.

That said, I dedicate this book to my beloved father who, as the reader will learn, is the true and only hero of this text. After all, this was the man who in my childhood took me for rides in the cabin of locomotives on local jaunts near Timişoara; who arranged for us to visit Timişoara's beer factory; who made certain that I personally met all four of the heroes that were the stars of my beloved local soccer team "Ştiinţa". Perhaps most impressively, however, my father invited a very attractive singer and dancer with whom—at the age of five—I had fallen hopelessly in love during our visit to a touring circus, to come to our home and have tea with us. If memory serves me well, my mother approved! Enough said!

Ann Arbor, February 24, 2021
(the 110th anniversary of my father's birthday)

CHAPTER ONE

Origins: The Virtues of Rootlessness

I was born and lived the first nine and a half years of my life as an only child in a Hungarian-speaking bourgeois Jewish family in an apartment at 1 Kutuzov Street in the city of Timişoara's central district. In the 1950s, Timişoara (Temesvár in Hungarian, Temeschburg or Temeschwar in German) was Romania's third largest city, with 142,257 inhabitants, of whom 75,855 were primarily Romanian-speaking, 29,968 primarily Hungarian-speaking, and 24,326 primarily German-speaking, with the rest an assortment of Serbian and Bulgarian speakers. In short, Timişoara was a polyglot place, as befit its multicultural history at the eastern edge of the Habsburg Empire.

The city also existed in the midst of a world that had coined the infamous term "rootless cosmopolitan," which became a euphemism for "Jew" and a way to denounce Jewish rootlessness, Jewish cosmopolitanism, Jewish *Bodenlosigkeit*—soil-less-ness—the history of Jews wandering from country to country, as an acute danger to the socialist glorification of a classless society. Though socialism in its ideal form was international and therefore borderless, the actual policies of socialist and communist parties and countries often bespoke a hostility to such openness and extolled a nationalist emphasis on home and hearth. To be sure, such a disdain for rootlessness as a threat to an idyllic and uncomplicated home life originated mainly on the right. Starting with the Romantics, who extolled the virtues and authenticity of a *Volksgemeinschaft*, the notion of a collective whole anchored in the concrete soil of a culturally distinct nation became common fare for many generations of the German right (where it remains alive and well to this day). "Blood and soil" gave this national collective its only legitimate identity: everything else was ephemeral, fleeting, uncertain. Of course, this notion wasn't unique to Germany; its equivalents can be found in all the countries of Europe and beyond.

The left, on the other hand, celebrated internationalism. "Workingmen of the world, unite! You have nothing to lose but your chains!" wrote Karl Marx and Friedrich Engels in *The Communist Manifesto*. The left's logic was simple: since workers are exploited internationally, they can defeat capitalism only by creating international bonds and international solidarity. Alas, it should have been obvious, by August 1914 at the latest, that this was wishful thinking. Instead of declaring solidarity with each other, Europe's socialist parties outdid themselves in their patriotic appeals to emperor and country. Articulating a kind of nationalism that in its essence was much more akin to the ideology of the political right than the left, socialist parties succumbed to the jingoist hysteria that led to the butchery of their respective working classes in Flanders Field and other slaughterhouses on the European continent.

"*Les extrêmes se touchent,*" as the French so aptly say. Among a number of issues on which the left and the right touch each other, few are more potent than those of nationalism, internationalism, and thus rootlessness. Under the banner of National Bolshevism, a considerable political movement arose in Weimar Germany that extolled a leftwing version of nationalism deeply hostile to any internationalism and more deeply rooted in a view of nationalism associated with the far right. Similar ideological strains existed in the Soviet Union. The Strasser wing of the National Socialist German Labor Party (NSDAP), better known as the Nazis, expressed views that were related to this overlap between left and right. We find this merger alive and well in many current manifestations, such as the anti-globalists and anti-vaxxers in virtually every European country and in the United States. One feature all these movements, no matter how disparate, share is a deep suspicion of Jews and their internationalism and rootlessness that often bleeds into antisemitism.

Marx's single greatest shortcoming was to conclude from his own cosmopolitan existence that nationalism was less of a uniting force for large groups of people of similar backgrounds and work conditions than was class solidarity. This proved wrong throughout the twentieth century and is socialism's most egregious failure. Lenin and his pals formed the communist movement by extoling internationalism. Starting with meetings in the Swiss village of Zimmerwald during World War I, and culminating in the formation of the Third International in 1919, they broke with the extant socialists over a number of tactical, strategic, and conceptual issues, none of which was more pronounced than the role of nationalism. This new formation embraced the virtues of internationalism, denouncing the social democrats for, among many of their alleged other failings, having succumbed to the siren song of nationalism, a bourgeois affliction. Yet, by the time Stalin emerged as the unquestioned leader of the Soviet Union in 1929, internationalism had proven to be a sham as far as the communists were concerned.

While the Soviet Union continued to hold up the fig leaf of the Third International, the organization itself became little but a puppet for Soviet national interests, and thus beholden to a highly nationalist mission. Socialist internationalism hadn't defeated the Nazis. Rather, Soviet patriotism, standing on the shoulders of much more primordial, soil-based Russian nationalism, proved decisive in the victory over Germany.

It is no secret that Jews played a disproportionately large role in the leadership of the European left, including within the Soviet Union. Beginning in 1948—the year I was born—Andrei Zhdanov, the leader of the Soviet Union's cultural policy, commenced an anti-cosmopolitan campaign that endured until Stalin's death in 1953. This anti-intellectual and nativist campaign dates back to a speech Stalin gave in 1946, in which he attacked Soviet writers, all of them ethnic Jews. This campaign against "rootless cosmopolitans" led to the purge of hundreds of devoted communists, not only in the Soviet Union itself, but in some of its satellite countries, most notably Hungary, Czechoslovakia, and my native Romania. In the latter, Ana Pauker (née Hannah Rabinsohn), a staunch Stalinist and the world's first female foreign minister, was brought down in a show trial in Bucharest (similar to such trials in Moscow, Budapest, and Prague) on account of her Jewish background, which made her an obvious agent of "international Zionism" and a spy for the United States.

With Stalin's death, the antisemitic frenzy within the communist world abated. But the suspicion of Jews on account of their rootlessness and cosmopolitanism never went away in that part of the world—and lives on in our current age of fake news and the rising fear of international conspiracies that inevitably involve the Jews in some fashion. Just think of George Soros, the epitome of this phenomenon in our contemporary world, blamed by far right and far left for every ill each and both consider to be crippling their respective ambitions and visions. The terms "rootless" and "cosmopolitan," though created by Stalinists in the late 1940s, continue to be associated with Jews. While writing this text, I turned to a friend, now a university professor, who was born in the 1970s and lived all his life in a small village in East Germany's hinterlands, far from any urban centers of intellectualism, until the Berlin Wall fell in 1989. I wanted to ask him whether Germans use the term *wurzelloser Kosmopolit* for "rootless cosmopolitan," as the phrase is rendered in English, or whether they say *entwurzelter Kosmopolit*, which would translate as "uprooted cosmopolitan," the way the French say *cosmopolite déraciné*. His response could not have been more poignant: "Oh, you mean as in 'Jews'?"

This phenomenon has existed all around the world, including in the United States, where Jews often have been suspected of not being loyal Americans, of harboring dual loyalties. Most American Jews bridle at the accusation of disloyalty. And yet, I have always hoped someone on either side of the Atlantic would call me a "rootless cosmopolitan" to my face. Why do I relish my status as a wanderer, an outsider, a profoundly and proudly rootless cosmopolitan? This book is an exploration of the ways in which this description fits my journey. Even though the term invokes loneliness and unhappiness, in my case "rootlessness" and "cosmopolitanism" embody a certain independence and agency, a sense of being orthogonal to the dominant culture, a tad askew, unaligned, disjointed, an outsider, an observer, a participant who, while not excluded from the group, manages to remain detached. Far from causing me loneliness and unhappiness, my rootless cosmopolitanism has widely enhanced my circle of friendships and given me access to cultures I otherwise never would have been able to penetrate. My rootlessness has caused me much joy and little anguish. I spent the first nine years of my life as a Hungarian-speaking Jew in an increasingly Romanian town in the country of Romania. Thankfully, I never experienced any antisemitism and enjoyed a happy childhood. But I could already see that my parents and I were not the norm, we were askew, we were not rooted in this place.

Just look at my name. On my Romanian birth certificate, I am listed as "Andrei," which is the Romanian version of Andrew. Throughout my life, every official document has borne this name, even though it carries no emotional associations for me. No one has ever called me "Andrei," other than left-leaning, Europhilic, American intellectuals who not only thought the name was exotic and sexy but believed that by calling me "Andrei" they celebrated my authentic non-American being. My parents and all my relatives and friends in Timişoara—even the Romanian ones—called me by the Hungarian "András," or, on occasion, the diminutive "Andris" though never its other "Bandi." When we arrived in Vienna, "András" mutated to its German variant "Andreas," which I was called with regularity during my nine years' stay in Austria. However, due to my yearly sojourns in New York over the summer months, "Andy" started to seep in so deeply that by the beginning of my studies at Columbia, it had become my preferred appellation, which it remains to this day.

Once we left Romania, I de facto had lost my Romanian citizenship. We then arrived in Vienna, where I spent nine years of my life waiting to leave for the United States. Austria embodied an important phase of my growing up, but the country also represented quintessential rootlessness for me. Officially, this duality marked my very existence: because I was not an Austrian citizen, I was documented as *staatenlos*, stateless. Being one of only two kids among hundreds in my secondary school who considered themselves officially Jewish, and having to find alternate supervised activities to occupy me while all the other students attended obligatory Catholic mass and one hour of Catholic instruction twice a week, also rendered my otherness quite palpable.

Even when I arrived at Columbia University in late September of 1967, my feelings of strangeness continued. Although this was my first appearance at an institution of post-secondary education, I was not technically a freshman, on account of having received three semesters' worth of advanced standing based on the *Matura* degree from my Viennese secondary school, the Theresianische Akademie. In my hubris—and egged on by my father, who was as ignorant and arrogant about these matters as I was—I rushed to finish this seemingly irrelevant and superfluous undergraduate degree so I could get on with what my father and I perceived as my real university education, meaning graduate and/or professional school. Accelerating my undergraduate education, which my European elitism construed as nothing more than gaining the same *Allgemeinbildung* that a *Gymnasium* education allegedly had already bestowed on me, constitutes one of the most profound regrets of my life. Cramming five semesters of work into four in my rush to eliminate the burden called "college" on my way to the real stuff, I did little else but study, without actually experiencing the culture of American undergraduate existence.

Despite my arrogant protestations that my Viennese education had sufficiently acquainted me with the writings of Homer, Vergil, Dante, and Goethe, the university, gratefully, compelled me to take Columbia's legendary year-long Great Books freshman courses, Contemporary Civilization and Humanities A, which shaped my life. But I was never a bona fide sophomore, nor a genuine junior, let alone a true member of the Senior Class of 1969, when I received my bachelor's degree.

My subsequent two-year stint at the Columbia Business School reeked of marginality in that I enrolled only to appease my worried father, who did not understand how one made a living with an advanced degree in sociology, history, or political science, and who compelled me to get a degree with which "one can do something."

Then came Columbia's fine doctoral program in Political Science, where I was anything but rootless, beyond the built-in insecurities of virtually all graduate students pretty much everywhere in the world. After receiving my doctorate, I joined the Center for European Studies at Harvard, where, quite opposite of feeling marginal and rootless, I became one of the mainstays of that amazing institution. The Center was a research-oriented entity that attracted Harvard faculty specializing in European studies, but also welcomed faculty from other universities to be resident fellows and pursue their research on Europe. I was one of those fellows, and even though I was a central figure at the Center and fully integrated into all of its activities, I was decidedly not a Harvard faculty member and did not have an appointment in any of that university's departments.

Since the Center did not pay me a salary, I had to become a professor somewhere else as well. During my 24-year association with the Center (I remained a fellow until 1999, when I joined the faculty of the University of Michigan), I held professorial teaching positions at three universities. First came Wesleyan University, a wonderful school, but close enough to Harvard Square that I commuted from Cambridge to Middletown, Connecticut, where I spent two or three nights per week in an unfurnished apartment, eating TV dinners, while maintaining my real home in Cambridge. My colleagues rightly believed this refusal to become a true part of the academic community in Middletown was problematic, and I was told between the lines that I would not be granted tenure, regardless of how stellar my scholarship and teaching were. Next came Boston University, where my teaching and research performance continued to be excellent but my allegiance remained across the Charles River at the Center for European Studies.

When I was offered the chairmanship of the Politics Department at the University of California at Santa Cruz in 1992, I hoped to shed my sense of rootlessness and affective marginality in the expectation that the width of a continent might sever my love for the Center and release me to fully embrace Santa Cruz. For many reasons—all my fault—this did not happen. Thinking of my mentor Karl Deutsch's brilliant measurement of a person's integration into a new environment, I failed miserably in that I never surrendered my Massachusetts license plate; I voted absentee in Massachusetts; I maintained my beautiful condominium in Cambridge; I kept my Cambridge dentist; I retained my tax accountant in Watertown; and I rented not only furniture in Santa Cruz, but even dishes and cutlery.

Much of this changed when I was offered a job at the University of Michigan in the fall of 1999. I obtained Michigan license plates two weeks after my arrival; registered to vote; acquired a dentist, a primary doctor, all in the town of Ann Arbor. I only kept my tax accountant in

Massachusetts—for superstitious reasons, lest I get audited by the feds. Most important of all, I purchased a house for the first time in my life, at the age of 51. To be sure, I had owned a condominium in Cambridge for 20 years, but in American culture a house bespeaks a greater degree of being anchored than a condominium.

Even in Ann Arbor, my orthogonality, rootlessness, and marginality did not disappear. Hired enthusiastically by the Department of Germanic Languages and Literatures, I saw from the beginning that, regardless of how warmly my colleagues welcomed me and how radically the concept of literature had changed over the past four or five decades, I was a trained political and social scientist in what, despite its avowed interdisciplinarity, was still primarily a department of languages and literatures. Three years into my tenure at the University of Michigan, the Department of Political Science extended an invitation to join at a fifty-percent level, meaning my appointment at the university would now be shared between German and Political Science.

Though I believe I am a respected member of the Political Science Department, my colleagues do not regard me as a bona fide political scientist. Nor should they. My work at Michigan, though prolific and published in fine venues, often involves topics distant from the core of the discipline of political science. Books on compassion and the phenomenon of dog rescue in America, on the comparative cultures of sport in Europe and the United States, on women's involvement in American soccer and European football might be wonderfully interesting, but they are not germane to the usual work of academic political scientists of the caliber populating that department at the University of Michigan. The disparate topics of my work might best be characterized as political sociology. Alas, the Department of Sociology offered me only a courtesy appointment, for which I am immensely grateful, but which, truth be told, is not the real deal and in no way makes me an accepted member of that department or its discipline.

Lastly, at a place like Michigan, teaching plays a decidedly second fiddle to conducting research and publishing the results. While I pass muster on the latter, I have truly excelled at the former, to the point of winning a number of coveted teaching awards. Though admirable in the eyes of my colleagues—as any hobby such as mountain climbing or hang gliding would be—teaching is not the activity that bestows true respect on a person in a place like Michigan. While most professors complain endlessly about their "teaching load" or "teaching burden," I have never, in my nearly 50 years of professorial existence, heard anyone complain of their "research load" or "research burden." Nor have I ever stood in a hotel lobby full of colleagues at a national association meeting and had one of them turn to me and say: "See that person by the elevator? Great teacher!" Never happened, never will. Conversely, I frequently hear: "See that person by the elevator? Just published a key article in the *American Political Science Review*. Go after them!" Bottom line: I have been completely marginal and tangential to all three of my departments.

This in no way means that my more than 20 years at the University of Michigan have not been glorious in most respects. I have loved the students, loved the teaching, loved the sports, loved Hill Auditorium, with its world-class performances that replicate Carnegie Hall's. Some things could have turned out more auspiciously with my two departments, but all in all both were civil if not warmly welcoming places. I was in though never of them. Bespeaking my rootlessness even at the University of Michigan, I once asked the dean of our college whether I might become a roaming professor, untethered to any department, who could teach in disparate places, including outside his own college of Literature, Science, and the Arts, something I already had done twice by offering classes in the School of Kinesiology.

His response was precious: "No, Andy! We have no positions for wandering and homeless professors! Continue being a wanderer in your work and spirit. That is called interdisciplinarity, and the college rewards that big time. But in terms of an affiliation, an anchor, you are compelled to do that work in something that our college and university call departments."

In his well-known essay "The Hedgehog and the Fox," the great Isaiah Berlin divides writers and thinkers into two categories: hedgehogs who see the world and their own work through one dominant lens, the honing and polishing of which forms their life's work; and foxes, who scurry about intellectually from project to project, their restlessness never permitting them to focus on one idea for any length of time. Berlin's own work centers on Leo Tolstoy, with detours into the writings of similar literary and philosophical giants of the Western canon. Not for one second do I compare myself to Isaiah Berlin's intellectual range and scholarly genius, nor to any person mentioned in his essay. I am merely using his insightful dichotomy to situate myself on the furthest possible end of the fox category.

One could also call me a jack of all trades, master of none. I started out working on German trade unions, which then expanded into a study of the related topic of social democracy in Germany and Europe in general. From there, influenced by my own experience, I began work on the so-called "new social movements," which culminated in my publications on the German and European left, the cutting-edge German party *Bündnis '90/Die Grünen* in particular. Concomitant with all three of these academic interests, I began publishing on the wide topic of German-Jewish relations by writing about the reception of the NBC television series *Holocaust* in Germany and Austria, the (in)famous *Historikerstreit* in Germany, and Daniel Jonah Goldhagen's immensely controversial book *Hitler's Willing Executioners: Ordinary Germans and the Holocaust.*

At this juncture, during the summer of 1986, partly as a result of the constant and debilitating battles I was fighting against what I perceived to be the antisemitism and anti-Americanism of the European left, I decided to investigate what I considered to be one of life's most enduring puzzles: *Why did Americans not follow or, at that time, play soccer?* Such a scholarly pursuit was possible only within the intellectually freewheeling and academically eclectic but socially comforting Harvard Center for European Studies, and would never have come about had my allegiances been to a conventional department of political science. The result was my most successful academic article, which has been translated into 15 languages. My study of sports also contributed to my becoming a fellow at the fancy Wissenschaftskolleg zu Berlin—the Institute for Advanced Study in Berlin—where I used the year to write two books, one of which was a continuation of the article written 13 years before. Published by Princeton University Press in 2001, the book became a kind of mini-classic in the world of sports sociology and comparative sports studies, neither of which holds any affinities to political science.

Always cognizant of the profound anti-Americanism in European discourse, particularly among left-leaning intellectuals, I wrote a scholarly article on this topic, the first of many, followed by a book that was translated into three languages. A longtime dog lover, though never a dog parent, I adopted in the late 1980s my first golden retriever and was stunned by the world of breed-specific dog rescue, about which I knew nothing. This new organizational form of volunteerism, which arose in the late 1970s and proliferated throughout the 1980s and 1990s, was, not surprisingly, dominated almost totally by women, since its core mission entailed the harnessing of compassion. In my earlier work on the German Greens and the new social movements, I had already come to realize that the single most important common denominator underlying all the policy reforms these actors wanted to achieve was compassion. After moving to Ann Arbor and adopting my fifth golden retriever, I published an article with a female colleague on the sociology of dog rescuers, leading to a book-length study of the topic, co-authored by one of my excellent female undergraduates.

Lastly, my continued interest in Jewish history and culture led me to write two books examining the world of Jewish students at the University of Michigan from 1897 to 1945, a particularly turbulent time for Jews in American and global history. As one Berkeley colleague scolded me: "Andy, I hate you. You've somehow succeeded in valorizing your personal hobbies and interests by rendering them into scholarly pursuits and academic publications. How have you gotten away with this?" My response was simple and to the point: "By remaining detached from departmental expectations and disciplinary norms; by creating my own intellectual and academic niches." In other words, by being rootless.

To this day, I loathe being asked where I am from because I do not know how and what to answer. When pressed, I mumble something like "I am from New York, but I was born in Romania" before desperately trying to move on. But am I really from New York? I lived there for two months for each of six summers between 1960 and 1966 and then spent eight years garnering five degrees from Columbia. This does not make me a real New Yorker, though I wish it did. I am a New Yorker only by default and for lack of an alternative. Timișoara was my birthplace, but that birth happened so long ago and has become so distant that I really do not see it as my home in any way. My fluency in Romanian, never great, and my Hungarian, once excellent, have deteriorated, and since my aunt's death in 1994, years have passed during which I did not speak a word of either language. Vienna? I would rather answer "I am from hell" than invoke that stunningly beautiful city as my home. I loved my 24 years in Cambridge, Massachusetts—I even got married there under the approving eyes of one of the city's justices of the peace—but I never ever saw myself as a Cantabrigian, and I hated all Boston-based sports teams too deeply and passionately to identify Massachusetts as my home. Santa Cruz barely qualifies as a one-night stand.

This leaves us with Ann Arbor, where I have lived since September 1999, where I own a wonderful house in a leafy and welcoming neighborhood, where I hold a rewarding job at one of the world's finest institutions of higher learning and even have purchased a plot for my wife and myself in a local cemetery. Still, I would never say "Ann Arbor" in response to the question of where I am from. I never came to know the city well enough to consider it my home and even though I have some close friends in town, I do not associate with them the city of Ann Arbor since all of them, too, hail from somewhere else and appear to me rootless in this town, just as I have always been.

Perhaps the answer is that I am from an imaginary New York, the New York that I constructed based on the observations and impressions I collected from the time of my arrival at Idlewild Airport in July 1960 until I left Columbia in 1975. Crucial for my construction of this New York was my passionate love for four of its teams, the Yankees, Giants, Knicks, and Rangers (please, do not even bother mentioning their upstart and peripheral counterparts, the Mets, Jets, Nets, Islanders, and Devils!). But what kind of ephemeral home is a location based on sports teams, no matter how beloved and important? Yes, I can speak with a *Noo Yawk* accent, intoning the requisite "co-awf-fee" and "cho-a-ca-late" and "doawg" and the silent "r's," with reasonable authenticity and credibility, but what does that mean? And yes, I adore New York culture and consumed it voraciously prior to the arrival of COVID-19. But that, too, is thin stuff in terms of comprising a real home.

But hold on. I do have a bona fide home: The United States of America. Yes, the whole darn continent, from the Atlantic to the Pacific, with Hawaii and Alaska included. I have made it my life's goal to visit all 50 states, not just touching down at an airport and moving on but spending a few days on the ground and seeing the sights. At the time of this writing, I still have four to go: North Dakota, Montana, Idaho, and Arkansas. Nothing makes me prouder than being told by strangers—students, colleagues, folks on airplanes—that they are surprised to find out I was not born in the United States because I speak such perfectly accent-free standard American English. Conversely, nothing depresses me more than the occasional person saying something like: "I detect a slight difference in your speech, not an accent, but some kind of an inflection, an annunciation, that is different; something along the lines of how Canadians pronounce 'about' and 'out' and 'again' and 'dollar.' Something that makes your speech slightly different from how normal Americans speak." Ouch! Such comments, rare as they are, have been known to ruin my day. They rob me of my most desired identity: that of being an American.

I was officially bestowed with this identity on Monday morning, September 27, 1971 when I was sworn in as a citizen of the United States at the United States District Court for the Southern District of New York in Lower Manhattan. It was a crystal-clear, crisp fall day with no cloud in the sky and bright sunshine bathing New York City's skyscrapers in a comforting warmth and a welcoming glow. I had arrived at home! No more statelessness!

Immediately after the swearing-in ceremony, I took a subway to Rockefeller Center where the closest office for obtaining a United States passport was located at the time. I think it quite telling that, for me, the single most important document testifying to my becoming an American and being at home was an item one usually uses to leave a place, not to establish roots in it. Upon receipt of this document a few days later, I proceeded to carry it (and its many successors) with me every single day for the past fifty years—to grocery stores, to doctor's appointments, to classes I have taught, to dinner dates with friends, to the movies, the theater, the opera, to concerts. (The only place I have never taken my passport has been to football games in Michigan Stadium; I worry that in the presence of 111,000 people it will get stolen or lost.)

While most Americans use their driver's license as a source of identification, I use my passport. This renders me a clear outsider. Upon showing my passport when asked for identificaton anywhere in the United States, the person often looks at me quizzically and responds with slight irritation: "No, I meant a real ID, please!" Americans do not identify with passports. To citizens of a vast country buffeted between two oceans passports are exceptional documents used only sporadically and for specific purposes. They are not documents used frequently in everyday life. In marked contrast, my only anchor in this rootless world has been my United States passport, an item whose only raison d'être is rootlessness since it is a document one uses solely for the purpose of traveling, of being unanchored, rootless. Of course, I use it for its intended purpose, too, but mostly for the immense solace, comfort, and security that nothing else comes close to giving me. My passport became my anchor, my rootedness!

1 Kutuzov Street

Everyone, in some sense, is susceptible to becoming rootless. If a person's identity can find its political expression in an institution called the state, then not having such a construct renders one homeless and nomadic. That has been the fate of the Jews since the destruction of the second temple in Jerusalem by the Romans in 70 CE. The Jews became an anchorless people in that they did not have a structure called the state and therefore lacked political and military power, meaning their rootlessness became their very identity. Thus, the wandering Jew.

My ancestors all hailed from what was the Hungarian part of the Habsburg Empire. But prior to that, all of them lived in what today would be Poland or Ukraine, from which they descended into Hungary because of that country's open invitation to Jews to create a middle class of merchants and professionals. For this to happen, the Hungarians pursued perhaps the most liberal and welcoming policies towards Jews anywhere in Europe in the early-to-mid-nineteenth century. Not having their own state, Jews depended on the rulers of other people's states to define their political existence. But states came and went. They shifted territories constantly. As my father always said, he hailed from a part of the world in which people did not move but countries did. *Staaten-los*, statelessness—just as my document of identification in my years in Vienna so clearly stated—by definition means rootlessness.

One of the only positive associations with rootless cosmopolitanism is the concept now known as multiculturalism. Though the meaning of the term isn't always clear, I would venture that a plurality of religions, languages, professions, classes, races, and genders must exist for a space to be labeled multicultural. By this definition, the world in which I grew up in the 1950s truly qualifies as multicultural, not only in relation to the city itself, or to our building, but to the narrow space of our apartment.

I am not sure which official named the short, quiet, leafy street on which we lived after the famed Russian general Mikhail Kutuzov, who defeated Napoleon in 1812 and stopped his invasion of Russia. Maybe the name was bestowed by the Soviets, who, with their Red Army, liberated Romania in late summer 1944. But upon my return to the street in 2012, it was still called Kutuzov, and the house appeared virtually identical to the house we had left in 1958.

The house was a two-story yellow stucco structure that must have been the property of an haute-bourgeois family before the communists' full assumption of power in Romania in 1948. A cast-iron gate opened onto a little garden where a bed of multi-colored roses always looked very pretty and reminded the visitor of one of Timişoara's beautiful parks, barely 100 yards away, which was appropriately called Rose Garden (or *rózsakert* in Hungarian, as my family always referred to it, or *Parcul Rozelor* in Romanian). In this park my father taught me to ride a bicycle.

The entrance to the house was a large wooden door on the right side. Upon entering the black-and-white tiled foyer, you followed a stone staircase a few steps down into the basement, where Mr. and Mrs. Hajdu lived. They were a Hungarian-speaking Protestant family, with

Mr. Hajdu some sort of handyman and Mrs. Hajdu a homemaker.[3] They spoke little, if any, Romanian. On the slightly elevated first floor, two doors led to two apartments. To the right, in the smaller unit, Mr. and Mrs. Ţunea lived with their lovely daughter, Livia. The Ţuneas were Romanian-speaking Roman Catholics who spoke fluent though faulty Hungarian because they hailed from the Banat region, Romania's westernmost province, of which Timişoara was the largest city. Mr. Ţunea worked as an electrician for the city, Mrs. Ţunea was a homemaker, and Livia, only known by her diminutive, Livicuţa, was four years older than I and had the most gorgeous dark eyes.

On the second floor lived another Romanian-speaking family, the Ţicalas. Their daughter, Doina, always sang arias from Verdi and Puccini operas, and I came to admire their son, Ţucu, for all the trouble he got himself into, and tried to emulate him as best I could, even though my mother and father warned me not to hang out with him because he was much older and smoked cigarettes in our small backyard. Unlike the Ţuneas, the Ţicalas spoke no Hungarian because they hailed from the "real" Romania, known as the Regat, and had come to Timişoara as adults. The Ţicalas were Romanian Orthodox. Lastly, rounding out this building's inhabitants, were my parents and I representing the city's middle-class Jewish community, whose members spoke predominantly Hungarian and numbered about 7,000 at this time. So the house on 1 Kutuzov Street represented a fair rendition of Timişoara's multicultural character in the 1950s.

The door to the left of the Ţuneas' on the first floor led to our apartment, which was decidedly larger than theirs. Here resided the three members of the Markovits family. My father—Markovits Lajos (always called by the diminutive Lajcsi) in Hungarian, Ludovic Markovits in Romanian, and Ludwig Markovits in German—was born in 1911 in the town of Satmar (in German and Yiddish; Szatmár in Hungarian; Satu Mare in Romanian). This town was then in the Hungarian part of the Habsburg monarchy, but it became known to Jews around the world by

---

3   I do not remember whether the Hajdus belonged to the Reformed (Calvinist), Lutheran (Evangelical) or Unitarian confessions all of which existed among the non-Jewish Hungarian speakers in the Timişoara of the time.

virtue of its famed Satmar sect of deeply observant Orthodox Jews, who, following the Shoah, established their headquarters in Brooklyn's Borough Park.

In addition to his native Hungarian, my father spoke perfect Romanian, which he used in his work as an economic planner in the Timișoara branch of the Romanian state's central bank, a job he attained by dint of having received a doctorate in business administration from the Commerce University of Budapest in 1937. (The title of my father's doctoral thesis, in an English translation of the Hungarian original, is "Palestine's Economic Development and Its Commercial Relations with Hungary.")

My father was the youngest of six children, the only child to attend the kind of secondary school the completion of which allowed access to university. By virtue of being Jewish, however, my father could not attend the fancy humanities-oriented *Gymnasium* that taught Latin and Greek; instead, he went to a commerce-dominated secondary school that only permitted him to enroll in something akin to a business curriculum at the university level. Not having the *Latinum* foreclosed my father's studying at a "real" university and thus precluded his becoming a medical doctor, a lawyer, or a graduate of any of the fields that my father would always longingly refer to as "intellectual." Carrying the title of "Herr Doktor" and "Domnu' Doctor" and "Doktor úr" was crucial to my father's identity. But having this degree from a commerce university always diminished the title's splendor in my father's eyes.

Both my father's parents, as well as four of his siblings, were deported to Auschwitz in May 1944. His parents and two eldest siblings perished in the Shoah; his sister, Margaret (Manci), and his brother Alexander (Sanyi) somehow survived and returned from hell. When the deportation of Hungarian Jews under Adolf Eichmann's command began, my father and his brother Benjamin (Benő) had the luck to find themselves in Romania. Having graduated from the Commerce University in Budapest in 1937, my father married my mother and started a new life with her in Timișoara, in Romania. Though he experienced horrible antisemitic persecution in the Romania of the early 1940s, he nonetheless escaped the Holocaust, for which he felt guilty throughout his life. As he would repeatedly tell me, were it not for the so-called Second

Vienna Award of August 1940, by which Nazi Germany and fascist Italy transferred northern Transylvania, including Satmar, to Hungary and left Timişoara in Romania, my father and mother would most definitely have been deported to Auschwitz.

One of the enigmas with which I pestered my father was why he and my mother didn't leave Romania after this award to join virtually their entire family across the border in what had now once again become Hungary. While Jews were not welcome citizens in Admiral Horthy's right-wing, authoritarian Hungary, they were not being slaughtered as they were in General Ion Antonescu's brutal Romania, where they experienced an extra magnitude of atrocities under the Iron Guard's murderous fascism. My father could never provide a rationale for staying in Romania, a decision that saved him from Auschwitz, aside from insisting that the Romanian fascists and antisemites were corrupt and venal, and therefore easily bribable, whereas the Hungarians were not, which meant the possibility of escape from the former was greater than from the latter. Otherwise, his only explanation came during one of our lunches at Columbia in the early 1970s, when he uttered the English words "dumb luck."

My father was a good-looking man, of medium height, with dark eyes and jet-black hair that turned gray later in life but remained thick and full until he died at the age of 79. He smiled prolifically and was disarmingly charming. Always a nifty dresser and unfailingly polite, he prided himself on being able to get along with everybody. His "diplomatic being," as he often called it, helped him overcome unpleasant situations and made him genuinely well-liked. His generosity was legendary and filled him with great joy and pride.

My mother, Ida Ritter (in all three languages though only called Ica by everybody which is Ida's Hungarian diminutive), was born in 1918 in Oradea (Nagyvárad in Hungarian, Grosswardein in German), the only child of an upper-middle-class couple who had her late in life. The family's social position meant they were conversant with central European culture, heavily grounded in its German variety. As the daughter of a worldly, assimilated, Jewish family, my mother was taught both German and French. She took piano lessons, as well as courses in etiquette.

Because of her social milieu, she was schooled by tutors specializing in the subjects she needed to master for her education to be officially recognized by the state. But, as indication of the contempt my mother's family harbored for all things Romanian and their esteem for Hungarian culture, my mother traveled across the border to Budapest every year to pass her yearly examinations at the Zrínyi Ilona Leánylíceum (Ilona Zrínyi School for Girls) as a so-called "magántanuló" (a private student). Passing these examinations—predominantly with straight A's in all subjects I might add—permitted her to advance to the next grade rather than take the tests in nearby Oradea, let alone Bucharest, the capital of the country of which she was formally a citizen.

There was another reason my mother was homeschooled: she was a sickly child who suffered from tuberculosis in her teenage years. Not until she attended university in Budapest did she actually enter a classroom. This was in 1936, when she met my father at a Jewish ball they both attended. This was a big annual dance organized by the Jewish university students of Budapest, often attended by the daughters of the Budapest Jewish elite, among them the three pre-Hollywood Gábor sisters (Magda, Zsa Zsa, and Éva), with whom my father, to his eternal delight, danced at one of these events.

My mother, intending to study philosophy and comparative literature, never really did so beyond her first year at university. When my father received his doctorate in 1937, the two married and moved to new quarters, away from neighboring Satmar and Oradea, where their respective families still lived, to unknown Timişoara, where an interesting business opportunity beckoned to my father. The cultural difference between my mother's milieu of assimilated and cosmopolitan haute bourgeoisie and my father's much more parochial and local petite bourgeoisie manifested itself almost daily in our lives. A clear division of labor also existed between the two in terms of who would engage me in which realm: my mother was clearly in charge of all matters of high culture, like playing the piano and learning about Homer, while my father conveyed to me the world of soccer, trams, and trains.

My mother's father died just before the war and is buried in the Jewish cemetery in Oradea, which I once visited with my father by taking the train from Timişoara and returning later that evening. My mother did not accompany us. Her mother was deported to Auschwitz in 1944 and was murdered there. My mother never talked to me about her parents. The little I discovered about them came from my mother's most intimate childhood friend, a lovely woman called Bözsi (the Hungarian diminutive of Elizabeth) Havas, whom I barely knew as a child but with whom I reconnected much later as an adult in Israel and London. She repeatedly emphasized that my mother's parents appeared to be like grandparents, as they were so elderly. She also mentioned how much my mother's parents protected my mother, not letting her join her girlfriends on any adventure that included any kind of danger. Bözsi also told me that getting tuberculosis at the age of 13 or 14 proved to be traumatic for my mother and adversely affected her entire life. However, being a chubby girl, my mother was also thrilled that, on account of her tuberculosis, she lost a great deal of weight and became the thin young woman she always had wanted to be.

My mother was an attractive woman who was my father's height; at five feet seven inches, that made her one of the tallest women in Timişoara at this time. Sporting thick, reddish-brown hair that she either let fall to her shoulders or pinned up in a bun, she also wore glasses that accentuated her deep intellectualism. Like my father, my mother smiled a lot, though I always detected a sadness that did not darken my father's face. I cannot recall her wearing makeup, other than a touch of a pink lipstick on the rare occasions she and my father went out. Sadly, when I think of my mother, I see her sitting in the living room in her dressing gown or, more frequently, lying in bed propped up by an array of pillows, book in her lap as she read, whether silently to herself or out loud to me. Many of our interactions consisted of my holding her hand while she lay in her bed.

As I got older, my mother's health deteriorated by the day. I do not think the doctors were able to pinpoint her exact illness, but her teenage tuberculosis clearly had deleterious effects. I fear she might also have suffered from what we now know as anorexia nervosa; she always obsessed about not wanting to gain any weight and become chubby again, as revealed by the only photograph of her I possess from girlhood.

And then there was Juliska, the Hungarian peasant woman who came to our place three or four times a week to help my mother with household chores. I never saw her hair because she always covered it with a kerchief, as married peasant women in many countries do. She also dressed differently from the women in Timişoara by never wearing pants and always wearing long, flowery skirts, the kind many young women on New York's Upper West Side and in Greenwich Village, as well as Cambridge and Berkeley and similar places across the United States, sported in the late 1960s. She mostly commuted from her village by bus and train, but on occasion her husband gave her a ride on a one-horse cart.

Juliska disliked Ţucu intensely. Once, when Ţucu and I were fooling around in our backyard, Juliska was hanging up the laundry to dry. Ţucu and I spoke in Romanian, and Juliska clearly didn't understand our conversation. I asked her with some irritation in Hungarian why she spoke no Romanian, even though she lived in Romania. Her answer: "Romanian is an evil language." This clearly reveals how, to many ethnic Hungarians, even peasants, living in Romania was a chore, a burden, something they hated because they found the Romanians inferior to themselves. And one way to show their contempt for Romania and Romanians was by refusing to speak the language.

My mentor Karl Deutsch argued that one learns a language "up" not "down," meaning minorities who deem themselves culturally superior to the majorities among whom they live will not learn the language of the majorities unless they find the culture of the majorities at least equivalent to their own. German settlers all over eastern Europe, including Romania, as well as Hungarians in Romania, never learned the language of the majority beyond the necessities of getting by in daily life. Deutsch maintained that Germans who settled in Argentina never ceased speaking German, whereas Germans who settled in Milwaukee did. The former deemed their Latin American environment inferior to German culture, which led them to cling to their own by speaking their old language. The latter, however, deemed the dominant Anglo-American culture at least equal to their own, which meant they loosened their adherence to German cultural norms and eventually stopped speaking German. Being German in Milwaukee attained a mere folkloristic identity of beer and sausages and Oktoberfest, rather than a sustained national and nationalistic one as in Argentina.

Life in the Markovits Apartment

Entering our apartment, one encountered a dining and living room that had a beautiful black wooden table. We ate our meals there every day, but much more important for me was the table's smooth, gliding surface, on which I could play an odd game called *gombfoci*—"button football" in Hungarian. In this game, buttons comprised the players, big buttons the defenders, smaller buttons the forwards, and the smallest shirt-button the ball, with matchsticks masquerading as the goalposts. One could not guide the players by pulling or pushing them but had to flick them adroitly into position or use them to strike the ball. If one struck a button belonging to the opposing team, one committed a foul, and the opposing team was allowed a free kick. I played this game endlessly until I became adroit enough so that I pretty much beat all the boys in the neighborhood my mother would allow into our home. Indeed, she even made an exception and allowed Țucu to visit me for the purpose of playing a match, which, to my eternal pride, I decisively won.

At this table, my mother would host her dinner parties, at which the women looked so pretty, with their red lipstick, high heels, nylons, and their furs, often featuring fox stoles on which the fox's head was still present. My mother would never partake of the food she had prepared but sat holding dry toast under the table in her left hand while holding one of her very rare cigarettes in her right, smoking it for all to see.

In the room's left-hand corner stood a beautiful concert piano, on which my mother and I played poorly and often, she voluntarily, I by virtue of her edict. Yet, one particular event will always leave this piano as memorable for me. After attending an afternoon piano recital with my mother in Timișoara's main movie theater, where all classical music was performed, the very young artist Gheorghe Halmos, known to my parents by his Hungarian name Gyuri, came to our house for a snack. I have no idea how or why my parents knew him, other than that he hailed from Oradea, my mother's hometown. Quite a few of my parents' friends were in attendance, as was Ella Philipp, my mother's occasional and my regular piano teacher, who shed her usual stern demeanor to swoon over the present star.

Even though Philipp never got me to play classical piano well and failed to teach me to read music at a meaningful level, my years with her honed my musical sensibilities to a degree they would never have attained merely by passively listening to records and the radio. More significantly, my lousy piano playing later came in handy to my learning to play banjo and guitar. At some point Halmos sat down at our modest piano and, to the delight of all, played heavenly music. Then I heard that Halmos was a student of a Budapest pianist named Annie Fischer. This name generated nothing but awe in the room. Much later in life, I heard Fischer play exceptionally beautiful Beethoven sonatas. Fischer and her artistry also became a topic of conversation in Ann Arbor, where I befriended the world-famous pianist Sir András Schiff—like Fischer a Jewish artist from Budapest—who has always made it a point of including a recital at the University of Michigan's Hill Auditorium during his United States tours. To my great pleasure, Sir András always took time to have a meal with me during these brief trips.

In the right-hand corner of our living and dining room were a phonograph and a Blaupunkt radio, with three plush chairs arranged in such a way that our family could gather to listen to either. Next to the phonograph was a shelf with a plethora of records featuring the music of Bach, Beethoven, Haydn, Mozart, Schubert, Schumann, Mendelssohn, and other nineteenth century German composers. Symphonies, violin concertos, cello concertos, piano concertos—all were present. Were it not for the occasional Dvořák (whose cello concerto I have continued to whistle on many occasions), Tchaikovsky (ditto with his violin concerto), and all of Verdi's and Puccini's operas, the collection would have been entirely German.

My mother, father, and I listened to at least one record virtually every evening after dinner, making Beethoven's symphonies and Mozart's sublime music second nature to me. On the wall opposite the piano was a shelf packed with books in German, featuring the usual suspects—

Goethe, Schiller, Hölderlin, Kleist, Grillparzer, Raimund, Nestroy, Kafka, Werfel, Mann, Feuchtwanger, Zweig—but also, to my delight, Karl May, who wrote fantastic tales of cowboys and Indians set in that mythic land called America. (Only later in life did I discover what a vile reactionary and German nationalist, with clear antisemitic streaks, this Karl May was. His many books were a must-read for all bourgeois boys in the German-speaking world and its central European satellites. A lasting benefit of having read these books with such passion and attention was my acquisition of a superb knowledge of the geography of the United States, particularly the regions west of the Mississippi, where many of May's stories take place.) The shelves also included books by Hungarian authors such as Madách, Molnár, Arany, and Petőfi, as well as classics by Homer and Shakespeare, both in Hungarian and German translations.

Were a skilled ethnographer to have entered the Markovits's living room between 1948 and 1958, she would have never realized this was a Holocaust-ravaged family whose male member had both of his parents and two of his six siblings murdered in Auschwitz, with only two surviving that hell, and whose female member, an only child, had her mother perish there. Such was the power of German culture in this Hungarian-Habsburg Jewish family, representatives of the central European utterly bourgeois *Bildungsbürgertum*. Hitler truly had no bearing on Beethoven in the Markovits family.

Exiting the room to the left, one came upon my bedroom. In one corner stood my bed, and in the other corner another bed, which, from early in my life, my father used every night. I never asked my father about this in all our life together as adults. My mother's constant illness required that she be given space all to herself, but I do not know anything more than that. I never felt any tension between them. After my father's death in 1990, so all parties would be exempt from embarrassment, I asked Bözsi and another of my mother's girlfriends whether they knew of any marital problems between my parents. Both emphatically denied this and reaffirmed my father's adoration of my mother, though I sensed his ardor took the form of esteem and appreciation rather than erotic or romantic enthrallment.

When I asked Bözsi about an attractive woman who was one of my father's colleagues at the bank, someone I had encountered once or twice in my life, Bözsi demurred and mumbled something about how men have these occasional flings at work, though she didn't know this to be true of my father, as my mother never complained, and most assuredly not about any philandering. Even my aunt Manci, my father's sister, who became my surrogate mother after my mother's death, revealed nothing of my parents' marriage, other than that they loved each other very much and complemented each other superbly. Like Bözsi, my aunt implied by a combination of body language and silence that my father might have had affairs at work. But these are post-hoc interpretations of a matter for which no one offered any convincing evidence. I never recall my mother and father fighting; never recall my mother crying about something my father might have done to her; and I never recall my father not spending the evenings and nights at home.

My father once told me a gentleman never intrudes on another's private space by asking indiscrete questions. Above all, a gentleman never brags about romantic conquests and does not talk about the women in his life, ever! Oddly, these are among the few of my father's dicta I have always upheld. I have never asked any of my male friends about their intimate lives and always waited for them to volunteer such information before I offered whatever advice or assistance I could provide. In the touchy-feely intellectual milieu of the Upper West Side in the late 1960s and early 1970s, when it was *de rigueur* to spill one's private life to virtual strangers as a sign of trust, I was often derided by friends, male and female, when I persistently refused to talk about my girlfriends.

A door on the right wall of this bedroom led to another room, in which there was some sort of double- or queen-sized bed, in which my mother always lay, even during the afternoon, and where I would spend hours and hours listening to her tell me stories and read me books like Homer's *Iliad* and *Odyssey*, which she read to me in German rather than Hungarian translation. (Last I looked, Homer wrote the work in Greek, but somehow, testifying to my mother's cultural snobbism, Homer in German was more authentic than in Hungarian.)

In 1955 or 1956, my father and mother took me to the town's main movie theater to see the film *Ulysses* starring Kirk Douglas. The film's showing was a major event in Timişoara, and I loved every minute of it, except when Ulysses (aka Odysseus) descended to Hades to meet with the deceased Greek heroes Achilles, Ajax, and Agamemnon. For some reason, their ghost-like depiction scared me so much that I had a number of nightmares, always requiring that my father (and occasionally my mother) come to my bed to comfort me. Of course, my mother read me all the Brothers Grimm stories in their original German, as she did Wilhelm Busch's legendary *Max und Moritz*. Throughout my mother's life with me, which sadly ended when I had not yet reached the age of ten and she the age of forty, she read to me only in German. Just like Homer, Shakespeare was nobler and worthier in a German rather than a Hungarian translation.

My mother was deeply bothered by her ignorance of English. While she always considered French a finer, more elegant language, she understood that English had become much more important, a notion seconded by my father, who spoke elementary English by dint of having studied it at the Commerce University in Budapest. Both agreed I was to learn English from early childhood. So off I was sent at the age of six to Mrs. Vágó, the English tutor to most of the Jewish kids in town. In wanting to write about her in this book, I was eager to find out how she knew English; only at this stage did I learn that Mrs. Vágó (to us children, she was known only as Vágó *néni*, Mrs. Vágó, with no first name) was the wife of the United Kingdom's honorary consul in Timișoara. This means she most likely spent the war years in the United Kingdom, where she picked up her fine English and where her husband must have acquired a sufficient knowledge of British culture and politics to become Britain's honorary consul in Timișoara, as distant and provincial a town as it was.

Mrs. Vágó must have been a good teacher because by the time my father and I departed in 1958, my English, though far from good, was far better than his. In her teaching, Mrs. Vágó engaged in methods I would now characterize as sophisticated, bordering on a seminar in comparative linguistics. Knowing my family's background, Mrs. Vágó assumed I knew not only Hungarian, but German as well. Thus, she informed me that unlike the German *der*, *die*, *das*, English has only "the" as the definitive article. This pertained as much to the obvious candidates of gendered nouns, such as *der Vater*, *die Mutter*, and *das Kind*, but also terms such as *der Löffel*, *die Gabel*, and *das Messer* (spoon, fork, knife). Here,

Mrs. Vágó signaled to me that the gendering of German nouns was not only to signify gender as conventionally understood in the "real" world, but as a classification scheme that gendered nouns randomly, having nothing to do with these nouns being truly masculine, feminine, or neutral. (There is nothing male about spoon, nothing female about a fork, and nothing neutral about a knife.) Then Mrs. Vágó told me that even though English was much less gendered than German and French, it was more so than our native Hungarian, in which the third-person singular is simply *ő* for all three: he, she, it!

The only story my mother read to me in Hungarian was Ferenc Molnár's gripping *A Pál utcai fiúk*, *The Paul Street Boys*, in which the weak and sickly boy, Ernő Nemecsek, tries to prove to his pals that he is no "cowardly rabbit" by entering the fray, and dies in the battle between two warring groups. It made me cry then and still does today. This book was obligatory reading for every Hungarian-speaking boy between the ages of five and twelve. The story remains poignant to me because it features the eventual success of male friendship over male competition and rivalry. Despite his death, Nemecsek prevails, not as a hero but as the little guy, the everyman, who takes all kind of abuse, even from his pals, but emerges as noble in the end.

Nemecsek's life and death fostered in me a compassion for the weak that has dominated my attitude and actions all my life. The pre-adolescent male friendship that forms the core of the book appealed to me then and still does, conveying an innocence and purity that the emergence of sexuality just a few years later steals for good. *The Paul Street Boys* represents a kind of desexualized *Romeo and Juliet*, with its Montagues and Capulets as the warring gangs, or *West Side Story*, with its Jets and Sharks. Then there is my continued love for rabbits, of which I have quite a few in their stuffed version—I pity them for an association with cowardice they do not deserve.

Even my passion for bears might have something to do with Nemecsek. Though often construed as fierce and powerful animals, to me bears were poor souls whom I saw being dragged with heavy chains by a ring piercing their sensitive noses and made to dance for people by being prodded with hot iron bars. This was a common sight in the Timișoara of the 1950s, and the memory still gives me the chills. Once, a smallish bear, maybe a cub, fell, and its brutal owner started kicking it relentlessly. I screamed so hard and got so upset my father had to rush me away. Frequently, the bears' abusers were Romani men who had to resort to such measures to eke out a meager living in a world that accorded them few, if any, meaningful employment opportunities. Communism's alleged universalism most certainly did not extend to the Roma in terms of giving them meaningful economic support. And it most decidedly did not shield them from the daily disdain and open hatred that most Timişoarans visited upon this group who were constantly treated as outcasts.

Racism against the Roma people was open and acceptable within every group in my birthplace, Timişoara—Romanians, Hungarians, Germans, Jews—including the Markovits family. Every mention of the Roma I heard was negative. Only later in life did I develop compassion for the Roma, especially when I learned about their brutalization by the Nazis.

A Romani woman who came to play a crucial and lasting role in my life was Azucena from Giuseppe Verdi's great opera *Il trovatore*. My parents took me to Timişoara's impressive State Theater on the city's beautiful main square, where the theater occupied one end and the massive Romanian Orthodox church the other. Though I seem to recall we saw a few plays there, I do not remember them at all, in contrast to the operas, which stayed with me for life. We saw the usual suspects: *Carmen, La bohème, La traviata, Rigoletto, Madame Butterfly,* and *Il trovatore*. In scene one of the second act of the last-named opera, Azucena (which means "Lily" in Spanish) tells her rapt audience of the horror that befell her when she witnessed the burning of her mother at the stake on the orders of Count di Luna. She does this in arguably one of the most moving arias for mezzo-sopranos, "Stride la vampa," ("The Flames Are Roaring"). Then Azucena recounts that, in revenge, she wanted to throw the count's baby into a nearby fire pit, but, amidst the commotion, picked up her own child and threw it instead. She then raised the count's baby as her own child. When Azucena re-enacts the throwing of the baby into the fire pit for her audience, she utters the word *fuoco*, which means "fire" in Italian, in dread. At that point in the production, a huge flame emerged from the pyre beside Azucena, which so frightened me that my parents had to take me home after the act, and we missed the rest of this wonderful opera. Since then, each of the many times I have seen or listened to *Il trovatore*, this scene has jolted me and given me the shivers.

Opera remained a source of great pleasure for me for the rest of my life. Together with sports, it provided the sole truly serene space between my father and me. Everything else was contested: grades, women, career, religion, politics, but never sports or opera. Once, after a particularly grueling fight with my father just before attending Mozart's *Così fan tutte* at the Salzburg Festival, where we were frequent visitors in the 1970s and 1980s, we sat down in our seats fuming at each other, full of anger and scorn. As soon as we heard the opera's heavenly harmonies, we spontaneously turned to each other and smiled warmly. I grabbed my father's arm when I noticed tears in his eyes; it was too dark for him to see mine.

Back to our apartment. Off the right side of the living room, a small corridor led to the kitchen on the right and to a bigger room on the left. In that room, sometime between 1951 or 1952 and 1954 or 1955, two relatively high-ranking Red Army officers (colonels, I believe) and their respective families lived with us. They used our kitchen and our bathroom, but they almost always ate by themselves; I do not remember them ever being present around the beloved black wooden table, which served as my sole place of nourishment as well as the surface for my button-football matches.

The first Russian couple had no children, which might have been why the husband showered me with such attention. The man's name was Josif, and I liked him immensely. He had this handlebar mustache I always felt like tugging at and a round face that always had a smile on it. Whenever he would come home, he would grab me, throw me in the air, and then catch me with his huge hands and press me to his powerful chest, which was covered by the Red Army's uniform. Befitting his high military rank, he wore fancy stars on his epaulettes, which I admired up close as he ran around the room with me, letting me sit astride his neck. I loved the smell of the sweet perfume or aftershave he wore, so distinct to Red Army officers and soldiers, and which we could smell all over town. Rumor had it that to counter the Soviet army's reputation of being dirty and unwashed, the troops used this sweet perfume to make themselves smell good to the natives.

"Andrei, Andrei," he would bellow, horsing around with me as my mother watched in fear. Once, when I was ill, Josif came home and suggested I be given a shot of his vodka, which my parents diplomatically refused. He always brought me Medved chocolate, which depicted a bear, my absolute favorite animal, on the package, since *medved* means bear in Russian, very close to the Hungarian *medve*. Josif was an immensely gregarious person. He hung out with my father, with our next-door neighbor, Mr. Țunea, and with Mr. Hajdu from the basement, though never with Mr. Țicala from the floor above us, perhaps because he did not exactly relish walking an additional flight of stairs.

All of them played chess; I remember Josif spotting a knight or even a castle at the beginning of a game against one of the local guys, and he would then invariably win with ease. These men conversed with a few words of Romanian, a few words of Hungarian, a few words of Russian, but mostly with the body language of male camaraderie—lots of backslapping, lots of hugs—and, of course, the language of football and chess. I sensed a genuine liking among all these men—not friendship, but a form of mutual enjoyment, however superficial.

Josif also taught me chess, which I came to play well enough by age seven to beat my father with some regularity, although I was always left wondering whether he let me win, just as he had let me win in button football a few years earlier. (By age seven, however, I had mastered this game to such a degree that demolishing my father and uncle and all adults was beyond doubt the result of my actual proficiency.)

Playing chess with my father throughout our lives offered us both a sense of calm and peace, perhaps even succor. Interestingly enough, in my adult life I only played chess with my father and no one else. The same pertained to him. Chess became our private game of sorts. For reasons never known to me, as soon as we sat down and commenced our games, my father would—without fail—break into the vast repertoire of Hungarian folk and pop songs with which he grew up and which he whistled or hummed until our game ended. Then, silence! He never sang or whistled these songs in any other context than chess! The two most memorable songs were "Az a szép, az a szép akinek a szeme kék" (beautiful, beautiful are those with blue eyes); and "Szomorú vasárnap," the Rezső Seress hit of the 1930s rendered famous by Billie Holiday's haunting cover, as well as by many other artists' under the title "Gloomy Sunday."

Written in a minor key, the song is so gripping that listening to it allegedly caused some people to commit suicide, especially in Hungary, where—for reasons I never understood—the suicide rate has been among the highest in the world ever since such statistics have existed. Indeed, the song has come to be known as "The Hungarian Suicide Song." There is no doubt in my mind that my deep lifelong affinity for the blues hailed from my father's soulful rendition of this truly haunting song during our chess games.

Josif was always driven to and from work in a type of jeep that he always called "Veelees," appropriately representing, as I much later learned, the Willys Jeep that the United States shipped to its Soviet ally during World War II. On occasion, Josif would persuade my mother to let me ride in his lap in the front passenger seat. This was blissful, and oh so cool! And then, from one day to the next, Josif vanished. No goodbyes, no farewells: he and his wife, whom I cannot remember at all, were gone. Much later, my father and I surmised he must have been demoted, possibly even purged, in the post-Stalin era following the dictator's death in March 1953. But these are just wild guesses!

Josif was followed by a horrible guy who rarely communicated with us, but who regularly beat his little daughter, who was around my age, with a leather belt. I remember hearing her cry almost nightly, and all we could do was turn up Beethoven or Mozart to drown out the disturbing sound and soothe our fear. For my father to have intervened in the affairs of a high-ranking Soviet officer in the Romania of the early-to-mid-1950s was out of the question. Thank God these people left fairly soon, with no Soviet military families following them into our apartment. Even though we repossessed this room, I barely recall its being used. I have no idea what it looked like. All I remember is feeling a sense of dread connected with the door to that room.

The way my parents related to the Soviets was very revealing of the culture of their social class. I heard nothing but contempt, derision, and even hatred for the soldiers of the Red Army: that they raped every woman in sight; that they could be seen wearing 20 or 30 wristwatches on their arms, stolen from locals at the point of a gun; that they were illiterate country bumpkins, utterly uncouth and uncultured; that they never washed (note the perfume story mentioned earlier); and that during air raids they never bothered to seek protection in shelters because life was so cheap to them that they did not mind dying.

I never heard anything positive about the Soviets, who were the only reason my parents and their Jewish cohort in Timişoara and far beyond were alive. Had it not been for the Red Army, the Germans, who had reached the outskirts of Timişoara, would have killed all 13,000 Jews living there at the time. (One reason for this agglomeration was that the Romanian authorities made Timişoara the central gathering-point for Jews from the Banat and other regions in southern Transylvania, with the possible future plan of having them deported to the death camps.)

Tellingly, I never heard one bad word about the Germans. I never heard anything positive about them either, but after what they had done to my family—I later tallied the loss at twenty-eight relatives murdered in Auschwitz and elsewhere—I am astonished that neither my father nor my mother expressed anything derogatory about the Germans. Quite the contrary: by listening only to German composers and extolling the writings of the German literary giants, my parents made it clear that the German language was superior to Hungarian, my mother's, father's, and my own native tongue. I am sure the Holocaust was so painful to my parents that they simply couldn't bring themselves to mention it to me— or possibly each other. The only time I saw my father upset enough to invoke the Holocaust—in a rage, his body trembling—was in my apartment on Manhattan's Upper West Side in the summer of 1975, when we got into a heated argument about the Israeli-Palestinian conflict and I presented the Palestinian side. Though I didn't advocate the Palestinian point of view, my father simply couldn't hear the difference. In a display of anger and fear I had rarely seen before, he screamed something to the effect that he never wanted to have Jews "baked in ovens the way my parents and my two oldest siblings were."

But with the exception of my father's sister, Manci, who did return from Auschwitz and who invoked its horrors almost daily, the Holocaust was a non-event in the Markovits family. This had much to do with a cultural snobbism essential to the partly assimilated Hungarian Jewish bourgeoisie. The Holocaust was much more present to my aunt Manci, who did not have my parents' cultural ambitions and pretensions, and whose German was poor. Aunt Manci never listened to Bach and Beethoven and did not read Goethe's *Faust* for pleasure in the evenings. Manci lost her husband in Auschwitz and never had children of her own, which meant I became her surrogate son. She had a creative mind she put to great use by inventing wonderful stories with which she would regale me for hours.

Had she lived in a different time and place, my aunt Manci could very well have become a published children's author. After the war, she married a wonderful radiologist who doted on and loved her dearly. And yet, when I would have a sleepover at their apartment, I sometimes woke to my aunt screaming, "*Anyuka, Anyuka, ne menj el, ne menj el*"—Mother, Mother, don't leave, don't leave!—and crying inconsolably. When I returned home, I would ask my mother and father what Aunt Manci was so upset about. My father would respond that he and Manci had lost the same mother. When I asked him why I never heard him scream at night as I had heard Aunt Manci scream, he replied that men don't cry. Not a word about the Shoah, nothing about how he never had to witness what Manci most likely experienced in Auschwitz: having her mother torn away from her at a railway station by brutal guards sending each one of them in different directions never to meet again.

Making me learn the best possible German was of such importance for my mother that she hired a native German-speaker to be my nanny and take me for long daily walks, mainly to the aforementioned Rose Garden and its environs. Frau Kommer, whose first name I never knew and whom I simply called Tante Kommer, was a statuesque woman with a beehive of white hair and a friendly face that hid her strictness. She never wore pants, dressed conservatively, and never missed a day, spending two hours with me every morning and some time with me every afternoon for nearly seven years, until I started elementary school.

Because of this immersion, I had no difficulties entering the German school, appropriately called the Nikolaus Lenau Schule (after the famous Romantic poet from the Banat). There I became one of the best students in my class, led by another German-speaking woman, Frau Kleefass, whom I later tracked down in Germany, and with whom I exchanged Christmas cards as a young adult. Rumor had it that Frau Kommer and her late husband were Nazi supporters during the war. This would not have been surprising since many (though far from all) of the local German speakers called *Schwaben* (Swabians, which was factually erroneous since their ancestors did not hail from Swabia but rather from Bavaria, the Palatinate, and Austria) expressed affinities for the Nazis and formed fifth columns, as was true of other German communities scattered across Eastern Europe. I asked my father in later life whether he and my mother knew anything about Frau Kommer's Nazi leanings. His answer confirmed my assumptions: "She probably was a Nazi, possibly a big one, but while your mother knew this, she simply did not care because Frau Kommer was known all across town as having the most beautiful German diction and great erudition in German literature and culture."

My parents' illogical contempt for all things Russian led me to construct the Markovits Theory of Intra-European Relations, which goes something like this: you hate all your neighbors, but those to your east and south you not only hate but disdain, you look down on them, you find them culturally and morally inferior and contemptible. (Witness Juliska's contempt for the Romanian language.) I am sure there are exceptions to this rule. While the Irish dislike the Brits, I do not think they find them culturally inferior. And I know nothing about how the Portuguese feel about the Spaniards, nor the Norwegians about the Swedes. However, if one looks at a map of Europe, this generalization pertains fairly well.

As was evident in the aforementioned descriptions of my parents'— particularly my mother's—admiration of German culture, this penchant was the legacy of the mid-to-late-eighteenth century, when, inspired by the writings and teachings of Moses Mendelssohn, the Jewish Enlightenment, or *Haskalah*, arose to form the steely spine of Central Europe's Jewish bourgeoisie. German became the lingua franca of all the middle-class, educated Jews of Central and Eastern Europe for 200 years. Any Jew of any cultural ambition anywhere in Central and Eastern Europe simply had to speak (indeed, read and write) very good, if not flawless, German.

This German-dominated worldliness was the most fundamental difference between the Yiddish-speaking *Ostjuden* of the Russian Empire and the eastern provinces of the Habsburg Empire, including Galicia and other parts of Central and Eastern Europe, and the German-speaking *Yekkes* of the West. *Yekke* hails from the German word *Jacke*, which means "jacket"; the term traditionally denoted Jews who lived in Germany proper and connoted a modern, secular person who followed the rules and was disciplined and straight-laced—the standard caricature of a German. This person represented the exact opposite of what everyday Jews, particularly in Eastern Europe, as well as their Gentile neighbors, believed a Jew to be: tradition-bound, religious, always skeptical of outside authorities, and even devious in some fashion by bucking the rules. I use *Yekke* here to describe a larger group of Westernized and secular Jews of Eastern and Central Europe outside of Germany's borders proper who disdained their brethren in the shtetls who did not wear "jackets," but rather kaftans and *shtramels*. While the *Ostjuden* found the *Yekkes* silly and supine in their extolling of German culture and their obedience to Gentile authorities, this negativity reflected a certain envy and even pity but not disdain. That remained the bailiwick of the *Yekkes* for their eastern Jewish brethren, whom they truly despised because the latter's existence threatened the former's tenuous acceptance by the non-Jewish world.

By having nothing to do with *Ostjuden*, the *Yekkes* hoped to salvage their newly acquired integration into the Gentile world. Auschwitz should have eliminated any of these illusions, but this was not the case with folks like my parents. As Marx and others presciently informed us, the lag of culture is one serious obstacle to progress. In the eyes of my parents, everything from the East was bad, and that included Romanians, Russians, Soviets, later the Chinese and even the Japanese, and most of all, unassimilated *Ostjuden* who never wore proper jackets. Yet another fine case for the Markovits Theory of Intra-European Relations!

Our Jewish Lives

Our Judaism was on some level shallow and on another level quite intense. We did not keep kosher (lean ham and spicy salami were particularly treasured delicacies in the Markovits household), and we did not keep the Sabbath. Of the many Jewish holidays, we celebrated only Rosh Hashana and Yom Kippur, with my parents fasting all twenty-six hours. We also held two seders—though without observing the rest of the Passover holiday—during which my father always invoked pogroms that would befall Jews when they opened their doors for the prophet Elijah. So we only opened a window!

My parents kept their families' *yahrzeits* most strictly, never forgetting to memorialize the deaths of any relative. Since my father recited the Kaddish not only for his two deceased parents—as did my mother for hers—but also for his two siblings killed in Auschwitz, plus various cousins, I remember seeing *yahrzeit* candles with considerable regularity throughout the year. Once, I recall my mother's particular gratitude to Josif for supplying her with candles, which apparently had become unavailable in Timişoara's state-owned and state-run stores, but were somehow available to officers of the Red Army.

My parents were also diligent about observing the memorial prayers (*Yiskor; Masker*) for the dead that were recited in the synagogue four times each year: at Passover, Shavuot, Yom Kippur, and Sukkot. These were the only times, other than for *Kol Nidre*, that my mother would venture to synagogue, when I so enjoyed looking up to the balcony and seeing her dressed elegantly and seated in the first row of the women's section amidst her girlfriends. My father and I would also attend Friday evening Shabbat services with some frequency, though never those on Saturday mornings. For some reason, *erev* Shabbat seemed more important for my parents, and perhaps for the community as a whole, than Shabbat itself.

Our temple—never called a *shul*—was built by the Austrian architect Carl Schumann, whose mentor was Ludwig Förster, architect of the famed Dohány Street synagogue in Budapest, Europe's largest and most beautiful. My father's pride in our synagogue, which he demonstrated every time we went there, had one particular basis: even though the building was inaugurated in 1865, it was re-inaugurated in 1872 by none other than venerable Emperor Francis Joseph I, who had traveled all the way from distant Vienna to the edge of his empire in order to dedicate this edifice to the Jewish community of Timişoara. The inculcation of such admiration and love for the great emperor would come to me in turn when we moved to Vienna in 1958. I encountered Francis Joseph's presence in some form or another pretty much every day of the nine years I spent in that city. My father would also never tire of mentioning that, among all the Habsburg emperors, only Francis Joseph I (1830–1916; emperor from 1848 to 1916) and Joseph II (1741–1790; Holy Roman Emperor after 1765 and sole ruler of the Habsburg lands after his mother Maria Theresa's death in 1780) were kind to the Jews.

The "Inner City synagogue," as it was called, followed the "neolog" interpretation of Judaism that had become so prominent among the Jewish bourgeoisie of Habsburg Europe: all prayers were conducted in Ashkenazi-accented Hebrew; women sat separate from men, with the former upstairs in the balcony, the latter downstairs in the main sanctuary. The cantor's praying was accompanied by a chorus and an organ, both of which were upstairs. My lifelong love of harmonies in general and choral music in particular hail from this glorious experience in Timişoara, where *Kol Nidre* for me became a quasi-operatic rather than a religious event. I will never forget Cantor Katz's beautiful rendition of the *bracha* for wine every Friday evening, when he turned to face the congregation from the *bima* and, with a beautiful gilded chalice full of wine in his hand, sang the blessing. Sublime!

All that I remember about our rabbi—Maximilian Miksa Drechsler, lovingly called *Matyi bácsi*, Uncle Matyi, by all congregants—was his kind face. But he commanded particular respect in the Markovits household by virtue of his having acquired not only a doctorate in philosophy from the Rabbinical Seminary in Budapest but for having studied at Oxford University. The other three synagogues in town are also worthy of mention. In the city's "factory town" district, there was the other neolog synagogue, an architectural gem built by the renowned Jewish architect Lipót Baumhorn and inaugurated in 1899. Two Orthodox synagogues built around this time, one by the German architect Karl Hart, as well as the Sephardic synagogue, round out the topography of Timişoara's public spaces for Jewish worship when I lived there in the 1950s. Only one of these edifices remains functional to the present.

My father taught me to read Hebrew so I could follow the prayers. Using the Ashkenazi pronunciation, he would sit with me over our dining room table, going over prayer after prayer, sometimes accompanying his reading with a warm melody. Only years later in Vienna, where I had an Israeli tutor for my bar mitzvah, did I learn the modern Hebrew pronunciation of these prayers, though to this day I often find myself regressing to the cadence and accent I learned from my father during my Timişoaran childhood. Indicative of my mother's gender and social standing, she was far too secular to read Hebrew. Instead, with some frequency she used a pocket-sized, 611-page book called *Mirjam: Imádságok zsidó nők számára*, which translates into *Miriam: Prayers for Jewish Women*, compiled and edited by Dr. Arnold Kiss, chief rabbi of Buda, the section of Budapest located north of the Danube. Containing not even one Hebrew word in the all-Hungarian text, my mother's copy was the book's 63rd edition, published in April 1922, meaning it must have been a popular book for the women of the Hungarian-speaking neolog movement among central Europe's educated bourgeois Jews.

Odd as it may sound, my Jewish upbringing in Timişoara was unimaginable without the prominence of sports—Association Football (soccer) in particular. On weekends, my father would take me to the grounds of my beloved Ştiinţa (Science), later named Politehnica, where we often met my father's Hungarian-speaking male Jewish friends and Romanian-speaking male non-Jewish colleagues from work. These outings provided an experience equivalent to that of a young American boy growing up cheering for his beloved baseball, basketball, and football teams. While there is nothing inherently Jewish in this, I cannot help but see an identical phenomenon in the lives of so many of my American-born male Jewish friends and colleagues, for whom this childhood experience, centered on their favorite sports teams, has remained an essential ingredient of their Jewish identity well into their adult lives. My father also took me to motorcycle races, where the sound of the revved-up engines fascinated me to such an extent that I made a habit of running around our apartment perfectly imitating the cadence of shifting gears.

Here I mean sports as a consumer, being a spectator and fan, rather than a participant in sports, or an athlete. If anything, the latter were disdained by many Jews, both *Ostjuden* and *Yekkes*, for similar cultural reasons, which held that playing sports, like engaging in most physical activities, was not a Jewish thing to do. Playing sports was a waste of time that should better be used for the study of Torah and other religious texts (for the *Ostjuden*), and for listening to classical music or reading literature (for the *Yekkes*). Both branches believed that the "people of the Book" had more important things to do than chasing a ball.

All this ran counter to Max Nordau's famous speech at the Second World Zionist Congress in Basel in 1898, when he coined the word *Muskeljudentum*, muscular Judaism, which was to separate the "new Jew" from the "old Jew" by dint of a physical prowess the latter never had. This spawned the creation of major Jewish sports clubs all over Europe and North America, of which names like Maccabi, Hakoah, Hapoel, Hagibor, and Bar Kochba are the best known. Jews became world-class athletes in swimming, water polo, fencing, soccer, boxing, baseball, and track, winning world championships and Olympic medals. As has been the case for all ethnicities, particularly bullied minorities like the Jews, sports stars were adored and welcomed as model representatives and strong protectors of the group. We all know what Hank Greenberg and Sandy Koufax meant to American Jews.

Indeed, Hank Greenberg's legend was so far-reaching that it must have reached even to Romania, because my father recounted to me in the 1950s that there existed a man in America who was so strong he hit baseballs way out of stadium. In other words, he was a *shtarker*, whom Jewish men could, and did, admire for a physical prowess they lacked. (By the time these images reached Romania, where baseball was unknown, the fact that hitting balls out of the park was part of the game had mutated into an interpretation of Samsonesque strength.)

To my father, there was an even more important *shtarker* than Greenberg, one whose sport my father and men around the world surely understood: Max Baer, the boxer who was heavyweight champion of the world from June 1934 to June 1935. But that was peanuts compared to his most dramatic feat: vanquishing the former world-champion Max Schmeling, Germany's star boxer and Adolf Hitler's favorite fighter, by technical knockout in Yankee Stadium on June 8, 1933. This made Baer a messiah-like hero to many Jews. More impressive still than defeating a German boxer who represented Hitler's National Socialism was that Baer did so wearing trunks displaying a Star of David, as he did for all his bouts. Even though Baer was only one-quarter Jewish, and even though he is buried in a crypt in St. Mary's Catholic Cemetery in Sacramento, California, for my father and millions of Jewish men of his generation, Max Baer was as Jewish as King David, and then some.

Still, the notion that the consumption of sports superseded its production in the valorization of Jewish male behavior remains. Aside from offering men a space for camaraderie, sports fandom also allowed them to use sports as a prop for intellectual pursuits such as remembering statistics and memorizing historical details, dispensing vast amounts of brainpower to master a body of knowledge akin to learning an entire language and its literature. Listening to Jewish men talk about sports is not that different from listening to them discuss the arcana of the Talmud.

Of course, the downside of this male bonding over sports was that it entirely excluded women. Never did I see my father more annoyed than when my mother dared ask him something during the radio broadcast of a soccer match or during a discussion of soccer-related matters with my uncle and their friends. Such displays of irritation never occurred with any other topic or event—not music, not politics, nothing! In Vienna and New York, where the television replaced the radio in the transmission of this holy ritual, women were just as unwelcome. Somehow the female voice and presence pierced this male sanctuary in a way that was intolerable!

One further sports-related incident where Jewishness mattered profoundly took place on July 4, 1954, when my father and I gathered around our radio to listen to Radio Budapest broadcast the World Cup final between Hungary and West Germany, played in the Swiss capital of Bern. The former, without a doubt the best national soccer team on the planet at the time, was a heavy favorite to defeat the Germans yet again, having done so by the score of 8-3 in the tournament's group stage. The Germans' upset of the Hungarian "golden team" (*aranycsapat*) in this game—forever celebrated as the "miracle of Bern" in Germany and bemoaned as its curse in Hungary—created a reaction in my father I will never forget. It influenced me throughout my life.

Far from being upset by the Hungarians' loss, as I expected him to be, my father turned to me calmly and said the result between these two teams representing evil nations was totally irrelevant to us. This event's only significance for us, so my father, was that it took place on the Fourth of July, the birthday of the only country in the world that was good to the Jews and where—God willing—I was going to end up some day, free of the burdens he'd had to endure all his life. This was the first time the United States of America assumed any kind of reality for me.

My pals in Timişoara were about a dozen kids with virtually identical backgrounds to mine: Hungarian-speaking Jewish boys and girls of neolog middle-class parents of various professions. Since communism diminished, though never alleviated, differences in wealth, none of us had more gadgets than the others, nor were our clothes and consumption habits different. We had our bicycles, which we rode in the city's many parks, and we lived fairly carefree and happy lives, largely unencumbered by our parents' pain from the nightmare of the Holocaust and their contemporary worries in negotiating the treacherous waters of a Stalinist dictatorship. I was a particularly cool and coveted figure among the boys for a while because my father surprised me with a soccer ball, the origins of which I never knew. This advantage disappeared after one of us kicked the ball into a window, shattering the glass and causing the man of the house to chase us for dear life.

All of my friends and their parents left Romania, as my father and I did in 1958, when the Soviet troops withdrew, or shortly thereafter. Their destinations varied, though most settled in Israel, the United States, Canada, and Vienna. I found out only much later that the Romanian government already had commenced a policy that it later augmented under the dictatorship of Nicolae Ceauşescu in the 1960s and 1970s: allowing folks belonging to ethnic minorities (such as Jews and Germans) to depart in return for payments in US dollars, with $2,000 per person being the normal price. Typically, this money was paid to the Romanian government by the respective emigrants' relatives and/or friends outside Romania. Or it was paid by the governments of Israel and the Federal Republic of Germany, which literally purchased the freedom of Jews and Germans so they could leave Romania and start new lives in these two countries.

I stayed in touch with quite a few of my pals, though I would not characterize any of these relationships as close, with two exceptions. Getta "Györgyi" Neumann, whom I already mentioned in the Preface to this book. Settling in France just outside Geneva, Getta has become the leading expert and guardian of all things Jewish in Timișoara, publishing a regular online newsletter in addition to various anthologies on this topic.

Then there is Hanna Doron, also mentioned in the Preface, my New York friend, who authored a wonderful book published in 2020, *Stories for My Children: A Memoir.* Hanna—always Anikó to me—is the older sister of my close childhood friend Jancsi, who was killed while serving in the Israeli Army during the War of Attrition in 1968. Through Getta's meticulous research on various Timișoarans, I know that many became successful in North America, Israel, Australia, and a scattering of countries in western Europe, pursuing careers in business, the law, arts, and in the academy at fancy places like MIT, the University of Chicago, and the Weizmann Institute of Science. None, however, had a more successful career than Ioan Holender, who became the longest-serving general director in the history of the Vienna State Opera, arguably the most prestigious institution of its kind in the world, and only the second Jew beside none other than Gustav Mahler to hold this august position.

My mother died on May 17, 1958, one day before what would have been her fortieth birthday. I was so distraught that my father and my aunt Manci did not allow me to visit her in the hospital. After consulting with our trusted pediatrician, my father and his sister also decided it would be best for me not to attend my mother's funeral. (This seems to have been a widely held belief in the mid-1950s, since I later learned that my wife-to-be, Kiki, was also detained from attending her father's funeral, on doctors' orders, in Vienna in 1956.) While I always understood the reason behind this decision, I never got a chance to say a proper good-bye to my mother and thank her for everything she had taught me. Instead, I do so at every *yahrzeit*: I have never missed one since then and will not to my dying day. The brightness of the annual candle and the rhythm of the Kaddish provide a proper framework for my communing with my mother. Occasionally, I would ask my father for the rationale for his decision not to allow me into the hospital or to the cemetery. Every time I did, his eyes welled up with tears and he turned away without saying a word, though he never cried. After all, men don't cry!

After we lost my mother in May 1958, my father and I lived in a blur. He sent me to the summer camp where I had gone the three previous years, but this time I became so upset that he returned two days later to stay with me. Here he was, an adult man among a mob of little kids and camp counselors who had taken vacation days from his demanding job to remain with his son at his summer camp! My father rented a small room next to the premises, and I moved in with him for the last few days of the session.

And then, on August 6, 1958, we got a huge surprise: my father's application to emigrate from Romania, which he had submitted for a number of years, was approved. We received a "Certificat de călătorie," a "certificate for travel"—not a passport but two sheets of paper—with the destination of Israel. We could take only two suitcases each and had to depart in short order. My aunt Manci moved in with us and supervised everything while crying constantly. And then an entire entourage of friends and relatives accompanied us to the railway station for our trip to the Hungarian border and then on to Budapest and westward to Vienna. This was a time when people in this part of the world simply did not travel abroad, and most decidedly not outside the communist bloc, unless they were departing for good, so the good-byes were dramatic and tear-filled. I do not remember much of anything other than my uncle Richard, Manci's husband, telling me a joke, as he always did, and always to Manci's annoyance.

My father and I boarded the train on September 1 and began a westward trek that was to involve a two-step immigration process, first to Vienna and then to the United States that was always my father's preferred destination and not Israel as stated on our travel document. The reason was completely simple and never a secret: He deemed the United States to offer me a better future than Israel. The train stopped in Curtici (Kürtös in Hungarian; Kurtitsch in German), the last Romanian locale before entering Hungary. Men from the Romanian border police and army boarded the train and started checking the passengers in our car. There were very few and most of them were neither Romanian nor Hungarian but foreigners—diplomats, most likely, or businessmen traveling from Romania to Hungary.

Three men came to my father and me and demanded to see our papers. One of the officials also asked us to open our four suitcases and place every item on the seats in our compartment. We did all this, and then one of the men asked my father upon perusing our travel certificates: "Where is Comrade Ida Markovits?"

My father responded that she had died on May 17 of that year.

"Oh," the man replied. "Then why is her name listed, and why is her photograph on the travel certificate on which your son appears?"

Something was clearly wrong, and things got testy. My father knew the head of police in Timişoara by virtue of his job at the bank, and he asked that the officer permit him to go to the stationmaster and give the police chief a call to clear up matters. This meant I was left alone on the train with two armed men, with the leader accompanying my father to the stationmaster. The officials were not particularly intimidating, but I was nervous beyond words and terribly frightened.

And then—sports to the rescue! One of them asked me which of the two Timişoara teams I liked. When I told him Ştiinţa, he smiled from ear to ear and said he, too, liked Ştiinţa. So we started to talk about the team's players and prospects for the season that had just commenced. After what seemed an eternity, my father and the officer returned, with the latter being annoyed for whatever reason. He assumed a gruff demeanor and told the two soldiers to go through every one of our items, and if need be rip them open to see whether we were smuggling any forbidden things like jewelry out of the country.

And then the nightmare happened. The man got suspicious of my most beloved teddy bear, whom I called Dovi—"little bear" in Hebrew—the only personal item I had taken with me on this monstrous journey.

The officer took a knife and slit the bear open, with the filling flying all over the place. He did not find any of the suspected contraband, but he had destroyed Dovi. I do not remember whether he apologized. It would not have mattered. Soon the train departed, and I cried inconsolably: 1958 would prove to be one tough year in my life!

CHAPTER TWO

A Paean to Tante Trude
(Who Might or Might Not Have Been a Nazi)

Leaving Timişoara in early September 1958 was nothing short of traumatic for me. My mother had died on May 17 of that year—one day shy of her fortieth birthday—and my father informed me sometime in the middle of August that we were to leave Timişoara in barely two weeks to go west, which meant saying a possibly final good-bye to all my pals and my beloved aunt Manci and uncle Richard. This was serious business.

After a two-day journey with a daylong stop in Budapest, where we stayed with one of my father's cousins, my father and I arrived at Vienna's Westbahnhof in the evening. There, we were met by one of my father's friends, whom he knew from his university days in Budapest. The man's name was István "Pista" Folian, but, as my father readily informed me, he had formerly been called Friedmann; true to the habits of the Hungarian-Jewish educated bourgeoisie, he had Magyarized his last name. A man of medium height, with a friendly face and kind eyes, he welcomed us warmly. Pista was accompanied by his wife Cigi who, per my father's repeated assertions, had been among the most beautiful girls in Budapest's Jewish society. She still appeared to be one elegant lady: lots of red lipstick, elegant pumps, a nice dress. She was the prototype of the woman my father always said had only one profession in life: being beautiful.

The Folians took us to a small hotel where they had booked a room for us. I have no idea who paid for this, because my father was not allowed to take one penny with him to the West. All I knew was that Vienna looked so big and majestic. Most of all, during our taxi ride to the hotel, I was impressed by the neon advertising on the buildings, something that did not exist in socialist Romania, most certainly not in provincial Timișoara. I remember one ad in particular: a neon sign for Osram, a major German company manufacturing a bevy of electrical items, including light bulbs, which touted its product to be as bright as the shiny day: *OSRAM, hell wie der lichte Tag.*

At this juncture, my father did not know where to go next: New York, where he could join his eldest brother, Alex, who had survived Auschwitz; or Tel Aviv, where his other older brother, Benő, had emigrated after the war. After all, Israel was the official destination of our journey, at least per our Romanian travel papers. My father was much closer in age to Benő; the two had shared more experiences than my father did with Alex or any of his other siblings, since only he and Benő had not been deported by the Germans and their Hungarian allies. Or maybe we should stay in Vienna? As it turned out, even at this stage my father was leaning toward New York, though with much hesitation and many worries. His life ended up being an uneasy amalgam between an idealized but failed New York (and America) and a disliked but actualized Vienna.

At this point one thing was clear: school had just commenced, and I had to be enrolled in fourth grade, which, in the Austrian and Romanian school systems at the time, constituted the last year of elementary school before the big jump into the tracked world of eight years in a *Gymnasium*. This paved the path for further education at university, or four years in a *Hauptschule*, which ended formal school-based education at the age of fourteen though often followed by a vocational education of some kind lasting up to five years. Since I had attended a German-language elementary school in Timișoara—Nikolaus Lenau Schule, *Şcoala Medie nr. 2*—for the first three grades, and since I had been tutored in German by my mother and Frau Kommer, my German was excellent, and my father expected me to make the transition seamlessly from my elementary school in Timișoara to an equivalent school in Vienna. But which school to pick? And how? And in such a hurry!

Enter my father's pal Folian, who had arrived in Vienna exactly two years before we did, leaving his home in Budapest in the fall of 1956, during the Hungarian Revolution. He had a son who was one year older than I was but with one big difference: when Folian's son, George, arrived in town, he did not speak a single German word. So the Folians had set out to find someone who would teach their son German, help him with his schoolwork, and prepare him for the all-important entrance examination for the *Gymnasium*, the gateway to heaven for middle-class Jews like the Folians and my father.

This person turned out to be a certain Hildegard Kohler, who lived at Lerchenfelderstrasse 139 in Apartment 11. She was a recently divorced woman who had a 14-year-old daughter and a shaggy dog and who was a part-time elementary school teacher with an elegant German writing style and a fine knowledge of arithmetic, both of which were major requirements for the entrance exam to the *Gymnasium*. The Folians prevailed upon Frau Kohler to have George live with her for an entire year, which was a double benefit to all: George was to learn superb German in an all-German speaking environment, master his school subjects properly, prepare for the big test, and enjoy a warm and safe home while his parents searched for, and found, the business and apartment that would constitute a successful new life. What worked so well for George should also work well for András, no?

My father contacted Frau Kohler the day after our arrival in Vienna, and they set up a time when he and I would go to her apartment, meet her, and discuss a possible arrangement. We took three trams from our hotel in Vienna's third district to the apartment building at Lerchenfelderstrasse 139. I was very impressed that the engineers on these trams performed virtually identical tasks to their counterparts back home in Timișoara, where one of my favorite pastimes had been to ride the city's trams and observe the engineers handling the manual shifts—speed stick with their left hand, brake stick with their right—with godlike dexterity and authority. I never wanted to be a fireman, but an engineer lording over the 6 line in Timișoara was an entirely different matter.

I was pleased to see that Vienna, too, had trams. But taking the Number 46, a much more modern train with closed doors that did not allow hanging on the stairs or riding in the caboose, which was so much fun on the older trams in Timişoara, put me off. This tram's engineer sat behind a glass door in an enclosed space that made watching his every move hard, if not impossible. I cannot describe my delight later that day when, upon our return to the hotel from Frau Kohler's apartment, we boarded a more old-fashioned tram that resembled the ones I knew from Timişoara. In this version, the engineer stood virtually unprotected inside the tram, working his speed and brake sticks close to the passengers. Only his uniform gave him away as the man in charge of our lives.

In this car, just like in Timişoara, there existed an open-ended caboose where folks lingered, often hanging from the steps while the tram was moving, even at some speed. Moreover, I noticed that in Vienna, too, young men used this open caboose to jump from and onto the tram while it was in motion. I was thrilled to be able to continue riding these old-fashioned trams, which were to disappear from Vienna's street scene a year or two after our arrival.

While intrigued by Vienna's trams, I was disappointed by the drabness of the buildings and streets we passed in both directions of our journey. Where were the majestic buildings about which my mother had told me so much, and which I expected to see in the former capital of the great Habsburg Empire? I remember my father's excitement upon passing a store called Julius Meinl, branches of which existed all over Vienna and Austria. As the tram sped by, my father asked whether I remembered that everybody in Timişoara called the main state-run and state-owned grocery store on the town's main drag "Julius Meinl" instead of by its official name, *alimentară de stat* (state grocery shop), even though that name and store had disappeared by 1948. Meinl stores existed all over the Habsburg Empire including in Timişoara. They were one of the constant reminders of this empire's cultural legacy, which lasted well into the second half of the twentieth century, long after the actual empire and the real Meinl had disappeared from these premises; communism was simply no match for this culture's staying power.

Having arrived at our stop towards the end of Lerchenfelderstrasse (where the street intersects with Kaiserstrasse), we left our tram and looked for Building 139. Stores ran along both sides of the street, and we located the proper building, which housed a seedy *Gasthaus*, a combination of a cheap restaurant and a neighborhood bar. We entered the building, which was dank and damp and dark with no elevator, as was true of most such buildings in Vienna, Budapest, Berlin, Prague, and many other Central European cities. We walked up two or three half-flights until we noted the number 11 on the door. We rang the bell and were greeted by the barking of a dog. Soon thereafter, a chubby but kind-faced blonde woman opened the door and welcomed us, all while trying to shoo away the big, shaggy animal.

We entered a small, dark hallway, then a narrow pathway which led to five doors: the furthest to our left was the toilet; followed by the next, which was the bathroom; then the kitchen; then two doors to our right, leading to the living room; and the remaining door, which led to the bedroom. We went into the living room, and Frau Kohler served us delicious homemade cookies with tea. She informed us that her daughter, Birgit, who was away at school, was 14 years old and lived with her. She and my father discussed how she had housed George in a small alcove off the living room, how she sent him to a fine elementary school just around the corner, how she taught him to speak, read, and write German, and how she prepped him for the big entrance examination to *Gymnasium*, the dreaded *Aufnahmeprüfung*.

George's parents would come most weekends to pick up their son so he could spend time with them, even as they were busy arranging their new lives in Vienna. I forgot what sum the Folians had paid Frau Kohler for this arrangement, but whatever it was, she and my father agreed I was to do the same as George had done: move in with her, attend the adjacent elementary school, and prep for the examination that was to be held in the spring of 1959. Frau Kohler smiled at me all the time and informed me that I would be so much easier for her to tutor than George since my German was so good. To my great surprise, she gave me a hug upon our departure and called me *Schatzi*, little treasure, which she was to call me for the rest of her life.

The deal was done: I was to come to her place the following Monday; she would bring me to school and pick me up thereafter, and my new life would commence. That fateful Monday arrived. Leaving our shabby but clean hotel, my father took me by my hand and we embarked on our tram ride to Frau Kohler's place. My father had packed a suitcase with my clothing and possessions—basically, I was to move away from him, at least until the coming Saturday. We arrived at Lerchenfelderstrasse 139, and only Frau Kohler's shaggy dog made me feel at ease, perhaps because my father disliked him (and all dogs) so much.

I hugged my father good-bye, and then Frau Kohler walked me to the elementary school located on Neustiftgasse. She brought me to my classroom, where I was greeted by the young lady who was to become my fourth-grade teacher. When I entered, I could not believe my eyes: on the front wall hung a photograph of Adolf Schärf, Austria's president at the time, and a huge cross with a Jesus figure hanging from it. What a contrast to the red star and the picture of Gheorghe Gheorghiu-Dej that adorned every classroom back in Timişoara! As I was to find out later that academic year, the staying power of the Austro-Hungarian curricular system, whether here or in Romania, was tenacious: with the exception of geography and history, which clearly had a Romanian flavor in Timişoara and an Austrian slant in Vienna, everything in my new school was taught in a virtually identical manner to the old school. My cognitive and intellectual transition from third grade in Timişoara to fourth grade in Vienna was basically seamless.

Other aspects of this transition proved much rockier. After Frau Kohler picked me up from school at noon or 1 p.m.—there was, and still is, virtually no afternoon school in continental Europe—she took me to her home (which was now my home as well) and served me a nice lunch. Then she walked with me into the park that one could see outside her window, a small, beautiful expanse called Kaiserpark, which, most importantly for me, had an enclosed soccer field similar to urban basketball courts in the United States, where I enviously observed boys a tad older than me passionately playing. Frau Kohler noticed my attraction to the game and turned me away, insisting—as she did all her life—that football was for proletarian boys and hooligans, not for gentlemen like me.

We then walked back to our apartment, and lo and behold, whom should I meet but Frau Kohler's daughter, Birgit, a pretty brunette who clearly did not appreciate my presence. She made a point of telling me that only she was to take the dog for a walk, that the dog was hers, and not for sharing. I respected Birgit's directive to such an extent that the dog became a non-entity in my life. I remember the dog dying a few months after my father and I moved in with Frau Kohler and Birgit, but I cannot recall that they mourned its passing. I have forgotten the dog's name, which is uncharacteristic of my later life, when I have come to remember the name of every dog I have been introduced to. It is people's names I now forget.

After Frau Kohler helped me with my homework, and after we had supper, and after she showed me the alcove off the living room where I was to sleep, I fell apart. I began to cry inconsolably, sobbing with such desolation that Frau Kohler had to call the hotel and contact my father, whom she asked to come fetch me, which he did. Rarely was I that happy to see him. And off we went to the tram, this time in the other direction from that morning, back to the hotel, which appeared so wonderfully welcoming that I hugged the late-night receptionist, a scruffy middle-aged fellow who hardly expected such affection from a stranger.

After that, my father proceeded to take me to school every morning and then picked me up at Frau Kohler's around 6 p.m. and took me back to the hotel. This routine went on until November or so, when Frau Kohler asked my father whether he would not be interested in moving in with us and sleeping in the living room, which had a fine bed. He would pay rent, and pay for her cooking and housecleaning, while we were basically her subletters.

And that is exactly what happened. My father moved in, and he remained well after my departure for college in New York in 1967. He continued to live as Frau Kohler's subtenant well into the early 1970s, even after he became a relatively wealthy man. Frau Kohler became my surrogate mother. I always remained *Schatzi* to her, until her dying day in Geneva, where she had moved in the 1970s to be with Birgit, who married a florist in that beautiful Franco-Swiss city. She never called me by my real name, "Andreas" in its German version, or "András" in its Hungarian, which my father used throughout his life. I was always *Schatzi* for Frau Kohler.

And I always referred to her as Tante Trude, even though her first name was Hildegard, which, at least to my knowledge, never contained "Trude" as an endearment. Tante Hilde or Tante Hildi perhaps, but Trude? I always used the formal *Sie* in addressing her, well into adulthood, though she, of course, used the familiar *Du* from the first time we met. My father and Frau Kohler always remained *per Sie*, as they say in German, my father referring to her always as Frau Kohler and she addressing him always as *Herr Doktor*, so much so that I remain convinced she did not even know his first name—Lajos in Hungarian or Ludwig in German—nor even his last name of Markovits.

Essentially, our landlady became my surrogate mother for my nine-year stay in Vienna. She took care of me when I was ill, cooked all meals for me, packed my school lunches, and washed and sewed my clothes. Frau Kohler even conspired with me when, at 16, I wanted to sneak the occasional girl up to my place in the afternoon, and she left the apartment, her own home, to spend a few hours in the neighborhood café reading magazines!

Frau Kohler was my most loyal ally. Not only did she leave her own apartment so I could bring girls home, but—much more importantly—always had my back in my frequently tense relations with my father. She mostly took my side, but in a diplomatic way so as not to annoy my father by confronting him, but rather to persuade him, to win him over with her intelligence and intuition. I confided in Tante Trude to an extent I never did with any other adult. She was even a buddy of sorts. One of my pal's parents caught him with cigarettes, which he was forbidden to purchase or smoke. Alas, he had somehow acquired five or six cartons of Chesterfields that he did not want to lose or give up. To the rescue rode Tante Trude. I told her the story, and she immediately found a place in our apartment where these cartons would be safe and my friend could always have access to them.

Who was this saintly figure, Frau Kohler? Remember: this all began because my father wanted to find somebody who could best prepare me for the difficult entrance examination to the *Gymnasium*, on which so much of my future depended. Frau Kohler performed that task brilliantly. Not only did I master this examination, I gained admission to what was arguably Austria's best-known secondary school, the Theresianische Akademie, where I commenced studies in September 1959, exactly one year after my father and I arrived as penniless refugees from Timișoara.

But already in that first year, Frau Kohler became so much more than a good tutor who happened to have a warm room in which I could feel safe and protected. In addition to being a teacher of German writing and literature and mathematics, she was our landlady and we her tenants. But the roles became oddly reversed very soon. In most measurable ways, my father and I became the bosses, with Birgit and Frau Kohler our subordinates. We were catered to; *our* needs became paramount. Frau Kohler became not only my surrogate mother, but also my father's loyal servant. To be sure, my father was immensely generous to Frau Kohler in his remuneration of her labors, for which he paid her in addition to the monthly rent, plus all the utilities and the monthly fees for our telephone, television, and radio.

Frau Kohler did not have a television set until we moved into her apartment. No doubt her material life improved immensely with our presence in her apartment. But we were the ones who were in debt to her. An arrangement that was supposed to have lasted one year, in which I was a temporary tenant in preparation for an exam, mutated into a nine-year stay for me until my departure for Columbia and a much longer one for my father, who stayed as Frau Kohler's subtenant for a number of years thereafter.

Out of nowhere, this saint appeared in my life, barely four months after my mother died and I had to leave my home and hearth and face an unknown future. Frau Kohler performed all the maternal functions traditionally associated with a mother in Western culture. Yet she was also an aunt-like figure, so much so that my aunt Manci, my father's sister, who joined us later in Vienna, rightly and understandably was jealous of my affection for Tante Trude.

I can remember only one instance when I had a disagreement, let alone a fight, with Frau Kohler (one has conflicts with one's mother, whereas one typically does not have conflicts with one's aunts). This single unpleasantness arose because I lent a pair of extra bathing trunks to a young Ghanaian student whom I met at the entrance of one of Vienna's main public pools. He wanted to take a swim but had no Austrian schillings and no bathing suit. Above all, he did not speak any German. So I came to the rescue with everything: money, English, and bathing trunks. We had a nice chat, and he was thankful to me for helping him.

When I came home and told Tante Trude the story, she grabbed this bathing suit out of my bag, as well as the one I had worn, and threw them both in the garbage. She offered no explanation. However, her eyes made clear that for her, a bathing suit worn by an African, which had contaminated the suit I had worn, could not be placed in the washing machine. Both had to be discarded by dint of being permanently unclean. To be fair to Tante Trude: I have no idea how she would have reacted had I lent my bathing suit to a white stranger. But I believe that her gaze would have been less fierce. And quite possibly, she would have opted to use the washing machine.

I was very upset, but I never said one word to Frau Kohler. Why? Upon later reflection, there were three reasons for my silence. First, in contrast to the arguments one engages in with one's real parents, I didn't see any point in confronting Frau Kohler on issues related to politics, culture, or society, so why discuss racism with her? Second, I did not want to upset her, as she might have drawn my father into the argument, and I dreaded that he might agree with Frau Kohler's action, which, in his case, would have led to a real showdown. And third, I genuinely loved Frau Kohler and had a great gig going with her on all fronts: food, drink, love, comfort. Why jeopardize such a fine arrangement?

The incident with the Ghanaian student did not represent a fight between Frau Kohler and me as much as it affirmed the deep racism that existed at the time in all of Viennese, Austrian, and European society, of which Frau Kohler was merely one innocuous member. And yet, what stuns me even now is that the constant and always difficult "Jewish question" never arose with Frau Kohler. After all, here were two Jewish Hungarian-speaking men from Romania who had moved into her apartment one day and somehow stayed for nine years and then some. I can barely convey how all-invasive and omnipresent the issue of antisemitism has been for European Jews, probably for all of their existence on that continent, but certainly since the Holocaust. Add to this a whole other dimension of fear, apprehension and complexity in the successor countries to Nazi Germany such as Austria and the Federal Republic!

Who is an antisemite; who is not? Who likes the Jews; who does not? How does this event or political development help the Jews; how does it harm them? Did this person look at me funny because he knows I am Jewish, or for another reason? The complex "Jewish question" never abates. But miracle of miracles: somehow the issue of Jews never came up with Frau Kohler! My father had no money to organize a bar mitzvah party for me on the second day of Rosh Hashanah in 1961, when—for the first time in postwar Vienna—a bar mitzvah was celebrated on one of the High Holidays. The big event was held in Vienna's Stadttempel in the Seitenstettengasse, the only real synagogue in town at the time. And right after the services there was a nice little afternoon party for Andy and his closest friends in Apartment 11 of Lerchenfelderstrasse 139, thanks to Hildegard Kohler.

Frau Kohler made us a hearty meal before every Yom Kippur and another meal after we broke the fast. She never cooked "Jewish food," but she also refrained from offering us any pork products, which represented such a staple of Viennese cuisine. The only time we explicitly did not eat at home was on the two Seder nights of Passover—we either went to my aunt Manci (once she had arrived in Vienna from Timişoara) or to our Jewish friends in town. Never did I speak to my father about anything Jewish as related to Frau Kohler, something we did in connection with pretty much everybody else, near and far. I never experienced an ounce of behavior or heard the most veiled utterance on Frau Kohler's part that could be interpreted as even vaguely antisemitic. And trust me: my antennae for picking up such slights have been sensitive throughout my life!

Remarkably, it never occurred to me until this writing that I had absolutely no idea what Frau Kohler did or thought during the Second World War, when she clearly was an adult and married to Herr Kohler. For all I know, Frau Kohler could have been among the Viennese mob that delighted in watching Jews on their hands and knees being forced by Nazi thugs to clean the streets with their toothbrushes. Her former husband could have been an active participant in the slaughtering of Jews on the Eastern Front. For all I know, Herr Kohler could have belonged to the SA or SS or other explicitly Nazi organizations, whose membership was higher per capita in Austria than in Germany proper. Such questions never bothered my father or me one bit. Frau Kohler was a non-Jewish Austrian woman who somehow floated above the entire Jewish Question that pervaded our relationship with everybody else. Very strange!

Then again, maybe not so strange after all. Rather, such obliviousness might have sprung from pure and unadulterated self-interest on my father's part, as well as mine. What could a confrontation have brought us? Would we have moved out had we discovered horrors in Frau Kohler's past? What if we had learned that Frau Kohler was an antisemite or—God forbid—a real Nazi? I really doubt this was true, but we chose not to find out because that was the convenient option, perhaps even the prudent one. Clearly, someone's racism towards others cannot compete with the love one has for oneself in terms of keeping a good thing going.

Despite the swashbuckling panache my father liked to exhibit with his irresistible charm and overt optimism, he was a hurting refugee who had just lost his wife and moved to a new place, which he regarded as temporary, since he was about to continue his emigrant's journey to a new continent. All this with a young child and no job. In such a precarious situation, one does not indulge in fact-finding missions about the possible antisemitism of a woman who provides comfort and shelter. I was a bereft little boy who desperately wanted and needed a mother and a home, both of which Tante Trude provided.

And what about Frau Kohler? What did she gain from this whole arrangement? At some point, I began to wonder if she and my father had a sexual relationship. After all, he was a single man and she a single woman living under the same roof in very close quarters. I never thought so, but during my last trip to Geneva in 2003, when I met Birgit for a nice meal, I asked her explicitly, assuming women talk about these issues more readily than men. And Birgit confirmed unequivocally that they did not! She said my father had plenty on his plate with his two girlfriends, Maria and Helga, the former of whom Frau Kohler liked, the latter less so. Frau Kohler's experience with her husband, Birgit's father, was so devastating that, according to Birgit, Frau Kohler had given up on men altogether.

Of course, the financial security must have been comforting for the Kohlers. Our presence substantially enhanced their material well-being. But was that all? Frau Kohler obviously respected my father immensely, and she genuinely loved me, but were those reason enough to take us in and cater to our every need and whim? Perhaps she wanted to help Jews because she was atoning for something dreadful in her past. Or she wanted to help Jews because she liked them. (Yes, rare as they may be, philo-Semites do exist.) Perhaps she had always wanted a son—or she had a son whom she had lost. This actually crossed my mind a few times when she gleefully abetted my boyish schemes, indulging me as mothers indulge their sons, but not their daughters.

For the Markovits men, the tally was clearer. Frau Kohler was a nonsexual wife who represented the third member of my father's troika of Viennese women: Helga—mistress; Maria—wife-like girlfriend; Frau Kohler—maid, nurse, cook, homemaker. For me, Tante Trude was a conflict-free substitute for the mother I had so recently lost, as well as a loving and trusted friend. I will never forgive my father and myself for never once inviting Tante Trude to join us in any of the thousands of meals that she prepared for us in my nine years of living in her apartment in Vienna. I never saw her sitting at the table with us, sharing with us the excellent meal that she had prepared for us. Instead, she served us our food and then left the room, always eating by herself, and often food of lesser quality than she made for us.

Unconscionable! Forever shaming! I only remember Tante Trude's presence at the table where my father and I ate at least two meals a day, sometimes three, when she helped me with my homework back in my first year in town preparing for my entrance exam to the fancy Theresianische Akademie. Frau Kohler was my substitute mother; she was my fun aunt; she was our landlord; she was our maid; she was our cook; but to my great chagrin and embarrassment she was never our equal.

Four Friendships:
Discovering America in Vienna

One of Frau Kohler's tasks was to get me to a level in mathematics and German that would allow me to excel at the infamous *Aufnahmeprüfung*, the entrance examination to Austria's elite secondary-school system called the *Gymnasium*. This written exam, administered at the end of fourth grade, decided whether, at the age of ten, a young boy or girl would be able to attend university eight years later. With only these *Gymnasia* conferring the much-coveted *Matura*, the Austrian equivalent to the German *Abitur*, the French *Baccalauréat*, or the British A-levels, which permitted a young person to proceed to studies at all institutions of post-secondary education, the tracking of the Austrian education system was beyond brutal.

Failure at this exam meant being tracked into a *Hauptschule* that, unlike the 8-year *Gymnasium*, ended after four years, necessitating entry into the job market at age fourteen in some kind of apprenticeship position or proceeding to a technical school or vocational program. None of these options offered anywhere near the cultural cachet or economic opportunities accorded by a completed *Gymnasium* education, never mind a successfully concluded university degree. Forget the material disadvantages that failing to attend a *Gymnasium* entailed. By virtue of our social standing, education and cultural capital, attending a *Gymnasium* was beyond a must. Passing this exam was compelling because crossing from the *Hauptschule* track to the *Gymnasium's* was at this time nearly impossible, as was entering a university without a *Matura*. (Both imped-iments have thankfully become much less rigid and foreboding over the past five decades.)

My failing this examination would have been a disaster on all lev-els, most of all in the realm of shame. There is no doubt in my mind that I would have borne the burden of failure at this exam for the rest of my life. To my relief and my father's delight and pride, I performed su-perbly. But this was not sufficient. My father was eager to have me enter Vienna's famed Theresianische Akademie (better known as the Theresia-num), which the son of his pal Pista Folian from Budapest, also tutored by Frau Kohler, had reached. Purely on practical grounds, the Theresian-um was one of Vienna's only schools that did not end the day around 1 or 2 p.m., as all other schools in Austria did at the time and has remained common elsewhere on the European continent. Secondary schools typ-ically commenced at 8 a.m., six days a week, and, following five or six classes interrupted by ten-minute breaks, finished at 1 or 2 p.m., with-out offering the students lunch or any kind of afternoon activities. Satur-day classes often ended at noon, with only four sessions of teaching. But the Theresianum offered an American-style setting in that about half the students spent the afternoon playing sports, engaged in other extracur-ricular activities such as music and drama, and doing their homework in a four-hour supervised study time. They then left for home at 7 p.m.

The other half of the student body consisted of full boarders who lived at the school and only went home every second weekend. Where-as the Folians had their son George become a full boarder at the school, my father realized this was out of the question for me, given the frag-ile nature of my psyche following my mother's death and our precarious situation living in a Viennese sublet as stateless refugees. But the half-boarder option was ideal. I would not need to hang around Frau Kohler's small apartment all afternoon, often without supervision because my fa-ther had a full-time job and Frau Kohler worked part-time at a garment store as a sales clerk, while her daughter, Birgit, did not appreciate my presence in their apartment.

But towering above these practical considerations was the Theresian-um's prestige, which was arguably more potent in countries like Hungary and the western parts of Romania (my father's domain) than in western Austria. Founded in 1746 by the Empress Maria Theresa (hence the name) with the express order to become an institution offering a superb education to the sons of the aristocracy, the school developed into a breeding ground for the Habsburg Empire's potentates—officers, judges, bureaucrats, administrators, in other words people of pedigree, accomplishment, and authority, whom my father and his family viewed with respect and awe from faraway Satmar in the hinterlands of the Empire's eastern provinces.

Even after 1849, when the Theresianum opened to commoners, the place retained an aristocratic aura that my status-conscious father admired. After serving as a so-called NAPOLA (*Nationalpolitische Erziehungsanstalt*, or National Political Educational Institution) under the Nazis, it was taken over by the Soviets in 1945, followed by the Americans. With both of these occupying powers departing Austria in May 1955, the path was set for the Theresianum to become a public secondary school. It did just that in September 1957, when it began offering classes as a special *Gymnasium*.

The institution became one of Austria's, perhaps even Central Europe's, leading secondary schools for boys. The specialness of the place consisted of its extraordinarily difficult admissions requirements, plus an added curricular challenge in that the Theresianum required not only the sciences and mathematics that were common in more technical secondary schools, but also Latin and other languages (though no ancient Greek) featured in more humanities-oriented institutions.

When the acceptance of George Folian made clear to my father that the Theresianum accepted Jews, the path seemed clear for my fulfilling my father's dream. But hold on. My father had conveniently forgotten—or suppressed—that George Folian had entered the Theresianum as a Catholic. As such, he attended obligatory mass and participated in the semi-weekly Catholic religion classes that were part of the Austrian curriculum in all *Gymnasia*. The Folians belonged to that large group of secularized Hungarian Jews, mostly denizens of Budapest, who sought full assimilation by Magyarizing their names (from Friedmann to Folian as already mentioned) and who distanced themselves from anything Jewish as best they could.

Indeed, we discovered in town second cousins from my mother's side who also hailed from Budapest, who had arrived in Vienna after the Hungarian Revolution of 1956, and who shed their Judaism by converting to Catholicism. This was anathema to my father. After these cousins invited us to dinner and my father learned of their complete distancing from all things Jewish, we dismissed them completely. My father seemed much more tolerant of his pal Pista Folian than of our relatives, perhaps because Pista proved to be such a trailblazer for my father, particularly by discovering and passing Frau Kohler and the Theresianum on to me.

Dr. Roger Kerber, an Unexpected Ally

Before I enrolled, my father decided to talk to the Theresianum's headmaster (or director in the Austrian nomenclature), a certain Dr. Roger Kerber, better known as Herr Hofrat, meaning Mr. Court Councilor, a common honorific in republican Austria, which had ceased to have a court of which one could be a councilor in 1918. My father sought this meeting to ask Hofrat Kerber whether I could enter the Theresianum while keeping my Jewish identity and faith. I can barely convey the enormity of the respect and trepidation my father brought to bear on this meeting. He was so nervous that he perspired heavily on each of the three trams we needed to take from our house in Lerchenfelderstrasse in Vienna's seventh district to the Theresianum on Favoritenstrasse in its fourth. I was numb with fear and worry.

With his finely groomed mustache and horn-rimmed glasses, Dr. Kerber, who, in addition to being the school's headmaster, was an expert teacher of French literature and language, struck an impressive posture, not to mention that he spoke in a regal baritone. My father must have been intimidated, but immediately upon our taking our seats in Dr. Kerber's office he got to the point: that he had been enamored of and impressed by the Theresianum all his life well before our arrival in Vienna; that he wanted me to become a student there, but feared that my being possibly the sole Jew among all the boys in the school would pose a problem. Moreover, my father did not want me to attend mass nor participate in the twice-weekly classes on Catholic religion.

Dr. Kerber's response was astonishing. He was completely understanding of my father's worries and concerns, in terms not only of the Theresianum, but of Austria as a whole. Even more memorably, he said something to the effect that Austria had not yet come to terms with its own dark past (he never uttered the word "Nazi"), which was nothing short of miraculous, as Austria had made the denial of its involvement in Nazi Germany the centerpiece of its postwar identity. This denial was not to be contested until the infamous Waldheim Affair in the 1980s and Chancellor Franz Vranitzky's moving speech to the Knesset in the 1990s. At the time of my father's conversation with Dr. Kerber, the exculpatory motto still held that pristine little Austria had been raped by big, evil Nazi Germany, with Austria becoming the first victim of the Nazi conquest of Europe. This massive distortion of history not only served the Austrians' self-image extremely well throughout the postwar era; it also placed Austria in an immensely favorable light in the world.

To be sure, world opinion always favors little countries over big ones. Few people hate Switzerland; the Scandinavian and Benelux countries are everyone's darlings. But to succeed as Austria has in bamboozling the world into believing that Hitler was German and Beethoven Austrian takes some doing, of which the perennial lie concerning Austria's innocence during the Nazi era is a central component. For the director of one of Austria's leading *Gymnasia*, well known for its deeply conservative orientation on the part of the faculty, the students, and their parents, to allude to the country's "dark past" was amazingly enlightened and insightful back in 1959.

Dr. Kerber promised my father he would personally vouch for my well-being in the school and see that I not be disadvantaged in any way because of my being Jewish. The issue of not going to mass was easily solved. Moreover, while my Catholic classmates had their twice-weekly religion classes, I would be away from the classroom having a free hour during which I could not leave the school's premises, but was allowed to do my homework or occupy myself in any way I chose. Quite likely, I would spend that hour with the few Protestant students who would not partake in the instruction in Catholicism taught by a priest. Indeed, Dr. Kerber continued, I would be granted leave from the school's afternoon activities once a week to travel to another *Gymnasium* in town, where all Jewish students of my age and grade would gather from all the schools in Vienna to receive instructions in Jewish religion, history, and a bit of Hebrew language. The Austrian state had to assure that all students received religious education; this was mandated by the nationally centralized curriculum. But no school in Vienna—excepting the Lycée Français—had enough Jewish students to warrant hiring a teacher of Jewish studies and Hebrew, making the pooling of students in one location a necessity.

After Dr. Kerber informed my father that I would start in the 1B and not in the 1A class, my father's and my happiness were complete. In the Theresianum at the time, the B classes commenced with English as the first foreign language and included it in the curriculum for eight years, with the A classes featuring French instead. Both classes began with Latin in the third grade (this was akin to seventh grade in American terms, since the first four grades of elementary school did not count in the *Gymnasium's* numbering of its eight years) and then added French for four years in the B track and English for the same amount of time in the A track. As befit the Theresianum's "specialness," Russian was added as a fourth language (alongside English, French, and Latin) in the sixth grade for the last three years of school. None of these were elective courses, which essentially were nonexistent in the Austrian secondary-school curriculum at the time, in which the kinds of courses, their numbers, and their content were strictly set by the Austrian ministry of education.

Having more English than French was triply important for my father. First, I had already received English lessons in Timişoara from Mrs. Vágó, making my English at this time quite good. Second, we were still on course to emigrate to the United States, where knowing English was vital. And third, even though my father admired French culture and loved the sound of the French language, his real love and gratitude was singularly directed toward the Anglo-American world, which he saw as our only savior from the two grand maladies of the twentieth century that had so burdened his life: National Socialism and Stalinism. His poor knowledge of English remained one of his true sources of shame and embarrassment, which he never overcame and which ultimately contributed to my father's decision to leave New York and return to Vienna, a wise move bespeaking ultimate defeat. Tellingly, his faulty and accented German never bothered him. Deep down, he took pleasure in grating on a German-speaker's aural sensibilities, a bit of a payback for the Holocaust.

The meeting with Dr. Kerber went so well that it changed my life. He was not only a man of immense erudition and obvious accomplishments, he was a real *mensch*, as I was to learn the Yiddish meaning of this word later in New York. (By dint of class and education, my father and mother not only were ignorant of Yiddish, but contemptuous of it.) Dr. Kerber could have been brusque with us; he could have been impatient, even demeaning. Here was a Jewish refugee from Romania who, instead of being unconditionally happy to have his son admitted to the famous Theresianum, came to bother the headmaster with his worries about his son's practice of Judaism, a topic of constant sensitivity and delicacy in all of Austrian life.

I did not see much of Dr. Kerber during my first four years at the Theresianum, other than as part of the many official functions he conducted as the school's director. Seeing Dr. Kerber would have meant I was being summoned to the headmaster for some trouble or malfeasance, which thankfully I never was. But commencing in September 1963, Dr. Kerber became my French professor. (As behooved title- and status-obsessed Austria, all *Gymnasium* teachers were called "professor.") His French was a native speaker's—his mother was French, which was evident from Dr. Kerber's first name since few, if any, Austrians of his generation were called Roger. (This was still a time when Austrian and German boys had names like Heinz, Horst, Hans, and Heinrich, not the contemporary Amadeo, Kevin, Daniel, and Dominik.)

Dr. Kerber was a demanding professor and a hard grader, but I found him immensely fair. During the four years he was my teacher, I performed well in his classes, and I owe my passable, on occasion even decent, French to Dr. Kerber's instruction. Indeed, having the ability to deliver a scholarly lecture in French, as I did at the Université de Montréal in October 2005, to the gratifying applause of an audience that never expected it, was due only to Dr. Kerber's great pedagogy in the 1960s.

Dr. Kerber was the only member of the Theresianum's faculty I later visited with some regularity on my trips from Columbia University back to Vienna to see my father. The first time, now retired, he invited me to his apartment for coffee and cake, I almost passed out. His address was on Hintzerstrasse, literally opposite the building where my teenage girlfriend, Daphne Scheer, had grown up and where I picked her up repeatedly and, on occasion, made out with her while her mother was away. Dr. Kerber's living room window looked straight across Hintzerstrasse into the Scheers's living room. Had I known this when I was Dr. Kerber's student at the Theresianum, I would have broken up with Daphne immediately, or at least insisted that I never pick her up from home or visit her there. Both Dr. Kerber and Daphne went to their graves never knowing this wonderful—but frightening—coincidence.

Dr. Kerber's effect on my life was gigantic even though our actual contact was minimal. He incarnates the person whom the fortunate among us have encountered at one point in our lives: a virtual stranger when measured by the time spent together, and yet a close relative in terms of influencing our trajectory. Such folks may not even be aware of the good deed they committed by an action they perceive as run-of-the-mill, ho-hum, or part of their usual modus operandi. Just think of the what might have been: Had Dr. Kerber been abrasive to us, or merely officious and formal, what would my father and I have done? Leave the Theresianum in a huff and not have me enroll there? Certainly not! We would have gone through with our decision under any circumstances. But had Dr. Kerber's demeanor been less welcoming, my already sky-high anxieties about attending this school would have shot into the stratosphere. And such worries might have crippled my chances for success. Dr. Kerber could not change my status as an outsider. Nor did he try. But his understanding of my father's and my predicament lent him a lasting humanity that proved auspicious for the start of my secondary-school career in a new and different environment.

In a strange way, Dr. Kerber's behavior in his office on the day my father and I visited always comes to mind when I receive a note from a student who has just taken one of my classes, thanking me for this or that gesture or remark that set them at ease and helped them to finish the class successfully. Some even mention that, by virtue of my encouragement, they decided to stay at Michigan and not transfer elsewhere. I find these comments more moving and satisfying than the formal teaching awards I have garnered. The prizes are a credit to my pedagogical skills, a testimony to my lecturing style, a reward for being able to convey knowledge to others. But they say nothing about my *Menschlichkeit*, my decency, my compassion, my ability to influence another human being's trajectory for the good, even without trying to do so.

For all I know, Dr. Kerber exhibited none of these benevolent characteristics to other students and their parents. Indeed, as the ensuing story about my friend Bill Gillespie will demonstrate, the Theresianum failed him miserably. I never ascertained whether Bill and his parents met with Dr. Kerber, as my father and I did, but even if they had done so, judging by Bill's total marginalization in his year at the school, Dr. Kerber must not have extended to them the welcome he did to us. Sometimes one gesture, one wink of an eye, one movement of the hand, can set a child on the path to success, as Dr. Kerber's compassion and understanding did for me.

The Austrian Gymnasium in the 1960s

At this juncture, a few words about the academic dimensions of the Theresianum and the Austrian *Gymnasium* are called for. The curriculum was basically a means for creating authority and order while stifling creativity and initiative. Everything was predicated on rote learning and the regurgitation of material on written and oral exams. Take Latin. The instruction entailed the translation of texts by authors such as Vergil, Ovid, Cicero, Caesar, and Tacitus. But we learned nothing about the world in which these men lived, what their lives were like, who their friends and enemies might have been, or in what context of Roman politics and life they produced their fine works. We did nothing but translate texts.

German class was no better. After spending an inordinate amount of time being drilled in grammar, punctuation, and the finer points of writing style, we were finally allowed to read some worthwhile literature.

But even in our later years, everything came down to our two-hour, in-class written exams, in which the highest credit was awarded for the reproduction of the schemes and formulas we had learned. I cannot remember one idea I was taught about Goethe's and Schiller's plays and poems. We learned some of these works by heart, but never engaged in a single challenging discussion about these giants of Western civilization. Not even the great Austrian dramatists Ferdinand Raimund and Johann Nestroy warranted an innovative approach in this curriculum. Not to mention more recent masters like Franz Kafka, Franz Werfel, and other important writers of the first part of the twentieth century; they simply did not exist. As for contemporary Austrian luminaries like Peter Handke (winner of the Nobel Prize in literature in 2019) or Thomas Bernhard (my absolute favorite), total silence. Nor do I recall our reading any female writers, most assuredly not Elfriede Jelinek, the Austrian who was awarded the Nobel Prize in literature in 2004. Ditto English literature—more bland stuff presented blandly!

Truth be told, French, under the leadership of Dr. Kerber, was not much better. Of course we were taught Antoine de Saint-Exupéry's *Le Petit Prince*, which, I am sure, is part of the curriculum of every French class in the world. Despite its wonderful style, I never warmed to the story, perhaps because of my dread of snakes and my equally great love of elephants—recall that the narrator shows the little prince a snake that ate an elephant! For that reason alone, I never liked the story, nor its author. But something Dr. Kerber mentioned stuck with me for life. Apparently, when the Nazi-allied Vichy regime declared the well-liked hero Saint-Exupéry one of its own, it came as a shock to Saint-Exupéry himself. Charles de Gaulle, the London-based leader of the Free French Forces, declared Saint-Exupéry a Nazi collaborator, and Saint-Exupéry, who had always held de Gaulle in low regard, became depressed and began drinking heavily. Always far more interested in politics and history than literature, I paid more attention to this comment by Dr. Kerber, which I am sure he made in passing, than to his interpretations of Saint-Exupéry's writing style.

But Dr. Kerber earned my everlasting respect and affection for yet another reason. Around this time, I became a huge fan of the French comic book *Astérix*; I devoured as many installments in the series as

I could, delighting in Astérix and his sidekick, Obélix, harassing the Roman Empire's legions in occupied Gaul. With the exception of the Nazis, there never existed an entity I hated more than the Roman Empire. Perhaps my hatred of Latin had something to do with that. Or perhaps the destruction of the Second Temple by Titus in 70 C.E. was another reason. Whatever the case, I loathed and still loathe the Roman Empire, even though it bequeathed to us the beautiful Romance languages, with Romanian being one of them. (The Romanians have always taken tremendous pride that the word "Rome" survives in the name of their language alone, as opposed to Portuguese, Spanish, French, or even Italian.)

My father knew of my passion for *Astérix* and welcomed it because I was learning French by reading the comics. When he mentioned this to Dr. Kerber during one of his three obligatory *Elternsprechtage* (parents-teachers conference days), Dr. Kerber's eyes lit up, and he told my father to encourage me (if such encouragement was ever needed) to continue reading *Astérix*.

When I had the chance to visit Dr. Kerber in his home after his retirement, I asked him why we never read *Astérix* in class, even though he liked the series so much and thought it of sufficient pedagogical value to encourage my father to keep buying it for me. He just smiled and said something to the effect that the Austrian and Viennese educational bureaucracy would never have permitted this to happen inside a classroom. Not even the headmaster of such a pedigreed school as the Theresianum, who also happened to be a French instructor, could take such liberties with his teaching of the material, thereby deviating from the centrally decreed curriculum.

History class consisted of nothing but mindlessly learning by rote the dates of battles and memorizing the reigns of various kings, queens, and presidents all over Europe, with an occasional excursion to the Americas and Asia. But we heard not one word of social or economic history, were given not the slightest understanding of larger trends, and received no inkling of political history in any meaningful sense of that concept. Much of the history we were taught concentrated on Austria and the German lands, which, given the school's location, made sense. But even here, the lacunae were pronounced and not accidental. The years between 1939 and

1945 simply never happened. Not one word about the Shoah, nothing about the *Anschluss*. The Austrian Civil War of 1934 between the rebellious Social Democrats and the governing Austro-Fascists received scant mention. (My taking the side of the "Reds" was not particularly welcomed, neither by the teacher nor by some of my classmates.)

Our history professor was a deeply conservative man with strong German nationalist leanings. Adding to this toxic mix was his glorification of everything related to the military: its battles, its discipline, its male bonding, its heroism. Even though the Wehrmacht received pride of place in his world—like all Austrian men of his generation, he had served in it during the war—he grew especially ardent when he talked of the German *Landser*, the German soldier, the equivalent of the American GI. In fact, he loved other militaries as well. He talked to me endlessly of the United States Marine Corps, whose members he admiringly referred to as "Leathernecks," thus revealing an admirable but telling acquaintance with a certain peculiarity of Marine terminology.

Despite all this, I did not dislike the man. He knew I was Jewish, as did everyone at the school, but I never heard him utter a remark I could even remotely construe as antisemitic. In an odd way, he wanted to claim me as a real Austrian—better yet, as a real German, certainly as a Gentile. He repeatedly asked me—and my father, on the days when our parents met with our teachers—whether my mother was possibly a *Volksdeutsche*, an ethnic German, of which there were so many in Timişoara. He did not want to accept her—and therefore me—as Jewish, and would have loved to know I belonged to his world. Today, this would be seen as an equally vile form of antisemitism as addressing me with an insulting slur; after all, he was showing a blatant disregard for my history and identity, and trying to appropriate me for his world and purposes. But I did not experience his behavior as hurtful, nor did my father. Rather than denying my actual identity, I interpreted my teacher's wish that I join his team as a compliment.

This man also taught geography. In principle, I loved this course, as I was hungry for knowledge about the world. But the focus was on the size of the countries, their exact populations, the names of their capitals, with little attention to their inhabitants' cultures, conflicts, or daily lives.

Here, too, the emphasis was on rote learning, with zero incentives for student originality. I will never forget my consternation—no, panic—when, on the first two days of my classes at Columbia, I was asked to write two papers for the ensuing class meeting. Writing papers? What was that? In my eight years at the Theresianum, I had never written anything close to an American term paper, which required the student read and research a topic, then write about it in an essay demonstrating what he had learned and hand it in to the teacher. Even at Austrian universities of the time, most examinations were oral, meaning one had to regurgitate the facts one learned at home and hope the professor and the committee approved. We never engaged in any research or independent thinking at the fancy Theresianum; all of our academic work consisted solely of memorization and regurgitation.

To be sure, the Austrian system allowed teachers little leeway in their teaching of the material. The system's degree of regimentation was second only to France's (in)famous secondary-education system, in which, the story goes, the minister of education in Paris can look at his watch and know exactly which formula is being presented in every sixth-form math class across France and, perhaps, in every school following the French curriculum across the world. Often in front of our eyes, our teachers were required to fill out forms in large books to prove to the authorities—the *Stadtschulrat* (Municipal School Council) and its superior, the *Bundesministerium für Unterricht* (Federal Ministry of Education)—that they had covered the prescribed material in a timely and orderly fashion. I recall the teachers always worrying about covering the *Stoff*—the stuff, the prescribed material—and rushing to do so as if someone were going to punish them if they fell behind or deviated in any way.

All this regimented learning fit with the militaristic discipline of the school. We were not allowed to speak during mealtimes. We had to follow the professors' orders, no matter how odd and ill-placed they were. We could not chew gum. We had to keep our hair short. We had to wear a certain shoe, into which we changed every morning and out of which we changed every night, lest we soil the school's pristine floors. Any kind of resistance or deviance was severely punished by measures such as having to stay late, even on Saturdays, copying texts, and, worst of all, receiving a bad grade in something called *Betragen*—comportment—which could (and often did) have seriously deleterious effects on one's grade reports, and thus on one's academic standing. To be fair, we were never beaten or physically punished in any way, as was still the case in the British public schools of the era.

All three people whose friendships I acquired during my years in the Theresianum—in addition to Dr. Kerber, if one can ever call one's former headmaster a friend—entered my life during my first four years at the school, the so called *Unterstufe*, the temporal equivalent to middle school. Tellingly, I did not establish any friendships in the next four years, the *Oberstufe*, the temporal equivalent to high school. The salience of these important friendships, all of which were formed before I reached the age of 13, can only become clear in the context of how the United States was viewed at the time by so many Austrians, in stark contrast to how I viewed America.

The United States barely figured in the Austrian secondary-school curriculum. We learned facts about the country in our geography classes: its population, the names of its largest cities, a few state capitals, a bit about its industry and agriculture, and that's about it. In history classes, the United States was somehow still an extension of Britain. America was—and still is today—viewed as part and parcel of that Anglo-Saxon world that has so troubled and fascinated continental Europe. The French and Germans in particular both have used the term "les Anglo-Saxons" and "die Angelsachsen" on a daily basis, often lending this inchoate amalgam a unity that it simply never had in real life. Of course, no American or Brit ever used this term to refer to each other or the alleged commonality between the two. We heard mention of the American War of Independence and maybe even a sentence or two about the Civil War and Abraham Lincoln, but the formal knowledge of America conveyed by Austrian schools was pathetically minute.

There existed, however, a more informal understanding of an America that was mighty and controversial and scary on some level, because *this* America represented an entity deeply antithetical to Europe. For most Austrians in my world, America was culturally inferior, but this very inferiority also represented a seductive quality that was dangerous and irresistible. How troubling to European elites that a European colony had constructed a political reality unique in all of human history, and then pivoted and rejected Europe via an armed insurrection called the War of Independence. Here was a polity in which the only sovereign was the individual (of course, a wealthy, white, male, slave-owning individual, but an individual all the same), not God, not a king, not a pope, not a bishop, not even a body of aristocrats.

Beginning on July 5, 1776, the European aristocracies came to disdain and fear this new entity, which meant conservative Europeans disdained and feared the United States and depicted it as an inauthentic newcomer, a parvenu that lacked the gravitas of Europe's established nations and their cultures. Many Europeans to this day claim the United States has no culture and no history! "What you call history, we call journalism," said one of my colleagues at a German university. Americans are not a *Kulturvolk*, to use the proper diction; they lack the depth to be one. Yes, they can create *Zivilisation* but never *Kultur*. They can create entertainment, but not culture. They are superficial, transient, and—yes—rootless, just like the Jews. No anchor, no depth and most importantly, no authenticity!

Not surprisingly, from the early nineteenth century until today, anti-Americanism and antisemitism have symbolically accompanied each other. The Jew and the American are all about money; only noble nations, like Germans, can create *Helden*, heroes; Jews and Americans are mere *Händler*, merchants; the Jew and the American lack soul; the Jew and the American lack roots; the Jew and the American are a mishmash of cultures and ethnicities, without a true allegiance to a single, solid core of values. These images are dominant in all of nineteenth-century German, French, and English literature, as my friend and colleague Jesper Gulddal has so eloquently argued and convincingly demonstrated.

The Romantics—so significant in the formation of German identity—hated America. Nikolaus Lenau, a poet from the Banat region in today's Romania, after whom, as will be remembered, my elementary school in Timişoara was named, bemoaned America's "horribly dull" nature, where one could not find a "brave dog" nor a "fiery horse, and no passionate human being." The land was so sullen and dreary it could not sustain any nightingales or songbirds of any kind. This barrenness of nature transposed itself onto American society and culture, the education system, and the people themselves, all of whom Lenau viewed as lacking imagination, burdened by small-mindedness, and enslaved by a practicality and mercantile outlook that was dreadfully insipid and vacuous.

Heinrich Heine also hated America, as did Hegel (though for different reasons). And much of the same cultural contempt existed in Britain—think of Frances Trollope and Charles Dickens—as well as in France, where Comte de Buffon's famous "degeneration thesis," which held that everything America touched degenerated into blandness and mediocrity, and that the United States was merely a degenerate Europe, gained immense popularity.

So much for the view of America propagated by Europe's aristocracies and all their conservative acolytes. What about popular culture? Here, the view of America became much more interesting, in that millions of less privileged Europeans had voted with their feet by emigrating to the New World and becoming Americans. And no European wrote more passionately or convincingly of that strange New World, no author exerted a greater influence in this realm in the German-speaking world and its central European reaches, than a certain pulp-fiction writer named Karl May.

I began to read May's books in Timişoara and devoured the remainder in Vienna, as did virtually all my male contemporaries, with some girls partaking as well. Having sold more than 200,000,000 copies of his work, May is, by sheer numbers, one of the most successful writers of the German language of all time. Though he barely left his native Saxony, and never actually visited America until late in his life (and even then ventured no farther west than Niagara Falls), a combination of imagination and the meticulous study of maps led him to write a series of amazing adventure stories.

At the center of these stories stands a character named Old Shatterhand, a native of Saxony and most probably a stand-in for May himself, who travels all over America. Early in the series, Old Shatterhand befriends an Apache chief named Winnetou, who becomes his blood brother. Winnetou is murdered, and Old Shatterhand spends much of his time avenging this act. The stories, almost all told in the first-person singular, extol the "noble savage," as exemplified by Winnetou and his Apaches, who fight with their few European allies (almost all Germans of some kind) against the evils of modernization perpetrated by various vile, often drunk, Brits, but also Irish and Jewish settlers, with their venal Comanches in tow. (I have no idea why May made the Apaches into holy warriors and the Comanches into murderous thugs, but there you have it.)

May's influence on the way German speakers have viewed America over the past 150 years cannot be exaggerated. Adolf Hitler was a huge fan and recommended May's books to his generals, with special editions printed for the troops at the front. The Nazis used May's depiction of the purity and heroism of the Apaches in their anti-American propaganda during the Second World War. But Albert Einstein was also a huge Karl May fan! To this day, travel agents offer packages for German tourists who want to visit the United States with the express purpose of retracing Old Shatterhand's and Winnetou's treks across the country.

During one of my many trips to Germany in the 1990s, I traveled to Bad Segeberg in the north-German state of Schleswig-Holstein to attend the annual Karl May *Festspiele*. I was one of more than 250,000 who came then—and have come annually since 1952—to celebrate May's writings about the American West. Words fail me even today as I try to describe the sight of thousands of middle- and working-class Germans dressed as Apache warriors and members of other Native American tribes. This phenomenon far overshadows incidents that have ignited debates on American campuses about cultural appropriation and the exploitation of Native American life. May's continued fascination for ordinary Germans occurs in a sphere completely apart from Germany's vibrant scene of elite culture, which, if it is cognizant of this particular Karl May event at all, must be deeply embarrassed by it. Then again, I am aware of no credible attempts to curtail the May *Festspiele*, nor any serious considerations that might lead to altering or ending these blatantly racist practices as would surely have been the case with comparable events in the United States, Canada, Great Britain, Australia, New Zealand and various west European countries such as the Netherlands and Belgium. The issue is straightforward: There simply are no Native Americans in Germany in sufficient numbers to shame the Germans into stopping this vile stuff reaffirming the fact that these changes only occur when the affected group has some physical presence in the country and thus possesses at least a modicum of voice and power. Karl May also wrote many books featuring adventures in North Africa, the Middle East, and the Balkans where a renamed Old Shatterhand here called Kara Ben Nemsi—also the author's alter-ego—performs comparable feats of heroism. Talk about Orientalism! Tellingly, I have never encountered Karl May festivals depicting Turks or Arabs in a similarly offensive way as has remained commonplace with Native Americans. These Karl May festivals have thrived in other German places beside Bad Segeberg and have been equally popular in a number of locations in the Czech Republic.

There are three additional realms of European popular culture in which the United States has been omnipresent since the 1920s, film, music, and cartoons, all of which ruled our lives as young boys at the Theresianum. We loved no films more than Westerns. I must have seen Gary Cooper's *High Noon* twenty times. In addition to Cooper, Hollywood stars such as John Wayne, Richard Widmark, and Burt Lancaster fired our imaginations. As for music, Elvis Presley ruled the roost, but to aficionados like some of my closer pals and me, Presley faced serious competition from Fats Domino, Carl Perkins, Jerry Lee Lewis, Johnny Cash, Chuck Berry, Chubby Checker, and British rockers like Cliff Richard and his band, the Shadows, and Tony Sheridan and the Silver Beetles (I wonder whatever became of them!).

In the world of cartoons and comics, few pleasures were more important than picking up the newest issue of *Micky Maus* at a newspaper kiosk every week. A magazine featuring Mickey Mouse and other Disney characters—most notably Donald Duck and his extended family—became a cultural marker for millions of youngsters like me. The German-speaking world enjoyed the good fortune of having an amazing woman named Erika Fuchs as the translator of these comics. Her quirky expressions, with their idiosyncratic syntax and neologisms, constituted a body of work that later attained the stature of true art. She invented onomatopoetic sounds that entered the daily diction of millions of German-speakers of the baby boom generation and beyond.

This was how I viewed America during my eight years at the Theresianum. Even though my English soon became far superior to that of any of my teachers', I was always criticized for speaking "American dialect" and not proper British English, as the teachers purported to do with their heavy Viennese and Austrian accents. One of them even docked me points for insisting on using American spellings on my tests, instead of the mandatory British versions. But my English was gauged to be so good that I never received anything below an "A" in any of my reports, even though some teachers would have loved to have graded me lower for my deviance in speaking a dialect.

"America" was thus a loaded entity at the Theresianum: uniformly rejected by the leadership and the faculty, which emphasized how the Theresianum was an institution for elites, and therefore had nothing but contempt for American culture, but also feared for the obvious attractiveness of American popular culture, which those in charge could not control. I will never forget our music teacher's reaction when I told him that I had just seen the movie *Porgy and Bess*, starring Dorothy Dandridge, Sidney Poitier, and Sammy Davis Jr.: "A joke that something as lightweight as that dares call itself an opera. Only in America can such a travesty happen! But the melodies are irresistible. I am ashamed to say so to you, but I really love them, though, of course, I would never go see this movie!" Of course some of my teachers in the Theresianum derisively called the Beatles an "Eunuchenchor" (a choir of eunuchs) by dint of their frequent (and brilliant, I might add) usage of falsetto voices. Remember that even though the Beatles were de jure British subjects, they were in the eyes of many de facto American by virtue of singing with American accents, being popularizers of the ultra-American cultural expression of rock 'n roll, and well, by being Anglo-Saxon, of course.

Three Amigos

I often felt alone in my love for all things American, fully aware that this love was not shared by most adults around me, including my father, who loved macro America, global-power America, liberal-democratic America, anti-Soviet America while sharing his milieu's contempt for and fear of micro America, popular culture America, rock 'n roll America, the irreverent America that was challenging Victorian bourgeois mores. But on my very first day at the Theresianum in early September 1959, when I nervously entered classroom 1B and was forced to mingle with thirty or so equally nervous ten-year-old boys, one student drew my attention. His name was Michael Freund, and he has remained one of my very best friends to this day. Michael was the smartest kid in class, not only gifted in arithmetic and science-related subjects such as zoology and botany, but also the best writer among us. Moreover, he was a talented artist, and developed into a fine amateur cartoonist.

At some opaque level, I sensed something Central-European Jewish about Michael. Although he attended Catholic mass and Catholic religion class, he sported darker features than most of the other boys. But beyond his physical appearance, Michael's "Jewish" persona became all the more evident when he invited me to his apartment, which was not far from our school, and I met his mother and father, both of whom seemed somehow Jewish to me. And sure enough, his mother began speaking perfect Hungarian with me while chain-smoking her unfiltered cigarettes. Though neither of Michael's parents were Jewish, they had Jewish relatives and friends. Michael's mother, in particular, with her perfect mastery of German, Hungarian, and Slovak, struck me as a veritable old school Habsburg cosmopolitan.

But what really drew me to Michael was his love of the English language and American culture. Michael and I shared nearly every interest, from Elvis Presley to politics, from Mickey Mouse and Donald Duck to Karl May's books, although I was shocked to discover that Michael never cared for sports, which I so passionately followed, nor classical music, which I loved. Not liking classical music in our upper-middle-class Viennese world was akin to heresy, but my admiration for contrarians allowed me to forgive him such trespasses.

Shockingly, when we returned to school in September 1961 to begin our third year, Michael was not there. His father had become the CEO of a major Austrian firm's Italian operations in Milan, where Michael had resumed his studies in that city's German school. I missed seeing him on a daily basis, but thankfully he returned to Vienna with some regularity over school holidays, and we would get together then. None of these visits was more memorable than one in the summer of 1965, when we went to a noted Viennese record store called *Drei Viertel* (Three Quarters), where a fascinating young man by the name of Edek Bartz was one of the key managers.

Edek had been born in 1946 in Karaganda, in the eastern part of Kazakhstan, to a Polish Jewish father and a Viennese Jewish mother. His parents brought him to Vienna in 1958, the same year I arrived in town with my father. Edek had an encyclopedic knowledge of all music, be it classical, jazz, or rock; and he initiated me, a casual follower of rock, into the genre's very core. (Later, he became famous in Austria and Germany by playing and curating all kinds of Yiddish music, including klezmer.) Michael and I would arrive at *Drei Viertel* and sit in one of its comfortable glass-enclosed booths listening to records for hours, with Edek supplying album after album. Here, during the late summer of 1965, we devoured Bob Dylan's recently released *Bringing It All Back Home*. Michael and I were mesmerized by every song on the album; repeatedly, we tried—with varying success—to take notes of Dylan's words. We replicated the same experience exactly one year later when we hovered over Dylan's *Blonde on Blonde* that had been released in June of 1966.

Nothing has connected Michael and me at a deeper level than our love for Dylan, the Rolling Stones, the Beatles, Paul Simon, the blues and—most of all—the Grateful Dead. When Michael visited me in the early 1980s at Wesleyan, where I was an assistant professor, we went to two superb Dead shows, one at the Hartford Civic Center and the other at the Coliseum in New Haven. Perhaps my most memorable meeting with Michael was in the summer of 1967, when we ran into each other at the Louvre in Paris. I was in a great mood because I had just returned from the United States Embassy, where I had scored a perfect 100 on the TOEFL test that Columbia University required me to take before it decided to admit me.

Michael and I met repeatedly during my visits home from Columbia to Vienna. His enthusiasm for American culture, along with his best friend's emigration to New York where he had entered a doctoral program in social psychology at Columbia's Teachers College, enticed Michael to apply for admission to the same program. After he was accepted, Michael moved in with this friend, and the two young men, along with their respective girlfriends, became my neighbors on the Upper West Side. Michael and I co-authored our very first academic article, which appeared in the fall 1974 issue of the newly founded *Österreichische Zeitschrift für Politikwissenschaft,* the foremost Austrian journal of political science. This peer-reviewed quarterly was among the first academic social science periodicals in postwar Austria.

After receiving his Ph.D. from Columbia in the late 1970s, Michael returned to Vienna, where he became one of that city's leading public intellectuals. He worked for the country's most innovative advertising agency, became a professor of communications at Webster University's Vienna campus, and for more than two decades edited the "Album" section of the weekend edition of Austria's leading, left-liberal, highbrow daily, *Der Standard.* "Album" was a compilation of articles on all aspects of culture, written by the paper's journalists and guest contributors. Michael's catholic taste has been boundless; he has published pieces on everything from the rock impresario Bill Graham to the evangelist Billy Graham, from the work of R. Crumb to a fine piece on Joni Mitchell, from Donald Duck to the catalogues of New York's finest museums. Few, if any, intellectuals, have made as wide a range of American topics known to Austrian audiences as has Michael Freund.

But all that came later. Even with Michael's brief presence at the Theresianum, my love for the United States usually went unrequited. Then, in the third trimester of my second year, our class was joined by the school's first bona-fide American student. Michael Guthrie, mentioned in this book's preface, was the son of Frederick Guthrie, one of the Vienna State Opera's premier singers, who, with his booming and haunting bass voice, had beguiled my father and me on many of our regular visits to this pantheon of operatic music. Even at this stage of his life, when my father was anything but wealthy, he made certain the two of us went to this famous opera house a number of times each season. In the mid 1950s, Mike's dad had used a Fulbright Scholarship to study voice at Vienna's Academy of Music, and, upon graduating from that school, was discovered by the legendary and controversial Herbert von Karajan, who hired him on the spot to become a member of the Vienna State Opera. Indeed, Frederick sang the prominent role of the night watchman in Richard Wagner's *Die Meistersinger* in that opera's first post-World War II performance at the State Opera on November 14, 1955, a few days after *Fidelio* graced the opera's stage, celebrating the vaunted company's return home from its post-World War II exile in the Theater an der Wien.

Though Mike always identified as an American and spoke flawless American-accented English, of which I availed myself at every possible opportunity, he had become a Viennese boy by dint of having joined his father and attended preschool, kindergarten, and elementary school in Vienna. He witnessed the signing of Austria's *Staatsvertrag*—state treaty—on May 15, 1955, while sitting on his father's shoulder in Vienna's legendary Belvedere Palace, where the ceremony occurred. This was arguably the most important moment in postwar Austria's history: the signing of this treaty began the country's independence from the four occupying Allied powers—the United States, Great Britain, France, and the Soviet Union—who had defeated Nazi Germany, and of which Austria was an integral part.

I liked Mike and spoke only English with him, but in many ways he was too highbrow for me. He knew nothing about American sports, for which I had come to develop a passion by virtue of spending summers with my uncle in New York and listening to all kinds of American sporting events on American Forces Network radio from Germany late at night in my bed in Frau Kohler's apartment. Michael, alas, also seemed equally ignorant about and disinterested in Austrian and European soccer, topics on which I had become the resident expert in my class, holding court every Monday morning following the weekend's soccer matches. (Mozart, Wagner, Verdi, and Puccini were all fine, but there was a limit to the interest they could hold for 12-year-old boys, no matter how cultured.) Above all, by being a full boarder, Mike never spent afternoons at the school with the half-borders like me, so I did not get to know him much outside of the short ten-minute intermissions between morning classes. Mike remained with us for the next academic year—meaning 3B—but was forced to depart thereafter on account of his alleged insubordination as a boarder. I had no idea of the reasons for his expulsion, but, as old men in Michigan, Mike confessed to me that he simply hated the Theresianum so much that he misbehaved on purpose every evening to the point where the school had to kick him out.

After Mike's departure, we remained in touch from time to time in Vienna, but then lost contact for fifty years, until the miracle of the Internet led us to rediscover each other living barely sixty miles apart in Michigan, he in Okemos, near Lansing, and I in Ann Arbor. This allowed us to meet regularly for monthly luncheons at an Olive Garden in Brighton, more or less half way between our two homes. I found out that Mike, having obtained his *Matura* degree from Kalksburg (the Theresianum's rival) in 1967, enrolled at Michigan State University, where he received both a BA and an MA in computer science. After a number of years in the United States Army, some of them spent in Asia, he returned to Michigan, where he joined the Department of Transportation. Mike became the resident specialist in geographic information systems and mapping, which made sense, given that he had always loved maps and was the best in our class in geography. Even though Mike remains too highbrow for me—no sports, no rock 'n roll, nothing but NPR— I am thrilled to have him close by because we share a world and an era I can discuss with virtually no one else.

Luckily, after I lost Michael Freund, an amazing new face appeared in the 3B class, on the very first day of its assembling in early September 1961: a blond American boy, sporting a buzz cut, wearing wire-rimmed glasses, and clad in a blue buttoned-down shirt with Levi's jeans and Keds sneakers. Wow! Such folks did not exist in Vienna at the time. I practically ran up to him and introduced myself in English. He beamed back at me and shook my hand firmly. "I am Bill Gillespie from the United States. So glad to meet you." We liked each other from the second we met, and we still like each other 60 years later.

By reason of the Theresianum's academic but also snobby reputation, Bill's parents decided to place their son in our school rather than have him attend the perfectly fine American International School on the outskirts of town. Bill's father, William Gregory Gillespie, was a colonel in the United States Air Force and had arrived in Vienna at the beginning of September 1961 to work in the US Embassy in Austria as his country's military attaché. The trouble was Bill spoke virtually no German, which soon became the bane of his existence at the Theresianum. Mike Guthrie and I tried to help him as best we could, but our limited resources were no match for the blatant neglect the school's faculty exhibited towards Bill. He received no extra tutoring and no empathy from the faculty or our fellow students, which meant he sat through hour after hour of instruction he could not understand. While I had never been completely at home in this school, the way the community treated Bill Gillespie instigated my real dislike for its faculty and students.

Bill was not actively bullied as that term is understood in today's America—nobody mistreated him physically or psychologically—but the neglect he suffered came pretty close. I reached out to him, and by late October we had become fast friends. Unlike my friendship with the two Michaels, Guthrie and Freund, Bill and I shared a passion for American sports. We talked a lot about the World Series between the Yankees and the Cincinnati Reds (which my Yankees won) and debated whether Roger Maris's 61 home runs that season should be listed with an asterisk (Bill) or without (Andy). During football season, we engaged in lengthy conversations about the amazing Baltimore Colts trio of Johnny Unitas, Lennie Moore, and Raymond Berry. Around this time, Bill invited me to his house in one of Vienna's fanciest districts, the nineteenth, right near the Vienna Woods. Since he invited me for a Saturday afternoon, he asked me to stay for the night. I had never heard of sleepover parties, because neither in Timişoara nor in Vienna—nor in New York City, for that matter—did I know anybody who lived in a place larger than a one-bedroom apartment, usually populated by the host, his siblings, and their parents.

When my father dropped me off at the Gillespies's home at Chimanistrasse 18 (a place I still visit during every one of my appearances in town), he and I felt something crucial in my life was about to happen. I always view that sleepover as my real entry to the United States, superseding the actual receipt of my green card in the summer of 1960. Until the Gillespies's departure in June 1964, I became a weekend resident in their house, spending Saturday nights there because Sunday was the only day with no school, so I did not have to get up early in the morning to take the tram from home to the Theresianum. For three years, I lived in America pretty much every weekend of the school year, even though I physically resided in Vienna. My father was pleased on two levels. I had made a true friend in Bill Gillespie, with whom I not only enjoyed myself but felt safe. And my father valued the social status and prestige that kicked in by virtue of his son being pals with a top American diplomat's boy who lived in a diplomatic compound in the fanciest district in town.

After spending a miserable academic year in the Theresianum, where I was his sole source of support, Bill transferred to the American International School for the two remaining years of his stay in Vienna. There, he excelled both academically and athletically, and picked up enough German that he became a fluent speaker. Away from the Theresianum's uncaring environment, finding comfort in the American International School, Bill actually learned German much more thoroughly and effectively than in a place where it was the language of everything from instruction to social interaction.

The Gillespie house became my America away from America, allowing me to enter permanently the actual America in the fall of 1967 without experiencing any culture shock. Of course, my spending summers in New York helped me acculturate to all things American, but without spending that much time with Bill in Vienna, I would never have become who I am. I came to speak accent-free American English; I became the master of teenage slang; I learned more American history than in all the history instruction at the Theresianum, where we never got beyond the perfunctory mention of George Washington, Abraham Lincoln, and Franklin Delano Roosevelt, none of these in a favorable light. I learned about chocolate chip cookies, devoured tuna-salad sandwiches with Hellman's mayonnaise, noticed that Americans drank milk with their meals (one of the customs I never adopted), and came to wear Keds sneakers and blue jeans, which were still not worn by Austrian boys at the time.

I played catch in Bill's yard, putting on a baseball glove for the first time. Bill got some of the other boys in the American diplomatic compound to play the game with us on a lot not far from his house. I was nervous about playing a game I had never played before, but excited as well. I felt totally accepted, unlike the uneasiness I felt participating in the pick-up soccer games in the Kaiserpark near our apartment on Lerchenfelderstrasse, even though I was not a bad soccer player. Never mind that I was a pretty poor outfielder and realized fairly early that the least talented boys were assigned to play right field, which became my steady position; no one made me feel unwanted or self-conscious. Late that fall, we began to throw a football to each other, with one of us being the quarterback and the other going deep as a receiver, à la Johnny Unitas and Lennie Moore. I remember watching the Army–Navy game of 1961 on the big screen in the Gillespies's basement, with the film reaching Vienna via some United States Armed Services connection in neighboring Germany at least two weeks after the game had been played in Philadelphia.

Then there was Schmutzi, the Gillespies's cuddly black poodle. Neither in Timişoara, nor Vienna, nor New York, where I always lived in small, cramped apartments, was having a dog imaginable. My father barely tolerated Frau Kohler's old dog on Lerchenfelderstrasse, and I deeply resented his undisguised relief when the dog died, relatively soon after our moving in. At the time, I too was nowhere as near to heartbroken as I would become later in life upon experiencing the death of a dog who in any way was close to me. I enjoyed nothing better than taking Schmutzi for a walk through the wonderful neighborhood of Grinzing, or playing with her in the Gillespies's generous yard, except, perhaps, her snuggling up to me when I went to bed in Bill's room full of posters of American war planes and aircraft carriers.

At some point, we began listening to the Kingston Trio on Bill's fancy stereo system. Bill loved music; he came from a gifted family in which everyone played the piano well, and his older sister Mary Jane was training to become a singer. We started to hum and sing the Trio's tunes, and one day, Bill acquired a cheap acoustic guitar. To imitate the Kingston Trio's sound as best we could, one of us had to pick up playing the banjo, the most American of instruments (though African in its origin). I immediately volunteered and set out to persuade my father to purchase one; generous as he always was, especially to me, he agreed. But there were no banjos to be had in Vienna in the early 1960s. So he cast his net across Europe, somehow acquired a banjo in Germany, and had it shipped to me in Vienna. Alas, it was merely a four-string and not a five-string banjo like the one Dave Guard played so brilliantly in the Kingston Trio, but it had to do.

I taught myself to play the banjo sufficiently well to join Bill's much more advanced guitar playing, and, lo and behold, we weren't bad. Our vocal harmonies were crisp, our playing enthusiastic, and we loved practicing and singing. Those Saturday evenings and Sundays became very important to Bill when his mother died after a long bout with cancer. Colonel Gillespie remarried, taking as his wife an Austrian woman named Maria, who, though she could not replace Bill's mother, was warm and kind and always smiled. Much later, during a trip I took from Columbia to spend Thanksgiving with the Gillespies at their home in Annandale, Virginia, Maria told Bill and me that, when they had guests to their house in Vienna for a Saturday evening dinner, folks would quietly tiptoe from the dining room to the closed door of Bill's room and listen to us play. Maria was allegedly so enchanted with our musical performance that she and a few of her guests began to learn the songs themselves.

It was via the Kingston Trio, whose every album I possessed and played constantly back at my cramped home on Lerchenfelderstrasse, that I fell in love with an aspect of American music that also pervaded the art of the Grateful Dead, particularly following their release of *American Beauty* and *Workingman's Dead*, in 1969 and 1970 respectively. The many overlaps between the songs both bands played beautifully bookended the decade of the 1960s for me and stayed with me all my life. Bill and I also began to branch out into the music and poetry of Bob Dylan via the harmony-rich trio of Peter, Paul, and Mary. One Saturday evening in late 1962 I appeared at Bill's place with a single by a British band called the Beatles, featuring two of their releases, "Love Me Do" and "P.S. I Love You." Bill and I loved both sides, and we began listening to the Beatles, continuing with the albums that appeared in 1963 and 1964, though we never dared perform any of their songs, sticking faithfully to the Kingston Trio's acoustic music.

Bill and I also went downhill skiing to a place called Semmering, one hour's drive south of Vienna, where, a few years later, I was to meet a lovely young woman named Kiki, who became the love of my life. Immensely athletic, Bill soon surpassed me in his skiing abilities, and this passion continued to the point that as an adult he became a part-time ski instructor in Colorado and various places around Washington, D.C. In the spring of 1963, Bill and I rented rowboats and then sailboats on an estuary of the Danube where the water was still. After we capsized one of the sailboats, leading to all kinds of trouble, I chickened out from any subsequent adventures in this realm. In notable contrast, Bill became an expert sailor, a pastime he continues to enjoy all over the Chesapeake Bay and up and down the East Coast.

Both of us were also war buffs and knew many details of key battles, none more intimately than D-Day. In 1962, we even went to Vienna's leading movie theater to see Darryl F. Zanuck's *The Longest Day*, which depicted the Allies' Normandy landing on June 6, 1944, featuring John Wayne and Richard Widmark, among many other stars of the time. I loved the movie so much that I went with my father twice more to see it. In that spirit, Bill and I played an Avalon Hill board game called D-Day. Of course, I never wanted to play the Germans. There was only one problem with my insisting I play the Allies: Bill was a much better player than I was, and I suffered defeat after defeat, witnessing my British, American, and Canadian forces get pushed back into the Atlantic Ocean by the stout German defenders. I often failed to reach Reims, never mind the Rhine, leaving poor France to continue its suffering under Nazi tyranny.

One day, I told Bill I wanted to switch sides and play the Germans. Sure enough, under his able leadership the Allies did indeed defeat the Germans and crossed the Rhine successfully, proceeding to Berlin, which did not appear on the board, but was clear to anybody who played the game. Rarely was I so exhilarated at suffering a loss as I was the time Bill beat me decisively in the board game D-Day, with my ineptitude leading to the Germans' defeat and Bill's skill assuring the Allies' worthy and much-welcomed victory.

Lest my psychic conflicts regarding this game continue, we ceased playing D-Day and picked up Chancellorsville, another Avalon Hill board game. That epic battle of the American Civil War was a much less emotionally—and existentially—contested space for me than D-Day. Even though I had intensely disliked the Confederacy ever since my father mentioned the Civil War to me back in Romania, its potential victory in this board game appeared less traumatic than the Nazis' driving the Allied troops back into the Atlantic Ocean. I much preferred representing the Union instead of the Confederacy, but losing to the latter was not as upsetting for me as having my Allies lose to the Nazis.

This game-playing made clear to me that, even though empathy and compassion are, by definition, other-directed and universal, all pain remains personal and highly particular. Bill understood that the Nazis were bad guys who were in some way more threatening to Andy and his dad than they had been to his own father, who actually fought them and their Japanese allies. Bill knew about the Holocaust before he met me, and he came to learn more about it through our friendship. Even though he intellectually understood my dilemma with the D-Day board game, I was sure that deep down he did not feel the full depths of my conflict. For my part, I often imagined later in life how an African-American kid in my shoes would have felt playing the same games. To him, losing to the Nazis wouldn't have been nearly as painful as losing to the Confederacy at Chancellorsville, which to me was unfortunate, but not traumatic.

Bill Gillespie remained my friend throughout my life. Upon his return to the United States in late 1964, he finished high school and earned a BA in chemistry from the College of William and Mary. He then spent 11 years as a chemist and program manager for the Bureau of Engraving and Printing, chiefly responsible for developing inks with which to print United States postage stamps and currency. He shifted gears in the late 1980s, becoming an expert on air quality and environmental issues, and finished his career with the Virginia Department of Environmental Quality, where he continued to lead inspections of air pollution sources and ran the air-monitoring network in northern Virginia.

Bill and I often went years without seeing each other but somehow managed to stay in touch. We went skiing together once at Waterville Valley in New Hampshire, and he came to my wedding to Kiki at the

Harvard Faculty Club in May 1998. I also saw him repeatedly during my two stints in Washington, D.C., when I was teaching in our nation's capital. I cannot assign a value to Bill's influence in making me an American before I truly came to live in America for good.

Michael Freund, Michael Guthrie, and Bill Gillespie appeared in my life in the first three years at the Theresianum; in other words, I met them all before I turned 13. All three were complete outsiders in the Theresianum; all were askew; all spent little time at the school; and yet all had a major influence on my life. In an odd way, I even include Dr. Roger Kerber as an outsider in terms of my experiences at the Theresianum. On the face of it, this is a silly thing to say of the institution's longtime headmaster. But in Andy Markovits's Theresianum, Dr. Kerber, too, was an outsider. He was half French, he had a soothing demeanor and, most assuredly, a state of mind that welcomed me as a refugee and a Jew—as a *Zuagraster*, to use the Viennese patois term denoting a party crasher. I will forever be in this special quartet's debt.

Even though I was basically a happy kid, my high school years were unpleasant enough that I severed my ties to the school immediately upon graduating in June 1967 and avoided all my classmates except Michael, Mike, and Bill. I never attended any of the reunions and never responded to any of my former classmates' attempts to establish contact. Once every decade or so, I would run into one or the other of my classmates by accident, but we would barely greet each other and then go our own ways, with the exception of one who became an artist and whom I did see two or three times in fifty years. I refused to set foot in the Theresianum's building until 2010, when I was a visiting professor at the University of Vienna and a dear friend and colleague from Germany came to see me, mainly so I could take him on a tour of my childhood haunts. I was pleased to oblige, which meant I had to include the Theresianum.

When we walked into the building on a sunny day in late June, I was surprised at how familiar everything looked and how little seemed to have changed in 43 years. But then, turning the corner towards the headmaster's room, I saw a number of young women walking confidently while happily chatting with each other.[4] I then noticed a woman's name gracing the headmaster's office. Lastly, we entered an area with a fax and photocopying machines and a few computer stations, and I was shocked to find one of these stations manned by a young fellow with hair reaching to the middle of his back, sporting a T-shirt that said, in English, "Up Yours," the requisite middle finger included. I almost felt like walking up to this young man and hugging him. These young women walking happily down the corridor, the woman's name on the headmaster's office, and this young man with his irreverent T-shirt and long hair almost liberated me from the oppressive feelings I had borne for nearly half a century whenever I thought about the Theresianum. I was beaming from ear to ear.

Then I took my German friend to my favorite ice cream parlor one block away from the Theresianum, which I had visited with some frequency when I was a student there. Somehow, the huge strawberry and chocolate collage tasted even more delicious than I remembered it.

---

4   In 1989, the school came to admit girls for the first time. As of September 2011, it added an elementary school and kindergarten, thus offering a fully integrated K-to-12 curriculum.

Daphne Scheer, Real Madrid and Internazionale Milano (Inter Milan): The Personal Meets the Political

Wednesday, May 27, 1964, was a cloudy day in Vienna. I went to school in the morning, fearing it might rain in the evening, when I was about to attend the most important sporting event of my life. The legendary Los Blancos (Whites) of Real Madrid, five-time champions of Europe and still chock-full of such talented, though aging, football luminaries as Ferenc Puskás (the leader of the Hungarian Golden Team that lost to the Germans in Bern in 1954), Francisco Gento, and Alfredo Di Stéfano, were about to play for the European club football championship in Vienna's Prater Stadion against the young Nerazzurri (Black and Blue) of Inter Milan, coached by the turgid but brilliant Argentinian strategist Helenio Herrera, and featuring such superstars as Sandro Mazzola (football royalty by virtue of being the son of the late, great Valentino Mazzola), Giacinto Facchetti, and Luis Suárez.

These players were living legends. Ferenc Puskás was the leader of the ill-fated Hungarian "golden team" that was clearly the very best national team in the world in 1954, yet succumbed to the inferior West Germans, an event that would lead each country's history onto a different trajectory: the former to the disastrous revolution of 1956; the latter to becoming Europe's shining success story. Until this game on the evening of May 27, 1964, my most lasting soccer memory hailed from that match on the Fourth of July 1954, when, as already mentioned, I gathered with my father around our Blaupunkt radio in Timişoara to listen to the broadcast.

The Vienna experience was further enhanced by my taking Daphne Scheer to the match. Daphne was a petite brunette, not quite five feet tall, with thick, curly hair and beautiful olive skin, slightly on the heavy side, all features I have found immensely attractive in women my entire life. I had met her in Hashomer Hatzair, the labor Zionist youth movement that had a chapter in post-Holocaust Vienna. It was one of three organizations available to Jewish kids in the Vienna of the 1960s: Bnei Akiva belonging to the modern Orthodox Mizrahi movement; Israel Hatzaira vaguely associated with the liberal Klal party, but essentially nothing more than a place for Jewish youngsters to get together on Saturday evenings and socialize around ping-pong tables before hitting the clubs on the sly; and Hashomer Hatzair, an openly Marxist organization that extolled Israel's kibbutzim and had as its adult patron Mapam, the more radical of Israel's two labor parties.

As befit such an openly leftist organization, the boys were never allowed to wear neckties or jackets, and the girls could not put on any makeup or wear high heels; these were accoutrements of the bourgeoisie that had to be shunned at all cost by Marxists of the left-wing socialist bent who extolled the collective existence of the kibbutz. Modesty was the motto, designed to spurn any bourgeois habits of consumerism and extol the ways of the proletariat, clothing included. My father hated all things Leninist, given that he had lived through the years of Stalinist Romania, but he harbored vague sympathies for Marxism's social democratic leanings, which made him steer me toward Hashomer Hatzair— Bnei Akiva striking him as too religious and Israel Hatzaira too fluffy and intellectually vacuous. After all, in Hashomer Hatzair we learned to speak some Hebrew, though purely the secular vernacular, as well as sing many Israeli songs and read the writings of many socialists, most prominently those of Ber Borochov, one of the founding thinkers of Poale Zion, labor Zionism. In short, we were engaged in intellectual endeavors my father immensely respected, regardless of the group's political bent— within reason, of course.

It was Hashomer Hatzair's decided intellectualism that made my father tolerate the organization's anti-bourgeois attitudes and behavior, both of which violated his core principles because he relished being an old-fashioned, established bourgeois with everything that entailed. Rendering the organization even more attractive was that its activities included long hikes in the local Vienna woods as well as other outdoor engagements, which meant the body was not totally neglected among all the mind-based activities of reading sophisticated texts and learning Hebrew songs by heart. We also went on two-to-three day trips where we stayed in various rustic lodges not far from Vienna hiking all day and then reading and discussing various pieces of socialist and Jewish history and philosophy.

Here, I met Daphne, my first serious girlfriend. She was the daughter of Viennese Jews who had fled to Palestine during the war and lived in newly formed Israel until the mid-1950s, before returning to Vienna. The Viennese Jewish community of the 1950s and 1960s—all 8,000 members—featured three groups of approximately equal size: the Jews of the Polish-Russian Pale of Settlement; the Jews of Hungary writ large, including Romania's Transylvania and the Banat region, from which my father and I hailed; and the returned Viennese Jews who, like Daphne's parents, had fled after the *Anschluss* in 1938, survived the war elsewhere, and found their way back to Vienna after the Allied victory. Daphne's father had died a while back—she never talked about the details—and she lived with her younger brother, Ronny, and their mother, who owned a women's clothing store. She was 10 months older than I was, being born in January, 1948 and I in October of the same year.

I could see that Daphne viewed our football-match date as special the moment she opened the door to her apartment and I spotted her wearing makeup and high heels, and inhaled the scents of perfume and hairspray wafting towards me. My heart sank when I saw how pretty she was: she was much more striking than would be appropriate for the drab culture of Hashomer Hatzair, where such displays of conventional bourgeois femininity were forbidden. But here we were, I in my casual trousers, button-down shirt and tie, but no suit jacket, Daphne in her high heels and proper little shepherd's checked wool suit, with match-

ing jacket and skirt, walking from her apartment building on Hintzerstrasse in Vienna's third district (which was, as already mentioned
in the previous chapter, literally across the street from my headmaster
Dr. Roger Kerber's apartment which, thankfully, I did not know at the
time) across Vienna's beautiful meadows. These meadows comprised the
lesser-known area of the city's famed Prater, an amusement park front-
ed by the world-famous Ferris wheel called the Riesenrad. I have never
understood how Daphne managed to walk through all that grass, sand,
and dirt in her high heels. But she did. On one level, I was immensely
pleased by how many of the men walking towards the stadium ogled
Daphne's sexy stilettos. On another level, I was embarrassed by how in-
appropriate they were, and how foolish Daphne and I must have looked
to the very men who leered lecherously at a young woman wearing high
heels. Still, at the deepest level, I felt she appreciated the significance of
my inviting her to an event that meant so much to me, and nothing reflected this more than her being decked out for the occasion, perhaps
even for me.

Obtaining tickets to this most prominent of games in Europe's football season was immensely difficult—and very expensive. This was the
first time in the postwar era that Vienna hosted a match of such international importance. My father somehow succeeded in purchasing the
tickets, and of course planned to go with me, as we had gone to soccer
matches back in Timişoara when I was a toddler and continued doing in
Vienna virtually every weekend of the season.

My father must have known how deeply in love I was with Daphne
when I asked whether he would kindly surrender his ticket and allow me
to take her instead. By toying with his unconditional love for me, I deprived him of a great pleasure that he keenly wanted to share with his
son, soccer and sports being the most important venues of communication between us, a bond that remained harmonious and uncontested
throughout our lives, even as we each traversed so many diverse locales.
Everything else was subject to terrible battles that were often brutal and
hurtful—arguments over women, school, work, and most importantly
of all, politics. But even as we navigated these troubled waters, we could
always find shelter together on the serene island of sports. No egos. No

envy. No jealousy. No tension. We sat side-by-side in many a stadium around the world, or on the couch of many an apartment, not saying a word yet feeling immensely close, even intimate. (I once read a study that men like to sit next to each other while women prefer to sit face-to-face. What a difference!) My father's willingness to give up both tickets to the match between Real Madrid and Inter Milan was neither the first nor last demonstration of his unconditional love for his son. Alas, later in my life I proved much less generous in my kindness to him, a failing I will always regret.

My entire involvement in this endeavor wreaked of egotism and self-ishness. First came the standard male notion that women should get involved—at least temporarily, though never too deeply—in matters close to us. And few passions were closer to most men—myself included—than watching sports. Because soccer was so significant to me, I assumed it would be so for Daphne; that participating in this event as a spectator would give her as much pleasure as it would give me. My preferences had to be hers, if only for an evening, despite her knowing nothing about the game, having no idea of the significance of this particular match, not even recognizing the two teams' names, and, most assuredly, not knowing any of the 22 players performing on the field.

Making the arrangement even less favorable for Daphne was the fact that she basically had no veto option. Knowing full well how important this event was to me, she must have been aware that she would have insulted me terribly had she declined the invitation. This was in stark contrast to another major event in Vienna that Daphne and I had attended a few weeks earlier. David Lean's epic film *Lawrence of Arabia*, starring Peter O'Toole and Omar Sharif, had opened in the city's premier movie theater to rave reviews. Both Daphne and I were eager to see the film. It was the man's role in those days to come up with the funds for such an occasion, but I did so with Daphne's full involvement and support. The soccer game was more of a *fait accompli*, an edict on my part rather than a mutually arrived outcome that was mutually desired.

Of course, not all dates have to be negotiated and agreed upon by both partners in order to be legitimate. This would exclude the wonderful dimension of surprise and spontaneity. But surely the occasion should be something the recipient truly enjoys and does not merely tolerate. I assumed Daphne would love me for inviting her to this soccer match, because she simply had to adore my passion for the game, my desire to share that passion with her, and, most significantly, my willingness to dump my father and take her instead. I tore apart this meaningful yet rare communal feeling between father and son for the simple reason that I wanted to impress a young woman who, truth be told, was not very impressed at the end of the day, because she knew nothing about soccer and didn't know how to dress appropriately for the event. This whole affair was merely a selfish gift to myself, which added little to Daphne's pleasure and well-being while most certainly diminishing my father's.

Still, the evening was not a complete disaster. For reasons having to do with politics and my hatred of all things fascist, I disliked Real Madrid, which was then identified as Francisco Franco's team. So even though I knew Real players such as Di Stéfano and Puskás much better than their Inter counterparts, I was heavily rooting for Inter. And when Sandro Mazzola scored a beautiful goal, I conjured up the courage to give Daphne a kiss the like of which I had never done before. I remain forever grateful to Sandro for having scored that great goal.

Daphne and I celebrated Inter's winning the European Championship by dancing around with visiting Italian fans before I walked her home, though this time she walked barefoot across the Prater's fields, holding her high-heeled shoes in her hand. I was ecstatic, both because of Inter's win and because of having Daphne hang on to me the whole way to her house.

Alas, that date did not impress Daphne sufficiently to make her love for me endure. A few weeks after the game, she dumped me for Eddy Penner, a rival I found to be undeserving, although in later years he became the head of the Department of Gastroenterology at the University of Vienna's medical school. After being dumped in his favor, I lost touch with Daphne. However, due to the small size of the Viennese Jewish community, I occasionally heard about her turbulent life from my father and others. Influenced by the counterculture of the late 1960s, she drifted from drugs to Maoism, and from one commune to another, studying pharmacology and philosophy, but earning a degree in neither.

In the course of the ensuing decades, I thought of Daphne often, with deep affection, not only because she was my first real girlfriend, but also because she was a genuine intellectual who became a victim of the famed 1960s, as so many people did, something folks like me forget about when touting that era as the source of many political and social advances in the liberal democracies of the West. I remember how Daphne always had a book in her purse, sometimes fiction, but often politics. When our group discussed the writings of Ber Borochov in the dank rooms of the Vienna Hashomer Hatzair, she did not back down from anyone, though she was never haughty or dismissive towards others during those debates.

I am sure that, as an active member of Vienna's student left in the late 1960s, Daphne read the requisite quantities of Herbert Marcuse, Theodor Adorno, and the other greats of the Frankfurt School of Critical Theory. I am also certain she must have been an active member of the Marxist study groups that enlivened the university environs of Vienna and many other European and American cities at the time. I even vaguely remember one of my Viennese professorial colleagues mentioning to me during a conference sometime in the 1980s or 1990s that there was this really bright woman called Daphne in his Grundrisse study group back in the day.

Part of this scene also featured drugs, of which Daphne partook, though I never knew what kind or amount. As became so fashionable by the early 1970s, communist groups of the most ideological variety decided to leave the freewheeling New Left behind and pursue a much more dogmatic Marxism, almost exclusively of the Leninist variety. This was the era of the so-called K-Groups in the history of the German Left with K denoting "Kommunist." These groups ranged from pro-Soviet to pro-Chinese to pro-Albanian (as late as the 1980s, I regularly encountered a sixtyish pro-Albanian agitator handing out leaflets announcing the imminence of a working-class revolution in the United States and other Western democracies at the Central Square T stop in Cambridge, Massachusetts). In Germany, Italy, and Japan (not accidentally, the formerly fascist troika), this element spawned violent terrorism, but no such factions emerged in Austria. Instead, Daphne assumed a leading role as a major activist in a Maoist student organization.

I have never understood why such intellectually gifted people as Daphne became Maoists. Trotskyists, yes! Anarcho-syndicalists, yes! Workerists, yes! Third World liberationists, yes! But Maoists? After we all knew about the disaster that was the Great Leap Forward? After we came to learn about the Cultural Revolution's singular brutality with its killing and shaming of innocent people? The only way I could vaguely understand intelligent Western students walking around waving *The Little Red Book* of Mao's sayings was by seeing organized Maoism as a cult. John Lennon brilliantly captured my feelings in the Beatles' song "Revolution" when he wrote: "If you go carrying pictures of Chairman Mao, you ain't gonna make it with anyone anyhow!"

In a strange way, I was not surprised that at some point in the mid-1980s, my aunt Manci went to purchase a blouse in a lady's garment store not far from her apartment in Vienna. And who should the gracious sales person turn out to be but Daphne Scheer, who had joined her mother as a full partner in the store. I had encountered similar stories among some of my West German lefty pals, who exited Maoism to settle into a solid bourgeois life. Many would contest my interpretation, but I have always viewed Maoism, apart from its revolutionary bluster, as the most *Gemeinschaft*-oriented and soil-bound ideology of the New and the Old Left. Of course, such settling down was supposed to happen in a collective commune out on the land, not in a lady's haberdashery store on a major Viennese street, but some kind of hearth-like telos beckoned for sure.

Interestingly, Daphne's future husband also hailed from this milieu. Though he was not Jewish, and though he and Daphne both denounced, even disdained, their Maoist past, it was in a Maoist commune of the late 1960s and early 1970s that they first fell in love. Another irony was that Daphne, whom I had met when she was adhering to Hashomer Hatzair's strict rules about not wearing makeup and perfume and in no way acceding to conventional female bourgeois fashion habits, ended up working in her mother's extremely conventional clothing store, precisely where my seventy-year-old aunt Manci would purchase her attire. This was not a store where the killer stilettos that Daphne wore to the soccer match would have been sold. No, this was a store that typified what the

Viennese so aptly call "*braves Wien*," good Vienna, decent Vienna, traditional Vienna, unthreatening Vienna.

As fate would have it, my wife, Kiki, and I eventually reconnected with Daphne—Kiki being another Jewish woman from Vienna, two years Daphne's junior, with many differences, but also some similarities such as Kiki's complete ignorance of and indifference to sports. Kiki and I even attended Daphne's wedding in the spring of 1996, when Daphne was already stricken by the illness that would kill her. The following year, with Eddy and Andy long in her romantic past, Daphne died tragically of lung cancer, not having reached the age of fifty, her death possibly a result of her chain smoking unfiltered cigarettes all her life, as was the practice among the counterculture activists in the Europe of the 1960s and 1970s. Anybody worth their leftist credentials at the time had to roll their own cigarettes, joint style, filled with Drum tobacco made by the Dutch company Douwe Egberts, wrapped in white paper.

Inter, the team Daphne and I saw win that magical night in 1964 (at least it was magical for me), reached the Champions League final in May 2010, 46 years later. As fate would have it, Inter triumphed once again, winning its third European championship. It did so in, of all places, the Estadio Santiago Bernabeu, Real Madrid's venerable home ground, where it defeated Bayern Munich, the perennial German champion often identified as one of Europe's "Jew Teams" (together with Ajax Amsterdam, Tottenham Hotspur, and MTK Budapest among others).

At the time, I was the Sir Peter Ustinov Professor at the University of Vienna, and, by chance, on May 22, the very evening of the game's appearance on television, broadcast from Madrid, I was having an early dinner with Daphne's cousin, Evelyn Klein, a noted Viennese psychologist. We scheduled our meal for 6 p.m. so that I would be safely in front of my TV set for kick off at 9 p.m. I wanted to meet Evi for the explicit reason of giving her a signed and dedicated copy of a book on Viennese football, to which I had contributed a chapter detailing my experiences at the city's football grounds in the late 1950s and 1960s. I dedicated my essay to the memories of my father, Ludwig Markovits, and Daphne Scheer who will remain forever linked by this Inter-Real match in Vienna in May of 1964.

The Rolling Stones Play Vienna (Resulting in Bodily Harm to the City's Jews)

In 1965, on their fourth European tour, the Rolling Stones finally made it to Vienna and were scheduled to play a gig in the city's Stadthalle on September 17. I had been an ardent fan of the group since I purchased their first LP, *The Rolling Stones*, the year before. Even though I favored the Beatles slightly more than the Stones, I loved the Stones' edgier sound and culture and, above all, their funkier rhythm and blues. The Beatles had their compositional genius and melodic harmony, but the Stones could boast gritty, in-your-face, two-guitar riffs, and Mick Jagger's onstage charisma.

As is true for millions of my generation, both bands remain an integral part of my life. In some respect, all new music represents an implicit rejection of the existing fare. Mozart's *Magic Flute*, which featured a German libretto, represented a cultural challenge to the hegemonic Italian-language operas of his time, including Mozart's own. Händel's and Liszt's popularity were akin to that of contemporary rock stars; one can find many such examples among instrumentalists and vocalists in every musical era. But not until the arrival of jazz and various dance styles of the 1920s and 1930s—the Charleston, swing, and boogie-woogie—did these new cultural forms attain a distinct identification with youth.

Clearly, this new phenomenon coincided with the invention of new means of communication, most notably film, radio, and the phonograph. The cleavage between generations became even more pronounced after the end of the Second World War, with the arrival of rock 'n roll, first in the United States and soon after in Europe, and indeed all over the world. It has become a commonplace to associate rock 'n roll with rebelliousness, sexuality, flouting the old, and extolling the new and outrageous. Little Richard, Elvis Presley, Carl Perkins, Chuck Berry, and Jerry Lee Lewis held the same cultural significance for European teenagers of the 1950s as they did for their American counterparts: these performers mesmerized young people, much to the fear and aversion of their elders. The Beatles, the Stones, the Animals, the Kinks, and virtually all English bands and musicians of that era became rock 'n rollers by virtue of having fallen in love with these American icons of the genre, whom they tried to emulate and transcend. Love for this music was almost a given in my world. But there was an added dimension of affection for me that most assuredly did not play a role for my counterparts in the United States, nor in Britain: Rock 'n roll was an English-speaking medium and—better yet—featured English of a decidedly American variety.

Virtually all British rock stars—including the Beatles and the Stones—employed an American accent in their singing, which they most assuredly did not when simply speaking. To me, this English-speaking, American-accented expression of sex, freedom, opposition, and rebellion provided two invaluable benefits. First, the lyrics enabled me to learn an English that was decidedly not that taught in the staid Austrian secondary schools of aristocratic ambitions and airs. I ruined a number of Elvis Presley and Chuck Berry albums by lifting and then lowering the needle hundreds of times so I could write down the words, which, in those days, never accompanied an album. I was ecstatic when, in June 1967, the Beatles issued their majestic *Sgt. Pepper's Lonely Hearts Club Band* album with the lyrics published on the back of the cover, the first time I can recall a band doing so. I remain convinced that my relatively nuanced knowledge of the English language and of key words and expressions harken back to this self-administered tutorial over many years in our small Viennese apartment.

But I derived a second benefit from immersing myself in the world of rock 'n roll: the music represented yet another visible dimension of the Allies' victory over the Nazis, the liberal democratic West's triumph over

Germany and its Central European appendages. In many respects, rock music fulfilled my secret wish to beat up or kill as many Nazis as I could, the same cultural and psychic function fulfilled by a film like Quentin Tarantino's much more recent *Inglorious Basterds*. I could not do this with Bach and Beethoven and Brahms on many accounts, not least because they are all German but also because their divine music does not lend itself to such fantasies, at least for me. I am sure that these violent wishes and images have much to do with rock music's aural difference to its classical counterparts as pertains to pretty much everything, from its relative compositional simplicity to its appeal to sexuality. Of course, opera is massively sexual; and of course it features, even fetes violence. To me, however, all its emotive dimensions have become intellectualized and confined. We sit completely still, not even whispering permitted, in a narrow chair in a sea of other people watching a stage. We do not actively dialogue or interact with the spectacle on stage though I have heard that on occasion at Milan's famed La Scala vocal fan battles develop in which cheers and jeers rain down on the singers from the galleries. Symphonic music has become even more cerebral and intellectual than opera. For reasons not quite clear, rock music always represented to me a triumph over all the evils and fears that I associated with National Socialism and Stalinism that so formed my early childhood in Romania. Of course, it also represented a solid rebellion against the German-infused high culture that especially my mother instilled in me during my childhood in Romania.

I will surely begin worrying about dementia when I forget any of the lyrics of the Rolling Stones' or Beatles' iconic tunes. I remember staying up late at night, my transistor radio hidden in my bed, listening to Radio Luxembourg, the Station of the Stars, which broadcast a feature called "Battle of the Giants," in which the DJ had two musical giants square off against each other, with the Beatles and the Rolling Stones being particularly desirable combatants.

My father, like millions of other parents, disliked both bands, but he felt genuinely threatened by the Stones' contrived bad-boy image and sexuality. While he tolerated the Beatles, and even came to concede to their immense musical talents certainly by the time they put out *A Hard*

Day's Night, the Stones remained unacceptable. With one notable exception: when my father saw the jacket of the first Stones' album, he perused the names of the musicians and, when he came to Mick Jagger, assumed a demeanor that bespoke pride, gratification, and astonishment, accompanied by a wave of his hand expressing an uncertainty, possibly even a worry. And sure enough, there it was: "This Mick Jagger, what kind of name is that? Might he possibly have been a Michael Jäger at some point in his life?," implying that Jagger was Jewish or at least of Jewish origin.

Men of my father's generation always held out hope that someone famous could be Jewish, however remote the possibility. Though "Jäger" clearly was more of a German than a Jewish name, Michael Jagger could be Jewish, especially if he hailed from England, where, my father assured me, such a name was totally uncharacteristic. I insisted Jagger was absolutely not Jewish, but my father never dismissed his hunch. When I took him to see the Rolling Stones in the Estadio Vicente Calderon, Atletico Madrid's home field, during the World Cup in the summer of 1982, and he got to see Mick Jagger emerge onstage wearing a see-through poncho protecting him from a driving rainstorm and hear him sing a thunderous "Under My Thumb" as the band's opening number, my father once again floated the possibility that this man's real name was "Michael Jäger," pronouncing both names in their German phonetic version instead of their proper English. A special and prolonged emphasis on *Jaaeeger* revealed a bit of Yiddish inflection, Yiddish being a language my father did not speak and contemptuously referred to as "*jargon*," a bastardized dialect of proper German, which, incidentally, my father never spoke well either.

But all that came later. The first Stones concert I attended, the one in Vienna in 1965, fell in the middle of the week, and with school in full swing, my father would never have permitted me to go. But a friend of mine had informed me that his much more enlightened father had purchased two tickets, and that he wanted me to accompany him. The temptation was far too powerful to resist. I had to invent some story so I could go see the Stones at the Stadthalle. On account of my excellent English, I tutored younger students in that language, which gave me a great opening to concoct a lie that would appear plausible to my father.

While it was not quite clear why I was to tutor this kid so late in the evening, my father, to my amazement, bought the explanation. All was clear for me to go see the Stones.

And what a concert it was. I will never forget Brian Jones's all-white three-piece suit, the pants not quite reaching his ankles. I loved his blond mane, also his guitar playing, which, at least on that occasion, I found more impressive than Keith Richards'. Even though the Stones' distinction has always been that they are a two-guitar band with no clear lead and rhythm guitarist, that evening Jones seemed to take over most of the solos, with Richards playing rhythm. While I valued a fine rhythm guitarist and found it upsetting when fans belittled that aspect of music-making in favor of an overly macho and showy lead guitarist, Richards appeared too subdued, almost lethargic, in the Stadthalle gig.

Maybe Jones's white suit and hair mesmerized me even more than did the always mesmerizing Jagger. I was also impressed by the stoicism of the rhythm section, comprised of the bass player Bill Wyman and the drummer Charlie Watts. In contrast to the peripatetic Jagger, Wyman and Watts did not move an inch; rather, they let their fingers, hands, and wrists do their superb work. I regard my admiration for Wyman and Watts at the Stadthalle as a precursor to my deep affection for Jerry Garcia, who also remained stationary while captivating his audience with his art, and whom I would not encounter until September 1969 at the Fillmore East in New York City, nearly four years to the day after I saw the Stones in Vienna.

The Stones ended their concert with a rousing rendition of "Satisfaction," sending my pal and me happily on our way home. Since our respective homes were not too far from the Stadthalle, we sang and danced down the deadly quiet streets of Vienna, a city which, at the time and in many parts still, succumbed to an eerie silence after 9 p.m. We broke that silence by singing loudly and dancing Jagger-like with the imaginary microphone in our right hands, bending down from the imaginary podium to the imaginary audience filled with imaginary gorgeous girls who looked up to us adoringly and ecstatically.

"When I'm driving in my car, and a man comes on the radio, and he's telling me more and more,'" I sang, bouncing as we turned right from Kaiserstrasse onto Lerchenfelderstrasse, where my apartment—in Building 139—was forty feet away. And whom should I run into departing from his parked car and walking toward our building, key in hand, but my dear father. I froze: I thought I was going to die on the spot. My father, barely three feet away, came toward me and smacked me. This was the only time in his life that he hit me. We walked up the stairs to our apartment without speaking one word. In fact, my father would not speak a word to me for three days; we ate all our meals in silence.

My father hit me in part because I lied to him. But he had caught me in lies previously in my life—and later as well—without hitting me. Chiding me, yes, maybe even punishing me in some fashion, but never hitting me. He had deeper reasons for his fury that night. My father would never have hit me had he caught me attending one of the great Wagner operas featuring Dame Joan Sutherland, the opera equivalent of Mick Jagger at the time, on the sly. My father loathed Wagner, not so much because of that composer's vile antisemitism, but because of the bombastic nature of his operas, which my father found too loud, too long, and too German. I, on the other hand, liked Wagner and would go to the *Staatsoper* by myself or with a friend to see one of his operas. My father was excluded from this culture, but he was not in any way threatened by it. He disliked Wagner: end of story!

Not so with the Stones. Not only did he have no affinity for their music, but—like most middle-class parents in North America and western Europe at the time—he instinctively felt threatened by the music's "animalistic" rhythm, its culturally inferior gestalt, and the obvious power and attraction it exerted over me. That the Stones and their music were Anglo-American, hence representative of the good guys, became irrelevant when my father saw his son prance around on the corner of Lerchenfelderstrasse and Kaiserstrasse late at night, appearing not fully human. For my father, his son loving and imitating the Stones was nothing short of a head-on challenge to everything he stood for and valued.

His anger and disappointment were almost too much for me. Characteristic of father-son relations in a bourgeois culture still so influenced by the Victorian age and its mores, my father and I never discussed the incident. What broke the ice between us was an important soccer match that our beloved team Austria was to play that weekend. Once again, sports—soccer in particular—came to the rescue in the complex relationship between Markovits Lajos and András (to use the appropriate Hungarian appellation).

Yet another incident mellowed my father regarding the Stones fiasco. The weekend after the concert, a photograph appeared in one of Vienna's leading newspapers, featuring the band seated in a restaurant in the company of two attractive young women, both of whom were—horror of horrors—daughters of Orthodox Jews from the Viennese community. In fact, I attended weekly Hebrew classes with one of the women. The uproar within the small Viennese Jewish community was immense. Even though the young women were not mentioned by name in the photo's caption, everyone in the community knew who they were, and the age-old question of how this incident would affect the community—whether this was good or bad for the Jews—emerged, in addition to the vilification of the young women for shaming their parents.

To this day, I envy those two women for having met the Stones, something which I, their most devoted fan, never managed to do, despite seeing them in concert 24 times, from New York to Boston, from Madrid to Berlin, from San Francisco to Detroit. That photograph also conveyed to my father the fact that the Stones were truly vital to my generation, and that the two girls, who most assuredly never received permission from their much more conservative parents, snuck around in all kinds of devious ways, not only in order to attend the concert, but to dine with the band in a fine Viennese restaurant.

Perhaps the women even spent time with the band beyond sharing dinner. I never dared ask my acquaintance. In some sense, whether they slept with any of the band members or not became irrelevant to me, because even if the Stones were not interested in these two attractive women sexually, even if the band members were just keen on spending an evening chatting with Viennese girls, I knew the girls would never have gotten to meet the Stones without deploying their physical beauty as currency. Lacking such currency, I felt handicapped on that count.

All this happened in a world in which I knew nothing of what was called "feminism" and had no idea that women's sexuality was often objectified by men, who used women's attractiveness, something I considered a source of great power, to harm them. To make matters still more complicated, the women's minds and education—not only their looks—did turn out to be important to the band. Having spent many summers in youth camps in England—camps that simply did not exist for Orthodox Jews in Austria at the time—the young women had acquired a deep proficiency in English, which allowed them to communicate with the band and act as translators for the Viennese journalists who were part of the dinner party and whose English was either nonexistent or inadequate.

Looking back, I wonder whether the Stones were even aware that these two young women were daughters of East European Jewish refugees, all of whom were victims of the Shoah. Did they ask the girls who they really were? Did they know about Vienna's brutal antisemitic history, which arguably rendered Hitler's arrival in the city on March 13, 1938, the most triumphant moment of his political life (after all, the boy who had made good in Germany had finally returned home to Austria)? Did the Stones know anything about Austrian antisemitism? Or any other antisemitism for that matter? Were the Stones aware that just miles from where they sat with these young women, a rightwing extremist in an antisemitic mob had, five months earlier, killed the Austrian retiree Ernst Kirchweger, making him the first political victim of the Second Austrian Republic? We will never know. What we do know is that the young woman's father slapped her after seeing her in the photograph in the paper, just as my father slapped me. She told me that when I ran into her in our next Hebrew class, thus proving that the Stones' first visit to Vienna indeed exacted bodily harm on that city's Jewish community!

Still, seeing that photo in the paper softened my father's antipathy toward the Stones and his anger toward his son. By the time he and I attended the World Cup in Madrid in the summer of 1982, both attitudes had evolved even further. In the subway on the way from our hotel to a match, my father suddenly turned to me and asked—*sotto voce*, almost childlike—whether it would be okay if he were to accompany me to the Rolling Stones concert later that week. After all, he said, he was an old man (71 at the time) who did not know even one of the Stones' songs, and he wanted to make sure I would not feel embarrassed by his presence. I barely believed my ears and joyfully responded that it would be my honor to take my father to a Rolling Stones concert in one of Madrid's huge soccer stadia.

Our relationship had changed profoundly in the previous 17 years. I had just completed five years of teaching as an assistant professor of government at Wesleyan University, where my father visited me repeatedly, and was on my way to Boston University with the rank of associate professor. The Stones no longer threatened to derail me from my academic career; they were not going to strip my father's son of his solid middle-class existence as a respected young professor; the band members were merely five guys who played superb music I enjoyed and that my father wanted to sample for one fine evening. Also, by then, the Stones had become middle-aged billionaires who, on occasion, pretended to be rebels but were increasingly unlikely to pull off the daring and provocative antics of their youth.

CHAPTER SIX

Arrival in New York: The Dream Meets the Reality

Even though my father and I had settled in Vienna as subletting tenants in Frau Kohler's apartment, and even though I had been accepted into my father's dream *Gymnasium*, the Theresianische Akademie, and finished my first year there, I always sensed Vienna was nothing but a way station to somewhere more permanent and better. That this was not wishful thinking was clear from the temporariness of our lives there: we lived in someone else's apartment; my father had not yet found a permanent job; and we were either at the Consulate of the United States or the office of the International Rescue Committee (IRC) every other day, being fingerprinted, filling out forms. America clearly beckoned.

Emigration entails both a strong pull and a push. The pull is the dream, the hope, the succor, and the safety the new place will bestow that the old place never could or did. Still, without the push, without some terrible reason, some unbearable hardship, most people would never leave their homes. Such a departure is immensely taxing on every aspect of human existence. Even more perplexing, the conceptual clarity of this dyad bears virtually no relation to its actuality as a lived experience. The pull becomes less shiny up close than it seemed from afar, and the push assumes a less foreboding dimension than it did originally. Reality, as is so often the case, becomes a muddling through, full of compromises and concessions.

Moving to the United States had always been a dream of mine, certainly since that fateful Fourth of July 1954 when my father informed me during the West Germany-Hungary World Cup Final in Bern, to which we were listening in our apartment in Timișoara, that the game's only significance was that it occurred on the birthday of this great and distant land, the place of all good. This fantasy was based on nothing concrete about the real United States of America, other than the occasional toy car I received from my uncle Alex, that distant and mythical New York figure, who had returned from the Holocaust and then emigrated to New York sometime in the late 1940s, before the Iron Curtain descended on the middle of Europe, hermetically sealing its eastern half from the rest of the world.

For my father, it was not so much the United States proper, but a mishmash of America, Britain, Canada, Australia—in other words, the English-speaking democracies, the Anglo-Saxons to use Franco-German parlance—that remained the only beacon of hope for those like us. The German-dominated world of *Mitteleuropa,* in which Jewish culture had played such a central role, had disappeared, and the very concept and all that it entailed had become untenable for a Jew after World War II. All that was left was the music, literature, and language my father required that I learn, not because he retained any affection for things German, but because mastery of a Western language could come in handy.

Even though my father did not mention the Holocaust, nor openly speak ill of the Germans, I felt his deep dislike for them in many instances of our daily life. Whenever he would see an item stamped "Made in Germany," he would mention with a kind of resignation bordering on hostility that no matter how hard one tried to rid oneself of things German they caught up with one, not least of all because of the quality of German products. Even though he respected German punctuality, he always commented on it unfavorably, as if such an obsession with being on time were inhuman; to my father, a fastidiously bourgeois person to whom punctuality actually mattered a great deal, the alleged laxness and spontaneity of the Italians seemed much more simpatico than the dreariness of German discipline.

What about my father's view of the Soviet world? His opinion of socialism or communism? Totally out of the question. He disdained anything from the East, which, to my father, was not European, hence savage. Throughout his life, my father repeated with gusto Count Metternich's famous dictum that Asia—a disdained entity—commenced at the end of Vienna's Landstrasser Hauptstrasse, which led to the city's eastern suburbs. My father hated and feared communism, which, after all, had cynically ravaged some of his Jewish pals, who heartily embraced the movement and went to work for the new communist regimes in Bucharest and Budapest immediately after the war only to be jailed, even maimed in one instance, or most certainly humiliated by the anti-Jewish purges of the Pauker and Rajk trials respectively. Social Democracy, the other option of the political left, was too weak, and too impotent in my father's life, to pose any real opposition to the two horrors of his world, fascism and communism, which he rightly saw as dialectically linked phenomena.

So the only hope remaining were the long-lasting liberal democracies of the English-speaking world. England, which my father adored and respected beyond words, was somehow off the table. Too elitist? Too non-Jewish? Too hard to assimilate into? I simply do not know. Canada might have been a possibility had my father known someone there from the old country. Australia was too far, even though his most beloved friend, Steven "Pista" Erdélyi, had emigrated to Melbourne with his wife. (My father never got to see Erdélyi in Australia, but in their older years they regularly met in places such as Hawaii, Thailand, and Bali.) So America it was, and with good reason: his brother lived in New York, and the Romanian quota had not been filled, meaning we could apply to enter the United States and become naturalized citizens.

I remember saying good bye to my friends in the 1B Klasse on our last day of school in late June 1960, expecting never to see them again. This was not terribly hard for me. Though popular on a superficial level among my thirty or so classmates, mainly by dint of my gregariousness—and, more important in an all-male population, my masterful knowledge of, as opposed to my mediocre performance in, most sports, soccer in particular—I felt not quite accepted, especially by the hotshots, the leaders of the pack. To be sure, I did not experience any overt anti-semitism at this stage, but, in an intangible but palpable way, I clearly was not part of the in-crowd.

My father, my aunt Manci, and my uncle Richard, all of whom had left Timișoara and joined my father and me in Vienna, along with a close friend of my father's—yet another Timișoarian—boarded the train to Salzburg, where, for reasons I never ascertained, the IRC had us begin our long journey to New York. Then came the good-byes as we boarded the bus to Munich. Once again, emotions ran high, just as they had barely two years earlier, when my father and I departed Timișoara, and all his friends and the few remaining relatives came to bid us farewell. The second leg in a never-ending emigration process, our westward trek, had commenced.

And yet, this departure felt different. My father and I were leaving for distant America. But no matter how vast the Atlantic Ocean appeared and how far away New York was for all of us, we were not crossing the Iron Curtain: we were not leaving a world to which one could never return. Whereas leaving Timișoara in September 1958 appeared final, leaving Salzburg and Austria in early July 1960, as huge and foreboding as this voyage seemed, did not strike us as a complete rupture from our previous life. My aunt Manci cried, but not with the bitterness and desperation she had exhibited two years earlier at our departure to the West from Timișoara. Sooner or later, she would come visit my father, me, and her older brother, Alex, whom she had not seen in nearly 15 years.

The only good-bye that felt final was the one I needed to say to Frau Kohler, my beloved "Tante Trude," the landlady of the apartment in which my father and I had lived as subtenants. The hug she gave me at the Vienna train station before my father and I boarded the train to Salzburg was one of the most heartfelt I have ever experienced in my life. In less than two years, she had come to love me deeply—to the chagrin and pain of her daughter, Birgit. The rootlessness of this generation of European Jews always helped me with good-byes because deep down I knew the chances of meeting these Jewish people again were real. Not so with my non-Jewish loved ones, whose rootedness in Vienna appeared a real impediment to our reuniting. Whereas I felt that Aunt Manci had good reasons to come to America, no such optimism emerged concerning Frau Kohler. This was not yet the age of trans-Atlantic tourism, and America was not yet on the regular vacation circuit of the West European bourgeoisie. Viennese folks of Frau Kohler's social station vacationed in Austria or, at best, traveled to Lido di Jesolo, Caorle, or Bibione, bathing resorts on the Adriatic beaches near Venice. America was still an unreachable entity to which one voyaged for good, not merely for a few weeks of sun and relaxation.

My father and I boarded a four-engine propeller plane at Munich-Riehm, the very airport where on February 6, 1958, Manchester United's plane had crashed while trying to take off from a slushy runway. That tragedy, in which 23 passengers, including members of the team, along with reporters and fans, died, had led to my becoming a life-long United fan. Also due to this tragedy, I had become anxious about flying, an anxiety I have never shed. I hadn't flown before, and neither had my father, other than traveling once with some of his colleagues from the Timişoara branch of the Romanian State Bank to headquarters in Bucharest. Entering the airplane, I was immensely nervous but excited. The plane's fuselage bore the name "Flying Tiger Line," which I later learned was the first scheduled cargo airline in the United States and a major military charter operator during the Cold War era for both cargo and personnel. I had a window seat and couldn't wait for the plane to take off.

And finally it did. I grabbed my father's hand, and its warmth and softness felt reassuring. The plane flew to London, where we landed and spent some time on the ground before traveling on to Shannon in Ireland, where we landed yet again and spent a longer time. I have no idea why the London stop occurred (might we have taken on passengers whom the IRC had slated to emigrate to the United States?); the Shannon stop made more sense since not all planes engaged in cross-Atlantic travel at the time had the capacity to fly nonstop from continental Europe to New York.

The plane's limited reach was reinforced by our landing at Gander Airport in Newfoundland, our first entry to North America. I wanted to deplane and stay, the cross-Atlantic trip having been terrifying because we were sitting near the engines and at dusk I saw the flame-like exhaust. This was normal, but not for a first-time flier leaving his home for the second time in less than two years. At dawn on that chilly, wet day, Gander looked desolate, with only a few military planes in the far distance. I longed to get off the flight, which, of course, we did not do. This brief experience in Gander, my first stop in life on North American soil, made me love the musical "Come From Away" that celebrated this airport's and small town's heroic welcoming of thousands of stranded passengers who in the wake of the tragedy of 9/11 were detained there unable to reach their final destinations in dozens of American cities.

New York, New York

And then, finally, in the early afternoon, we landed at New York's Idlewild Airport. I will never forget the approach: the Manhattan silhouette, the Long Island coastline, all in the bristling sunshine of a cloud-free day. Maybe I wasn't so sorry, after all, not to have disembarked in Gander. We walked down the steps and into a nondescript building, where my father once again grabbed my hand: "This is it!" he said. "This is America! This is our final destination. We have arrived."

And then we met the Immigration and Naturalization Service officer, whose entire demeanor spelled WELCOME TO THIS COOL PLACE, at least to me. Here was this middle-aged man sitting in an elevated glass booth, looking down at us and our papers. He wore a white short-sleeved shirt with an open collar revealing a white crewneck T-shirt. His outer shirt had a pocket on the left side with all kinds of pens and perhaps even note cards in it. And on this pocket was a nametag with an Italian name, something like Mangione or Marsala or Mantoni, definitely starting with the letter M. He became forever ensconced in my memory as the kind Mr. M. Previous authority figures for me were stern men in ties, never with open shirts, often with scary uniforms buttoned close to the wearer's neck. And the name plate on Mr. M's shirt was amazing! No Romanian policeman, Soviet officer, or Viennese official had his name attached to his shirt for all to see.

On top of all this, the man was chewing gum. As my father and I stood looking up at him, the officer blew some pink bubbles, revealing to me that he was chewing Bazooka bubble gum, the very stuff the Theresianische Akademie and my father and all well-heeled Vienna and bourgeois Europe had decried as vulgar and unbecoming in a young gentleman like myself, so uncultured and uncouth—so AMERICAN—which meant my pals and I loved it beyond words.

And then, in the corner of his booth sat a transistor radio, emitting words that clearly belonged to the broadcast of a live sporting event, which, I already knew, must have been a baseball game since Americans did not listen to broadcasts of soccer matches. Could I have landed in a cooler country than this, where an authority figure who held our lives in his hands appeared and behaved in a manner you would have liked to imitate but were never allowed to?

I also got to use my English—which was already passable and possibly better than my father's—with this man who made me feel important and accomplished. To top it off, when he welcomed us to the United States and told us where to go to meet his colleagues from Customs and pick up our bags, he gave most of our documents to my father, of course. But he also handed a few sheets of paper to me, as if to say, you, too, apart from your father, are welcome in this new place. From that moment on, all my experiences with authority figures in the United States—and my life in this country as a whole—have been basically positive in notable contrast to many of my fellow immigrants, particularly from non-European countries, not to mention African Americans. How crucial in one's highly impressionable life as a child are such chance encounters. I always wondered what my relationship to America would have become had we met the officer next to this wonderful Italian-American New Yorker, who, unlike Mr. M., would have been dour, unfriendly, rude, scary, and not blowing pink bubbles.

After getting our luggage and meeting with a New York-based IRC employee, who had us fill out more forms, we were finally able to leave the restricted area and enter the waiting area to be met by my uncle Alex. I was expecting a dashing and buoyant man, welcoming us to this dashing and buoyant New World. Instead, after some searching, I saw my father hugging this smallish, gray-haired, balding man with sad eyes and a shuffling gait. Uncle Alex—"Sanyi" to the Markovits family—hugged me warmly, but I sensed his sorrow. He barely smiled at me, even though he clearly was delighted to meet me. He appeared a broken man, which is exactly what he was, having lost both his parents, his four sons, and his first wife in Auschwitz and now was living in an unhappy marriage with his second wife, who had lost her first husband and only son in Auschwitz as well. How do folks like this continue to live I have always wondered.

After such tragedies, many victims of such unspeakable crimes never regain any pleasure in life; they carry on, but they become shells of their former selves, hollowed out by the pain of their losses. Though my father had experienced the usual brutalities of war while living in Timișoara, he was spared the hell of Auschwitz. My aunt Manci, who, like her brother Alex, went through Auschwitz, survived the death marches, and was barely saved by British troops from dying of typhoid in Bergen-Belsen, still smiled and was jovial despite experiencing horrors that marked her deeply. Somehow, collective tragedies as profound as the Holocaust still manifest themselves differently in each individual.

Uncle Alex and his second wife, Lulu, owned a small candy store on the northeast corner of Broadway and 92nd Street, which did not make them rich, but paid the bills. They lived in apartment 14J in the building above the store. But their one-bedroom apartment, which had a fine view of midtown Manhattan, was furnished with nothing more than two twin beds in the bedroom and a table with four chairs in the dining/living room. There was a clock radio on a stand in the bedroom, and an identical clock in the living room, which also had a mattress in the corner for the occasional guest. No pictures on the walls, no television, no plants, no decorations of any kind, no books, no alcove in which to sit and read in the evenings, nothing for decades, until 1972, when the couple moved back to Europe and discarded their failed life in New York.

They were, however, not one iota happier in Vienna than they had been in their barely furnished apartment in New York. The couple had no friends in either city. Alex never regained the standing he enjoyed before the war. He smiled rarely, and his sole joy was going to his Orthodox synagogue on West 91st Street between Broadway and Amsterdam

Avenue, which, alas, he did not do often enough. When the weather was nice, he and his wife would spend the occasional Sunday afternoon sitting on the bench on the dividing median on Broadway near their apartment building and their store, silently inhaling the fumes of the hundreds of cars passing in both directions. This was their pastime, their relaxation, their vacation!

After meeting Uncle Alex at Idlewild in Queens, we stepped outside into the bright New York sunshine and hailed a cab for the ride back to his place in Manhattan. A huge, bright yellow Chevy Impala with all kinds of numbers and words marked on its side pulled up. Out stepped this young Black man, who placed our bags into the cab's trunk and then beckoned me to sit beside him in the passenger seat so my father and his brother could have more space in the back. As the driver started the car, this amazing rock 'n roll music blared from his radio, with commentary from a crazy-sounding DJ whose words I could not fully understand, but whose enthusiasm and showmanship dazzled me.

All the windows were open, and the young driver, like the immigration official, chewed gum, and was one-arming the car, maneuvering it along this three-lane highway—the Van Wyck—incessantly switching lanes. Then we found ourselves on this massive bridge—the Triborough—which, though impressive on its own, was rendered even more so by revealing the Manhattan skyline in the distance. Rock 'n roll, big yellow car speeding down a busy highway, colossal skyscrapers along the skyline, a young Black taxi driver willing to engage me in conversation—this was one cool place.

To me, Black people were mythic figures like the great Pelé and a few of his other Brazilian soccer-playing colleagues, Didi and Vava, whom I had seen in books, though never on TV, vanquishing the best football nations during the World Cup of 1958, when Brazil won the first of its five trophies. Black people were also Louis Armstrong, Duke Ellington, and Count Basie, whom my father liked and respected for reasons that were never clear to me, particularly since I do not recall ever listening to their music in Timişoara or Vienna. Still, my father mentioned them often and only with the greatest respect and admiration; ditto Josephine Baker, whom both my mother and father alluded to on occasion.

I also recall my father being pleased that something good had happened for Black people in distant America in 1954, though I had no knowledge of the Supreme Court, let alone the landmark desegregation case it decided then. But no one came close in my father's admiration, even affection, to Ralph Bunche, one of my father's heroes by dint of his elegance, his eloquence, and his brilliance as a political thinker. However, most important for my father was Bunche's mediating role in the founding of the state of Israel and the subsequent armistice with the Arab states, for which Bunche received the Nobel Peace Prize in 1950. That was all I knew about Black people as an 11-year-old.

We could not stay with my aunt and uncle in their Spartan apartment, so next thing I knew we arrived at a hotel on West 47th Street, right in the middle of the Times Square area. I have no idea who arranged our stay there, whether it was my uncle, my father, or the International Rescue Committee, but when we checked into our room, I saw from my father's face that he was less than pleased. While as Europeans we did not know about air conditioning and never expected such a luxury, we did know a thing or two about rundown bathrooms and ugly lampshades.

The unbearable heat that greeted us that first evening made us learn about American amenities such as air conditioning very quickly. But more important, the heat made us leave our room and walk around the neighborhood, which was a life-altering experience for me. Barely ten steps from 47th Street, Broadway was lit up in all its glory. I thought I had left planet earth. Night had turned to day—and what a multi-colored day it was! I had never seen anything like this before. Yes, Piccadilly Circus in London was bright and exciting, but I saw Piccadilly later, when I was 13 or 14, and so it would always remain in the shadow of my first experience with the far more bustling and brilliant Times Square.

What a contrast to Vienna's measly *"OSRAM, hell wie der lichte Tag"* ad, which had wowed me upon our arrival there from dark Timişoara in 1958. In Manhattan, I was overwhelmed by the movie marquees, the theater awnings, the mass of people walking the streets, the women smoking in public, to my father's dismay and my delight (I found this terribly sexy and seductive). And then, somewhere between 43rd and 44th Street, there on Broadway, rose the gargantuan CAMEL ad in which the man smoking the cigarette puffed smoke into the night air every ten or so seconds. What a country! My father simply could not tear me away from staring at this amazing construct.

Hungry, we went into a Horn & Hardart redolent with the smell of stale onions and cold coffee, and my amazement continued. Here there were no servers, no waitresses or waiters, only machines dispensing food. Thank God my father found a restaurant official to whom he gave some paper money so we could receive the necessary coins to feed the food machines. Jetlagged out of my mind and surely awestruck by New York's vista from the Triborough Bridge, not to mention the smoke-puffing CAMEL man on the huge wall of a neon-lit building, I ate the first egg-salad sandwich of my life. It has remained one of my favorite sandwiches to this day.

The next morning, my father and I commenced our trek to various offices that I do not remember, since they all looked alike to me, though with one major distinction from their counterparts in Romania and Austria: the folks working in the American offices were not scary. They all reminded me of the wonderful Italian-American immigration officer who had admitted us into the country: informal, gum chewing, in some ways irreverent. In one of these offices I encountered my first African-American official, the first time I experienced a Black person being my superior or controlling something I wanted and needed. My father, I am sure, also felt less threatened by these American officials than he had back in Europe under any of the many regimes that had ruled his life. But he also construed this American informality as indicating a lack of competence and authority, a theme that became a constant throughout his life: America, the casual and informal; the gullible and naïve, all wonderful traits, but dangerous in that they bespoke a weakness and lack of resolve. This, to my father, was particularly troubling since he feared that America's mighty enemies would prevail by dint of their being much better equipped for the proper deployment of power by virtue of their uncompromising discipline and compelling ideologies.

We spent our days visiting many of my father's immigrant friends all over four of the five boroughs—none had moved to Staten Island, which I would not visit until much later—with many subway rides to Queens, Brooklyn, and the Bronx often taking more than one hour each way.

While I loved riding these trains and came to learn all the BMT, IRT, and IND lines by heart, my father seemed annoyed by the immense distances this city imposed on its citizens. Most of his friends, none of whom I knew, seemed settled in their new environment. All the men had jobs; they all made a decent living. And yet, even though most had lived in New York since the late 1940s, and none longed to return to the Europe they had left in disgust and despair, none seemed truly happy.

I remember noticing my father's pensiveness and preoccupation on our long subway rides back to the Hotel Ashley from various visits to Rego Park and Flushing in Queens; Borough Park in Brooklyn; and the Pelham region in the Bronx. He loved what he perceived as America's benevolent and indispensable role in the world, but he seemed increasingly doubtful whether this would be the right place for us. Though a man of rare kindness and generosity, my father was also a vain man for whom status and standing were immensely important. I cannot convey strongly enough how he cherished being called *Domnu' Doctor* (Mister or Master Doctor), or *Tovarăşul Doctor* (Comrade Doctor in Romanian), *Doktor úr* (in Hungarian), and the constant *Herr Doktor* in status-obsessed, quasi-feudal Vienna, where titles (the more the merrier) preceding any name were de rigueur to being accepted as a person of any consequence.

Well, there weren't any doctors in New York other than the medical variety. And nobody showed the slightest deference to an immigrant whose English was rather poor, which bothered my father no end. I had never seen him embarrassed until we arrived in New York. Angry, yes; disappointed, yes; desolate, yes particularly after losing my mother; but never embarrassed. Not a single day went by in which I did not feel my father's deep insecurity concerning his lack of proper English, and his limited knowledge of American history, customs, and culture. He felt totally uncomfortable and out of his element.

Nothing made this clearer than an incident the telling of which will make me shudder forever. I have no idea to which restaurant in our neighborhood of Times Square my father invited a dear friend whom he had not seen since this man left Romania for Cuba in 1948. He had married a Cuban woman, with whom he fled first to Miami, then to New York, after the Cuban Revolution. This friend arrived at the restaurant with his wife, both of them fancily dressed, as were my father and I. Even though we had a reservation, we had to wait in line. Always an impatient man, my father was surely upset that he was made to wait with guests in tow, which he found rude and demeaning. He approached the maître d' to slip a ten-dollar bill into his pocket so we would be seated immediately.

And then came the tragedy: my father must have missed the man's jacket pocket or his hand, and the bill landed on the floor for all to see. I feel my father's embarrassment every time I think of this event, which is often, because I deem it the decisive moment that revealed to him that no matter how much he loved the United States and what America stood for in his own history and the world's, he would never become totally comfortable in the "real" America.

Such a mishap would never have happened to my father in Central Europe, where I had witnessed him bribing countless waiters and maître d's to great effect, getting a better table in no time, even with other people waiting. He had performed many identical—and related—moves on European terrain, and he pulled them off smoothly and with authority and panache. Not in New York, where he simply did not know the proper codes of bribery. And even if he had, his deep insecurity at not having mastered them would have inevitably led to this embarrassing mishap. This public humiliation left a life-long mark on my father as it did on me. While we never spoke about it in our lives, I know that my father suffered not only from this humiliation but that it happened in front of me, his biggest fan, for whom—like many fathers to many sons—he appeared invincible during my childhood, only to become mightily fallible throughout my adult life.

Even though my father was an immensely well-mannered and courteous man who never swore or used bad language, and who always wore a suit and tie, he had a definite swagger about him, a decided male coolness that served him well with women and everybody else in Europe, but that he simply could not muster in New York. Much later, during one of his many visits to see me at Columbia University, he admitted sheepishly and with immense shame and regret that his pedestrian Central European *Schmäh*—a wonderful Viennese word for charm, sleight of hand, impishness, jive, all under full command of its user—was no match for

New York's power and might. His German, though never good and spoken with many grammatical errors and a Hungarian accent, was still much better—certainly in 1960—than was his English; he often relied on me as his translator, even when I was 11 years old.

Sometime that summer we received our green cards, which meant we had become resident aliens of the United States of America. Ah, green cards: the road to bliss and happiness! The dream of millions all over the world! At this time, the United States Immigration and Naturalization Service handed these out much earlier in the lengthy immigration process than was the case later. Hence, we received ours a few weeks after arriving in the United States. This meant our path to United States citizenship became a reality, as it did for me in 1971. For my father, the green card was essentially a permanent United States tourist visa that permitted him to visit the country annually, provided he would never allow 365 days to pass between each visit. And this he did regularly between 1960 and 1990. For thirty full years, my father followed the letter of the law but abused its spirit, which intended the green-card holder to live primarily in the United States on her or his way to becoming a United States citizen: in other words, to have the United States be the person's primary home, not its yearly tourist destination.

Then, in March of 1990, on what turned out to be my father's last visit to the United States, I was waiting at Boston's Logan airport for him to exit the customs area with the brilliant smile and warm eyes he always exhibited when he first glimpsed me at the various airports where I had picked him up over the years. But, as he came toward me in the waiting area, he was literally crying. "They took away my green card," he said dejectedly. "They said that I clearly showed no intention of ever living in this country and that I could always come to visit as an Austrian citizen by applying and receiving a permanent tourist visa at virtually no charge and with total ease. And that I could always come to America by dint of my son's being here as a citizen." But this was no consolation for my father. He had lost his gateway to permanence in America; he had lost his exit option from Europe. He had lost part of his identity, in which an imagined and attainable America had received pride of place! He died barely three weeks later.

By the middle of August 1960, my father had come to contemplate our return to Vienna very seriously. One crucial component weighing in that decision was my status as a student in the Theresianische Akademie, which, to my father, was equivalent to the Lycée Henri IV in France or an Eton-Harrow-style public school in England. We looked at comparable schools in New York during our two-month summer stay, but my father couldn't find anything of that caliber he could afford. He decided to synthesize the best of both worlds: making sure I would get a superb secondary education in Vienna, but also making sure I would retain my access to America by never losing my green card. I was never to let one year lapse without spending time in the United States, which I did by spending every summer until my secondary-school graduation with my uncle or friends in New York.

My father's decision to depart from the actual America but retain the imagined America by making it the world in which I was to thrive confirms the fact that the stickiness and power of culture, language, and habits—the aspects of one's life that comprise convenience and security—almost always trump desire, longing, and idealism, all of which are highly risky and uncertain. No one who ever interacted with my father doubted that he truly disliked Central Europe and never regarded it his home or the venue of his future. He adored the United States and attributed the world's good fortunes—most certainly his—to America's existence. Had it been an issue of affective preferences, my father would have stayed in the United States and New York, both of which he loved, and not have returned to central Europe and Vienna, both of which he disliked, if not hated.

And yet, his complete comfort in and knowledge of the cultural codes of the latter, and his insecurity in and fear of those of the former, made the choice to return to Vienna, where he lived as a rootless transient for the ensuing thirty years, a logical one. Vienna was the closest replica to the Budapest in which my father had thrived as a student in the 1930s and in whose culture, particularly the urbane Jewish manifestations of it, he felt so at ease. Not by chance were all of my father's friends in his thirty-year life in Vienna just like him, Hungarian Jews of a certain Budapest-infused urban cosmopolitanism.

In the course of that summer, I got to know New York City well. My father and I visited all the usual sites—the Empire State Building, the Statue of Liberty, the Cloisters, Fifth Avenue, Central Park, the Circle Line boat trip around Manhattan Island, Coney Island, the Bronx Zoo—and I loved riding the subways whenever and wherever I could. My father, perhaps foolishly, had such confidence in me that, when I did not want to spend time in the Hotel Ashley's lobby during yet another of his meetings with a Hungarian-speaking Jewish refugee from Romania, he brought me to Times Square Station and allowed me to ride the IRT local train (later named the Number 1) all the way up Broadway to the end of its line past Washington Heights into the Bronx and then return to Times Square. I committed all the train's stops to memory, which came in handy seven years later when I began my studies at Columbia and lived in Furnald Hall, with a window opening straight onto the 1 train's 116th Street station.

Through some arrangement—maybe the IRC's or a friend's—my father and I spent a few weekends outside the city with lovely families all of whom had two traits in common: they were not Jewish, and they all spoke at least some German. I remember the warmth with which they welcomed us for a one- or two-night stay, and I will always cherish the opportunity this provided me to experience American suburbia. During my first weekend of this sort, somewhere near Montclair, New Jersey, I spent the first night in my life in a private house inhabited by one family, with a dog and a two-car garage. Here were all the icons of middle-class suburban life. From Timişoara through Vienna and all the way to New York, I had never lived in a house, only in apartments.

Not until I joined the faculty at the University of Michigan in the fall of 1999 did I live in a house in a neighborhood that could be classified as vaguely suburban, though we are proud to have sidewalks and therefore feel entitled to consider ourselves as living in something akin to a real city. These weekend stays did not make me love the American suburbs, but they did not make me hate suburbia the way my contemporaries at Columbia and virtually all my friends throughout my life did with such a passion. Hating suburbia became de rigueur to the identity of every self-respecting American friend or colleague with any intellectual ambitions. To most of these people, American suburbia—together with Wonder Bread—had become the quintessential symbols of the vacuity and inauthenticity of American bourgeois life, to which any other was preferable, including European bourgeois life, which received a free pass, if not outright admiration from my American academic friends and colleagues. For reasons I never understood and chalked up to the innate Europhilia of most American left-liberal intellectuals, these sentiments were anchored in a deeply-seated sense of cultural insecurity regarding their American upbringing.

I remember how a number of these families were taken by my Viennese-accented German, which they experienced as particularly cultured. This was in sharp contrast to what was to develop in Vienna at the Theresianum, where my now increasingly American-accented English would be derided as an undesirable "dialect" to be dismissed in favor of real English, which, naturally, was solely that of the British variety, though spoken with a pathetic Viennese accent the local-born instructors of English never managed to overcome.

During our occasional weekends in the suburbs, my father discovered a phenomenon that a few years later provided his lucrative livelihood in Vienna: supermarkets. Such wonders did not exist in Central Europe at the time, and my father was impressed with them, so much so that we spent hours in a number of stores—I remember an A&P either in the New Jersey or the Westchester suburbs—with my father taking copious notes on the various aisles and their displayed wares. Unbeknown to us, a Hungarian Jew living in Vienna at the time, and a frequent visitor to New York to see his siblings in Brooklyn, was also fascinated by supermarkets and was to establish the first such store in all of Austria. My father was to join him as a partner in 1963, and together they created an immensely successful supermarket chain in Vienna called LÖWA.

To my father's eternal credit, he took me to a baseball game in Yankee Stadium, where the hometown team played its archrival, the Boston Red Sox, though I knew nothing of this rivalry at the time. Two aspects of this expedition bespeak my father's deep love for me and his wish that I become an American, even if this would elude him forever. First, my father understood baseball's cultural currency for a young boy in America; and secondly, he was willing to take me to a game and sit with me for hours, even though he didn't know the game's rules, its players, or its history. He was determined not to let his ignorance be an impediment to my acculturation into American life.

Indeed, every subsequent summer in which my father and I spent time together in New York, we would see a Yankees game. The last one I recall was in 1976 after I received my doctorate from Columbia. He had come to know some of the rules by then and even knew the fielders' positions although the game's nuances eluded him. Still, he loved sitting next to me, soaking up the atmosphere.

With school back in Vienna about to commence in early September, it was becoming increasingly certain by late August that we would be heading back to Europe. Instead of flying, my father chose to travel with me on the SS *United States* so I could experience a huge ocean-liner and spend four glorious days aboard such a floating city. But when it came time to say good-bye to New York and board the ship for Le Havre, I threw a temper tantrum, which I rarely did as a child. I was kicking and screaming that I did not want to return to Vienna, that I hated it there, that I wanted to stay in New York and go to school there and live my life in Manhattan, probably in the middle of Times Square, right in the Hotel Ashley.

It was then that my father announced a pact he kept for the rest of his life: I was to go with him to Vienna, and I was to continue to attend the Theresianum every year from September until June, but I would return every summer to New York City and either stay with my uncle or someone else. I was to spend a number of weeks in New York every summer until I graduated from the Theresianum and it was time to go to university, which, again per my father's assurances alongside the docked SS *United States*, I would attend in America, no two ways about it. This deal became a reality to its very letter. On his deathbed in Vienna in April 1990, my father invoked what we had come to call the "SS *United States* pact." He assured me it was the absolute best pact or deal he had ever made because it put me on the immutable path of making America my real new home.

Columbia 1968:
How the World—and Andy—Changed
in a Single Year

In September 1967, I departed Vienna for New York to commence my
tertiary education. In contrast to past summer trips, this one was for
real and for good. After listening to my father's parting speech at Schwe-
chat, Vienna's airport, I boarded the plane that was to take me to London's Heathrow, where I switched flights for JFK. The journey had become routine for me since I had undertaken it every summer between
1960 and 1967, though occasionally with Frankfurt and Paris, instead of
London, as the intermediate stop.

Due to my uncle's proximity to Morningside Heights—a mere ten-
minute bus ride from 92nd Street, straight up Broadway to 116th Street—
I got to know the Columbia campus well through my summer stays.
I had even entered the hallowed space of Hamilton Hall, where Columbia College had its headquarters and where, on the first floor, the dean
resided. Here, I had my interview with a hip, young assistant dean with
whom I discussed in great length the make-believe tennis match in Mi-
chelangelo Antonioni's provocative film *Blow-Up*, which first appeared,
to much acclaim in intellectual circles, in 1966. The assistant dean must
have been impressed with what I had to say, because Columbia decided
to admit me. On many levels, my traveling from distant Vienna to Columbia entailed fewer hurdles and unknowns than the journey most of

my classmates undertook, even the ones from the greater New York metropolitan area, let alone Idaho or Michigan, because I actually knew the place, at least the looks of its buildings and the shape of its campus.

But leave it to European elitism to erect obstacles where none should have existed. For my father and me, college was nothing but an unpleasant burden that one had to overcome on one's way to real university, where one studied real subjects and prepared for such all-important professions as medicine and law. College offered only a liberal arts education, which was nothing more than the *Allgemeinbildung*, general education, that a fine *Gymnasium* like the Theresianum amply provided. One needed not go to university to learn Greek philosophy, German poetry, and Central European history! One already knew those by virtue of one's *Gymnasium* education and simply by being a cultured person.

If I could redo one aspect of my life, I would be rid of this arrogant pretension that deprived me not only of a fine all-round college experience, but of learning important subjects in the depth and breadth they deserved. Since I knew from my letter of admission that I would earn advanced standing at Columbia by reason of my *Matura*, I declared myself a sophomore rather than a freshman. Hence, freshman orientation would not apply to me! Who needed such useless nonsense about what courses to take and where to eat and what to do! I knew this already by virtue of being this educated European boy. No freshman anything for me, thank you very much, least of all anything called "orientation." This was kindergarten stuff, not a university's.

I flew to New York on a Tuesday so I could register for classes on Wednesday and begin them on Thursday, the day Columbia's semesters began. I carried $1,500 in cash, since I needed to pay my tuition and room and board and my father did not have a United States checking account. (Checking accounts barely existed in continental Europe at the time; weekly wages and monthly salaries were paid in cash-filled envelopes, and my father and his peers constantly walked around with large wads of currency in their pockets. As late as the 1990s, I would be reimbursed by my German or Austrian hosts at universities and other institutions with large sums of cash for all my expenses plus honoraria.)

My uncle Alex had a checking account at the Chemical Bank branch on Broadway between 91st and 92nd Streets, but neither my father nor I wanted to inconvenience him. My last two summer stays with my uncle had become increasingly cumbersome. I was no longer a little boy, but a young adolescent who wanted to explore New York at all hours, especially at night, which my uncle made all but impossible. And the paucity of furniture in the apartment rendered the place dreary, if not depressing. I forgave my uncle everything because of the horrors he had experienced in the Shoah, but staying with him for six weeks at a time became tense and unpleasant. I did not even ask him to meet me upon my arrival at the airport now named JFK instead of Idlewild as it was when we first met seven years before.

I took a taxi and arrived at 116th Street and Broadway, the main entrance to Columbia University. Lugging my two huge suitcases onto College Walk, I hung a right at the School of Journalism and descended the steps beside the statue of Thomas Jefferson to reach Furnald Hall, in which I was assigned Room 214 as my new home. I entered the beautiful atrium of the dormitory through the large glass door and received my room key from the person working at the desk, who told me that because the elevator was not working I had to take the stairs and that he could not help me because he had to stay at his post.

I looked around the lounge and saw but one person, who was sitting on a couch reading *The New York Times*. I noticed that he wore a T-shirt that said MICHIGAN in blue—a lovely coincidence, given where I ended up finding a home many decades later—whereupon I asked if he would give me a hand with my two suitcases. He said yes, and this was the beginning of my lifelong friendship with Allen Drescher, who was about to start his senior year at Columbia. Hailing from a Jewish family in Port Huron, Michigan, Allen later went on to Columbia Law School. After that, he found himself in Oregon where he became a successful lawyer and respected judge.

Two months after our encounter in the atrium of Furnald Hall, Allen invited me to spend Thanksgiving with his family in Port Huron, which became the first Thanksgiving of my life. During that visit, Allen took me to Congregation Mount Sinai, his family's synagogue in Port

Huron, to introduce me to its Rabbi, Charles Rosenzveig. A Holocaust survivor from Poland, Rabbi Rosenzveig impressed me on many levels. As fate would have it, nearly 30 years later I authored the "West Germany" chapter in the anthology entitled *The World Reacts to the Holocaust* that the rabbi co-edited with noted Holocaust historian David Wyman, published by the Johns Hopkins University Press in 1996. When I moved to Ann Arbor in the fall of 1999, I became very active in the Holocaust Memorial Center that the rabbi founded and directed at a beautiful location in Farmington Hills. There, it continued its pivotal role as a fine center of education and outreach well after Rabbi Rosenzveig's sudden death in December 2008.

Classes and Travails

After paying all that cash to the Registrar and obtaining my Columbia University identification card on Wednesday morning, I went to the Foreign Students Office, where I had an appointment with an official who was to determine how much, and what kind, of advanced standing the College would grant me based on my *Matura*. A kind man who was intimately familiar with foreign secondary-education systems, including the Austrian *Gymnasium's*, he proceeded to waive all language requirements, plus all natural science requirements, yielding almost three semesters' worth of credits that Columbia was to grant me as advanced standing. When I noticed he did not waive the famed Contemporary Civilization and Humanities requirements, I grew annoyed.

"Sir," I said, "I do not need to read Homer! I know this already!"

I will never forget his priceless answer: "Mr. Markovits, I do not care if you were Homer himself! Every student at Columbia College must take these two pillars of our curriculum. No debate!" Thank God for this man's stout decision not to wave these two great courses, which formed the basis of my entire academic career.

But my prospects did not look promising on that Thursday, the first day of classes, in the fall of 1967. At 10 a.m., I entered a classroom on one of the upper floors of Hamilton Hall to commence my college career with a course on microeconomics. The teacher, a young man of Indian origin, handed out some information a student next to me informed me was called a "syllabus." I looked at this document and began to sweat. Students were to hand in problem sets every Tuesday, which they then received back on Thursday with the teacher's corrections, which they had to hand in again the following Tuesday along with the new set. Problem sets as homework? And at such a clip? Surely, this must have been some error or misunderstanding.

The teacher then explained to us the essence of microeconomics and how this subject differed from macroeconomics, for which I was not to have my first lecture until the following day. He proceeded to engage in some basic concepts of linear programming, which was to form the basis of the course, which dealt with the maximization of a firm's desired output or revenue, given certain constraints. He ended the class by handing out a problem set we were to complete and return by the following Tuesday.

Oh my God! I had no idea what hit me. I expected college to be a leisurely activity in which one hung around in lovely cafes, flirted with girls, played chess, and debated lofty ideas until the wee hours of the morning. In my fantasy, attending classes was optional but discouraged because only stiffs bothered to show up for lectures. At some point, one passed an examination or two by having crammed the material word-for-word and reproduced it orally in front of a professor whom one did not know and who couldn't care less about his students. One would acquire all the material one needed to know for these exams by various cheat-sheets or supplemental materials published by cram courses that sprouted alongside universities for the sole purpose of helping students master these exams. In other words, I had the continental European model in mind.

From the microeconomics class I rushed to my first Humanities A class, where once again a syllabus awaited us with tons of meticulous detail. At least the first few classes appeared to be devoted to Homer's *Iliad*, my domain if ever there was one—I was a central European *Bildungsbürger* with a Theresianum *Matura* to prove it, never mind my mother having read this book to me repeatedly back in Timişoara.

Since my Humanities A class met five days a week, we were asked to write a one-page paper for Friday on the tensions within the Greek army as it embarked for Troy. Did such conflicts exist? Everybody knew Paris was an arrogant idiot for eloping with Queen Helen of Sparta and incurring the wrath of the Greeks, but what division existed among the Greeks themselves at this early stage of the ten-year conflict? We had never discussed any such conflicts in the Theresianum. Nor could I recall my mother ever having said anything along these lines.

Worse: I was asked to write a one-page paper overnight on this topic. Who had ever heard of such an assignment? And then came the clincher: The paper had to be typed! Typing was what secretaries did, not cerebral boys like me! I had never typed a single letter in my life, nor had my father. My sense of shock accelerated in the afternoon, when, in my first Contemporary Civilization class (dubbed From Plato to NATO), we discussed passages in Plato's *Republic*, about which we were asked to write a three-page paper, to be submitted at our Monday meeting. This paper, too, had to be typed.

I was in a panic. Even though the time was quite late in Vienna, I called my father in desperation. His first response was: "Surely there must be some girls there who can type these two papers for you." (His basis of thought: typing was for girls attending secretarial school, not for young men who had attended the Theresianum.) My reply: "Dad, there are no female students at Columbia!" (At the time, neither he nor I knew anything about Barnard College across the street.) This was not a good sign: my father's blocking for me, which he had done so brilliantly all my life, proved ineffective in this situation.

I ran to the Columbia Bookstore and purchased a standard Smith Corona portable typewriter, as well as the first book I could find that offered instructions in typing. That evening, I went to the Furnald Hall study room, preferring it to the loneliness of my dorm room and hoping to find some inspiration and succor in other students' presence. The opposite occurred when I noticed how a dozen or so students typed away on their papers with ease and speed and skill. Obviously, American high school graduates could type, whereas their European counterparts decidedly could not because this studied ignorance and inability underlined their status as elites for whom the mastery of useful subjects was unnecessary and unwanted.

I stayed up all night trying to type my Humanities paper, but grew so frustrated that I decided to print my work in capital letters, praying the teacher would accept it. When the time came to hand it in, I sheepishly explained to the teacher that I could not type and therefore was handing in my work in handwritten form, but that henceforth I had every intention of mastering the art of typing. To my surprise, the teacher was understanding and accepted my work, the only paper out of twenty or so that was not typed. What a mensch! Professors as understanding and kind human beings rather than ogres like in the Theresianum who meted out punishment with joy when stuff was askew and did not meet with regulations. Amazing!

But there was still the more elaborate Plato paper for Monday's CC class, which had to be written and typed over the weekend. On Sunday morning, the phone rang. It was my father from Vienna, who somehow had mobilized my uncle to get me a typist in the form of one of his neighbor's daughters, who would type my paper for a fee. I finished writing my paper in the late afternoon, then took the bus to my uncle's place, where he walked me from his apartment in 14J to 14B or 14C, where a lovely family resided who introduced me to the daughter who was going to type my paper.

So, old Europe came to my rescue even at Columbia, in the combination of my father's machinations and a young woman's typing abilities! While she was typing, I ran down to my uncle's candy store and purchased a box of Lindt chocolates that I was going to give her in addition to double the amount of money she expected. In the end, everyone was thrilled, and I departed back to Columbia, smiling for the entire length of the ride up Broadway on the 104 bus.

My smiles, however, soon turned to frowns when I received my first grades on these assignments: C-minus on the Plato paper, and C on the Homer paper, with devastating comments on both. Columbia had taken all but two days and one weekend to cut arrogant Andy down to size—he who hadn't thought it necessary to attend freshman orientation, he who wanted CC and Humanities waived by dint of his formidable *Bildung*. All my feelings of superiority due to my Central Europe-an education and cultural capital went out the window and in came the realization: this was a whole different world to which I had better adapt in a hurry if I was to survive, let alone succeed. Work was going to be my only salvation here, not European arrogance based on a classist no-tion of *Bildung*, nor any amount of that Viennese mixture of charm and guile we called *Schmäh*.

I felt the way my father must have felt when he realized in the sum-mer of 1960 that nobody in America was going to call him *Herr Doktor* as a matter of course, that old-world titles and demeanor meant nothing here in terms of gaining access to the goodies of life. But unlike my fa-ther, who had surrendered to his ignorance of America's cultural codes by the time he was so utterly humiliated by his inability to bribe the maître d' in that restaurant, I was determined to prevail. To be fair, I was a good deal younger than he was, and much better equipped with all the necessary resources for success, not least my fluency in English. When-ever I have been asked in the past fifty years what Columbia University taught me, I always mention first and most prominently, well ahead of my five diplomas: How to type!

Even though I was working every waking minute on my five cours-es (with most of my peers taking only four), as well as improving my typ-ing skills, never sleeping more than five hours a night, if that, I decided to celebrate my birthday by doing something truly collegiate: going to a football game (*not* of the Association, that is soccer, variety but decided-ly its American gridiron cousin). My nineteenth birthday was on Friday, October 6, and so I decided to travel to Baker Field in the Inwood section of Manhattan on Saturday afternoon to watch Columbia play Princeton.

I had watched lots of baseball during my summer stays with my un-cle, but this was my first opportunity to watch football since I had nev-er spent the other seasons in the United States. Oddly, this was also the first time I felt a divide on the Columbia campus. I could not put my fin-ger on my impression at the time, but this divide became patently obvi-ous when I asked Allen Drescher, who had been so helpful to me upon my arrival at Furnald Hall, whether he wanted to accompany me to this football game and his answer was a brusque "no." Ditto a few other students I had started to get to know in my classes and via the lounge of my dormitory. They clearly showed no interest. Worse, for reasons I was to discover only later, I felt they were actually a tad hostile toward football.

So off I went by myself, taking the IRT Number 1 all the way to the very tip of Manhattan Island. Even though Columbia football was nowhere close to big-time college athletics, I enjoyed everything: the collegiate atmosphere among the spectators; their preppiness in clothes and demeanor; the colors; the bands; the mascots—the Columbia Lion and the Princeton Tiger. I found something wholesome about this playful, competitive, but unthreatening atmosphere, especially in contrast to the vile and often violent soccer crowds in Vienna I was used to. Princeton won easily, 28–14, foreshadowing that our university's football team would lose a lot more than it would win during my eight years at the university and that Columbia football would gain distinction from the length and frequency of its losing streaks rather than its successes.

But that afternoon, I thrilled to the superb play of Marty Domres, the Columbia quarterback. Domres exhibited his immense talents even against a stout Princeton defense, demonstrating why he later became a first-round draft choice for the National Football League, where he flourished for nine years. Best known for replacing the mighty Johnny Unitas as the starting quarterback of the Baltimore Colts in the 1972 season, Domres was one of the rare Columbia football players who garnered national attention in college and the pros. And I reveled in the kudos I received on my American acculturation and knowledge from an elderly Columbia fan sitting next to me. In our conversation about Columbia football and Marty Domres, I floated the idea that there was something special about playing quarterback at Columbia since the legendary Sid Luckman, who led the Chicago Bears to four NFL titles in the 1940s, had also played quarterback for the Lions. The man complimented me on my knowledge of football history, which came as a surprise to him, given my age. Better still, he never guessed that I was not a native-born American youngster, but rather a European teenager who had arrived at Columbia University barely three weeks before the game.

A few weeks later, midterms rolled around. I studied hard for all five of my exams, but perhaps none harder than my microeconomics class, in which I felt most insecure. Nervously, I entered our classroom and awaited the teacher's passing out the exam. Once he did so, he lingered a few minutes while the students commenced their work—and then he left the room! I could not believe my eyes. Back at the Theresianum, I was used to having each written test proctored by extra faculty, in addition to the subject's regular teacher, with students occasionally frisked before the exam and made to sit far apart to minimize cheating. After all, cheating in Austrian schools embodied arguably one of the most honorable activities a student could perform because it was never only for personal benefit but also as a service to the common good. One did not only cheat to gain individual advantage but also to help one's classmates who were struggling with the exam. And at Columbia the teacher just left the room?

I looked around and noticed that none of the students spoke to each other or attempted to cheat by exchanging information. What kind of world was this? About 10 minutes into this silence, having hit a snag with one of the problem sets on the examination, I reverted to my 12 years of European primary and secondary schooling and leaned over to the student on my right, whispering for help. The look he gave me was a composite of utter disgust, as in "you scum, you lowlife, how can you do this?," and total contempt, as in "you idiot, you imbecile, aren't you at Columbia now?" My shame and embarrassment were beyond words.

Indeed, this was the only examination in my eight years at Columbia that I failed. When, at the end of the hour, our teacher returned and we handed him our blue books, I noticed that the young man who had rebuked me for trying to cheat sported a large SDS button on his shirt, beads around his neck, and longish hair. At least from his outward appearance, he was a man of the left, someone who presumably sympathized with socialism, some form of redistributive justice, and a collectivist correction of competitive capitalism based on individual striving and achievement.

But the sentiment of compassionate socialism clearly did not extend to the competitive atmosphere of collegiate learning, in which each man was out for himself, earning rewards and recognition in the form of grades based on individual achievements. Whereas the struggle in European schools had always been between the students as a collective versus the professor, in America the struggle was among the students for the professor's benevolent judgement and reward. (Lest I focus solely on the individualism and competitiveness of American students in contrast to the collectivist bent of their European counterparts, I should also mention the paramount importance of fairness that constitutes a moral category for many American students. If you get two candies, I should get two candies, and if I get two, you should get two. If I get two and you only get one, that's not fair! In addition to this devotion to fairness, honor plays a role. You simply dishonor yourself by cheating!)

The first semester ended by my traveling to Vienna over the Christmas break to visit my father and family, in the process meeting a young woman who—23 years later—was to become my beloved partner for life. After this trip, I returned to Columbia for final examinations. I studied day and night to attain decent grades, knowing that great grades were out of my reach. The study period was made harder by my having fallen in love with this pretty woman back in Vienna, to whom I wrote many letters at this time. My only solace in those trying weeks was hearing the soothing and sexy voice of Alison Steele, aka the Nightbird, on WNEW-FM, to whom I listened virtually every night, hoping she would play some sweet Grateful Dead tunes. More often than not, she fulfilled my wishes. With three B-minuses and two B's, my first term at Columbia ended mercifully not a second too soon.

With my cognate requirements out of the way, I could enroll in the political science courses that were to constitute my major. I loved the rich offerings from which I chose three courses under the "comparative" rubric of the government department, one taught by Dorothy Guyot, who became my only female teacher since Frau Kleefass had taught me in my elementary school back in Timișoara and the kind woman who was my fourth grade teacher in my first year in Vienna. There were no female faculty at the Theresianum. CC and Humanities continued unabated since they were each a yearlong course.

Back in Vienna, one of my father's friends suggested I contact a Robert Austerlitz, a linguist specializing in Uralic and Altaic languages who, this person thought, was chair of the linguistics program at Columbia and a wonderful man who would love to hear from me. In early February 1968, I called Linguistics from my dorm room and asked to be connected with Professor Austerlitz.

Robert Austerlitz, Polyglot Professor and Friend

"Horselips here, how can I help you?" came over the telephone.

Horselips? I was not going to question this because I thought I had simply misheard the word "Austerlitz." We began to speak, and suddenly Austerlitz said he had received a note from his pal in Vienna that this Viennese kid was going to contact him, but I did not sound remotely Viennese, rather more like somebody from New York's Upper West Side. I loved the man right away! No, I said, I was indeed this kid from Vienna, whereupon—testing me, perhaps—he switched to a heavy Viennese dialect, to which I responded in kind. Connection made!

"Come to my office on the second floor of Philosophy Hall next Wednesday at 5 p.m. so that we can chat a bit and then go out for dinner," he said before hanging up.

The following Wednesday, I arrived at his office wearing a tie and jacket, as one properly should when invited to meet a professor and go to dinner with him afterwards. I was greeted by this five-foot-seven-inch bundle of energy, sporting a gray beard, wearing a denim shirt open to the navel and flip-flops on his bare feet, and smoking a filterless cigarette—Chesterfield, of course. When I told him the languages I spoke, he responded to me in each: Hungarian, flawless; Romanian, ditto; German, superb; Viennese dialect, authentic; standard American English, fine as well. He was not only impressed by my mastery of these languages but clearly saw me as a soulmate with whom he could engage in all these languages on a sophisticated level. Even my workmanlike French passed muster with him.

Austerlitz was the son of an American mother with Bohemian roots and an Austrian father hailing from Moravia, thus solidifying his Habsburg pedigree. Though born in Bucharest in 1923, he grew up in Braşov (in Romanian, Brassó in Hungarian, and Kronstadt in German), a city very similar to my birthplace of Timişoara in its multilingual, multi-religious, and multicultural composition. Austerlitz "returned" to the United States in 1938 at age 15, seeing the country for the first time in his life. Having had a Hungarian-speaking nanny, he spoke that language, as well as perfect Romanian, German, and English simply as a matter of growing up. He attended a German elementary and a Romanian secondary school, where he picked up perfect French in addition to Latin.

I never ascertained whether Austerlitz was related to Fred Astaire, who, as is well known, was born Frederick Austerlitz, and whose parents changed their name to Astaire, fearing that "Austerlitz" was too reminiscent of the famous battle. Fred Astaire's father was named Fritz, as was the famed editor-in-chief of Austrian Social Democracy's daily newspaper, *Arbeiter-Zeitung*. This paper was a daily staple of our reading in Vienna, due not only to its high intellectual content, but also because one could avoid the antisemitism of the Austrian press if one read this paper as opposed to others. Even though my father was anything but a socialist, he was most comfortable reading Social Democracy's daily paper and, once an Austrian citizen, voting for the country's socialist party because he viewed the two extant bourgeois parties simply off limits for a Jew. This Fritz Austerlitz, unlike Fred Astaire's father, was in fact related to Robert Austerlitz, though in what capacity I do not remember. Robert never got to meet Fritz. But he was obviously pleased and excited to hear that I knew of Fritz and held him in high regard as one of the great figures of what came to be known as Austro-Marxism.

Already at our first meeting, Robert asked me to give him a summary of what made Austro-Marxism "Austro." I was to do so in Viennese dialect, which I promptly did. Now it was my turn to serve in this speedy ping-pong match: "What is the deal with Horselips?" I asked him. Ah, he said. One of his Berkeley colleagues once informed him that his secretary had left a message that a certain Professor Horselips from Columbia University wanted to speak to him. So my assumption in our first phone call was correct: "Austerlitz," if pronounced quickly, did indeed sound like "Horselips," probably to many more people than this Berkeley secretary and me. Austerlitz loved to play with his name. Once, while we were sitting in his office waiting to depart for dinner, a young Frenchman whom Austerlitz did not know appeared and introduced himself. Austerlitz replied: *"Enchanté! Et moi, je m'appelle Robert Austerlitz, comme la bataille."* To which the Frenchman memorably replied: *"Mais non, monsieur le Professeur, comme la victoire!"*

Austerlitz was still wearing his flip-flops as we traversed the Columbia campus towards Broadway on our way to a Cuban restaurant called Ideal on the southwest corner of 108th Street and Broadway. When I reminded him of this—after all it was early February in New York City—he informed me that he was never cold after having spent two years at the University of Helsinki in the early 1950s. He had studied Uralic languages (such as Finnish and Hungarian) in Helsinki, and Altaic languages (Turkic and Mongolic) in a number of places, later becoming a professor of Uralic and Altaic languages and one of the world's leading linguistic experts in this field. In Helsinki, he fell in love with a Finnish girl who later became his wife and with whom he had two children. The family lived near Teachers College on 120th Street and had me over for a number of meals during my Columbia days.

For the first of many times dining at the Ideal Restaurant, I ordered black beans and rice for my main meal and guava with cream cheese as my desert. Austerlitz was the life of the party in this small bodega-like establishment where everybody knew and loved him, especially the convivial Cuban owner, with whom he sang a few songs after dinner in perfect Cuban Spanish. Austerlitz spoke all these languages without any foreign accent by virtue of having perfect pitch. His musicality was beyond impressive. He took me to hear the New York Philharmonic in Avery Fischer Hall at Lincoln Center later that term, my first classical concert as a Columbia student. The evening featured Antonín Dvořák's Symphony No. 9, *From the New World*, one of my all-time favorite pieces of music. On our way back to Columbia walking north on Broadway, Austerlitz began whistling and scat-singing lengthy melodic lines of the bassoons, oboes, clarinets, and cellos. I had never heard anything like this and thought this was only what world-class conductors might do.

After Austerlitz found out I liked jazz, we went one evening to an establishment on New York's famed 52nd Street, roughly between Seventh and Fifth Avenues, which had been the world's jazz mecca from the

1930s until the late 1950s. Jazz gods like Miles Davis, Thelonious Monk, Charlie Parker, Art Tatum, Fats Waller, and Billie Holiday, among many others, often played there. While this concentration of genius had disappeared by the spring of 1968, when Austerlitz and I went there, we heard two superb bands play first-rate music. And this time, too, on our way to the subway for our trip up to Columbia, Austerlitz reprised some of the trumpet and saxophone soli in an uncannily precise manner. It was during this subway ride back to Morningside Heights that he also informed me of his playing the organ in Texas and jazz piano in New Orleans while serving in the US Army in the 1940s.

The last time I saw Austerlitz that spring semester was on the evening of Monday, April 29, when we went to dinner at Ideal. Afterwards, I walked him back, not to his home on 120th Street, but to Fayerweather Hall on the Columbia campus, where he took up a position between the building and its occupying students on the one side and their opponents, the conservative Moral Coalition, on the other. We hadn't talked much about politics, being too busy gabbing about history, music, languages, and accents, but I knew that Austerlitz cared deeply about Columbia and its students and wanted to be a peacemaker as best he could. I bid him farewell around 10:30 p.m. and, after making the rounds outside the five occupied buildings, returned to my dorm room. I did not have a good feeling. The next thing I knew, I was awakened by screams that the cops had commenced their assault on the five occupied buildings.

I will discuss these monumental events a bit later in this chapter. Here, let me note that my friendship with Austerlitz was the highlight of my second semester at Columbia. Getting to know him made me genuinely happy and even proud in that a world-famous 45-year-old professor must have enjoyed the company of a 19-year-old undergraduate to whom he owed nothing more than a civil 20 minutes during office hours. Perhaps somewhere Austerlitz came to see certain parallels between his Habsburg upbringing in Braşov and his academic life at Columbia and my journey from Timişoara via Vienna to New York. Clearly, what attracted me to this man was not only his obvious genius regarding his aural abilities with languages and music. His delight in, and mastery of, American popular culture grafted onto his undeniably impressive European *Bildung* also constituted an attractive combination for me, rendered all the more special on account of its rarity among academics and intellectuals.

Getting Acclimated at Columbia

In my second semester at Columbia, I discovered another source of lasting joy: Columbia basketball! Led by two sensational players, Jim Mc-Millian and Heyward Dotson, both of whom were African American, and by a fine senior center named Dave Newmark, who was Jewish—all three products of New York City's public high schools, with Dotson a Stuyvesant graduate who followed his Columbia days with a Rhodes Scholarship at Oxford before becoming a prominent New York lawyer—the Lions captivated the campus with their exceptional play and won Columbia's only Ivy League championship in men's basketball. The team featured a stellar 20–4 record that included major victories against national powerhouses such as Louisville, St. John's, and West Virginia, the last in a tournament played at Madison Square Garden. One of my classmates invited me to join him to watch the Lions play their bitterest rival, the Princeton Tigers. What rendered the atmosphere in University Gym so electric, even ecstatic, was the small size of this venue. It looked like a glorified high school gym to me, not the basketball stadium of a major university, and Columbia beat Princeton 69–60.

We played Princeton twice more that year, and on the final day of the season, we lost, creating a tie for first place between the two schools. This necessitated a winner-take-all playoff that occurred at St. John's University. The entire Columbia campus—faculty and students—were focused on this big game. I listened on the radio in the lounge of Furnald Hall along with dozens of students. We went nuts when Columbia demolished Princeton 92–74, and for the first time I experienced the immense communal power of pride and joy conferred by American collegiate sports, which, thirty years later, became a staple of my life at the University of Michigan. I will always cherish that I was on campus for the only season in Columbia's history when the school won an Ivy

League championship in men's basketball, was nationally ranked, and made it to the second round of the NCAA post-season, later known as the Big Dance.

Dotson, Newmark, and McMillian all went on to the NBA after graduating with their degrees from Columbia. But only McMillian succeeded. Joining the pedigreed Los Angeles Lakers in 1970, he replaced the legendary Elgin Baylor. With McMillian starting as the team's small forward, the Lakers embarked on a 33-game winning streak during the 1971–72 season, setting a record that no team has ever accomplished in the league. To crown it all, the Lakers won the NBA championship that season, making Jimmy Mac not only an Ivy champion but also an NBA one.

In 1973, the Lakers traded McMillian to the Buffalo Braves where he played until 1976. At the time, I was living in Boston and found out where the Braves were going to stay during their visit to play the Celtics. I wrote a note to Jim, hoping he would respond. He did, and we had a bite to eat in the cafeteria of his hotel, which was close to the Boston Garden, where the Braves had lost to the Celtics. We reminisced about Columbia, and I was surprised when Jim, out of the blue, shared with me his deep disappointment at being traded by the Lakers to the Braves. Never was it clearer to me that, despite the claims that these sports are nothing but businesses, the teams' actions deeply affect real human beings who exist behind the veil of the millions of dollars they make. Jim payed the tab and we hugged good-bye, never to see each other again. Jim McMillian died in 2016; Heyward Dotson passed away in 2020; only Dave Newmark of this trio is still alive—he resides in Berkeley and we are friends on Facebook.

Clearly, the most significant societal event that was to inform the end of my first year at Columbia was the student revolt of late April 1968. This is not the place to share my thoughts on the reasons for the revolt and its consequences. Pertaining to the latter, I have published on the effects of "1968" in Europe and the United States. Here, I will only reiterate the gist of my findings and analyses: that this year and its events in the advanced industrial societies of the world, of which Columbia was central in the United States, ended the century-long Victorian era of bourgeois morality, comportment, and habitus.

These events commenced what I have called the "discourse of compassion and inclusion" that continues unabated in our contemporary world half a century later. Everything changed: how we relate to women, to ethnic minorities, to animals, to nature; how we speak; how we dress; how we view authority; how we live our daily lives; what we eat; what we drink; what we smoke. This is not to say that everything 1968 wrought is wonderful and without problems. Far from it! But in the *longue durée* of the democratic struggle, 1968—and, with it, the events at Columbia— represent a major milestone of palpable improvement.

My own "1968" event commenced on April 24, the morning after the first buildings were occupied, when I received a phone call from Mr. Blau, our immigration attorney, with whom I had no direct contact since my father and I arrived in the United States in the summer of 1960 and received our green cards in his office in midtown Manhattan. I had informed his office of my presence in the United States every summer, and I did so again when I started at Columbia in September 1967, though I never spoke with him personally on any of these occasions. Attorney Blau informed me in no uncertain terms that I had better not occupy any buildings and get charged with trespassing or worse, if I valued retaining my green card and not getting deported from the United States. I will never forget his parting words: "Remember, you are not a U.S. citizen yet! Once you are, you can do anything you damn please, even hang out with these Commie bastards. But not yet, son, not yet!"

I have often debated whether that call prevented me from participating in the occupation of any of the five buildings. Mr. Blau's warning served as a massive hindrance; but an even more powerful deterrent might have been the sacrifice, both financial and psychological, my father incurred by sending me to Columbia. I simply had to succeed at Columbia and not risk being thrown out, no matter how strongly I felt about some of the issues the protesters espoused. Being expelled from Columbia—and quite possibly the country—would have devastated my father in ways I could not even begin to imagine!

But truth be told, I was also a tad skeptical about the protesters' culture. I had attended a few SDS meetings throughout the year and made the acquaintance of some SDS members, apart from the young man whose glaring disapproval of my attempt at cheating on the micro-economics midterm examination will haunt me for the rest of my life. I found most of them shallow in their knowledge of history and events in our contemporary world—for example, virtually none of them had a clue as to what was happening in the Czech Republic at this very time—and even of the relevant literature.

While I was by no means an expert on the writings of Karl Marx, let alone the major Marxist authors, I seemed to know more than many of my SDS-sympathizing peers. I could not shed the impression that some young men participated in this movement to socialize, to pick up groovy girls in sexy miniskirts, to be cool. In retrospect, I completely misgauged at the time that this event's importance lay precisely in the cultural dismantling of bourgeois values and mores and not whether its activists knew their Marx or not. It was precisely the challenges to bour-geois codes of behavior rather than the acuity of intellectual insights that really mattered then and gave "1968" at Columbia and elsewhere its his-torical importance and legacy.

I must immediately add that I never got to know even one of the African-American protesters and radicals whose culture and motiva-tions were vastly different from what I experienced among the white students I met. And I never felt comfortable with this group's glorifica-tion of dictators like Ho Chi Minh, never mind Fidel Castro. Hating American policy and advocating for the peoples it repressed and mur-dered? For sure, I am with you. But deifying and romanticizing dicta-torial leaders merely because they opposed the United States was objec-tionable to me then, and has remained so in my complicated encounters with much of the New Left in Europe and the United States over the years. The Western left's penchant to embrace, even glamorize, dicta-tors does not only hail from a hatred of capitalism and its leader, Amer-ica, but also from a disdain for liberal democracy's bourgeois drabness. It is this dimension, more than many others, that have rendered the far left and the far right so attractive to many Western intellectuals over the years. Among many bad things, bourgeois democracy is boring in a way that communism and fascism, certainly in their movement stages, are decidedly not.

I, however, met two Teds who were exceptional. First, there was Ted Kaptchuk, who left the SDS leadership in 1968 on account of his graduating that year. An East Asian culture major, Kaptchuk deeply understood the Viet Cong, their Viet Minh predecessors, the corruption of the Diem clan in the South, and many other aspects of the conflict. Listening to some of his speeches was enlightening on many levels. This guy had gravitas; he was a true intellectual.

And then, one evening, after returning to Furnald Hall from Butler Library, where I liked to work in the ornate reading room, I heard a man speaking eloquently about repression to a group of about 15 students sitting in my dorm's lounge. This was the first time I had heard the term "Frankfurt School" and names such as Max Horkheimer, Theodor Adorno, and, above all, Herbert Marcuse. I also heard the man talk about how these German-Jewish emigrés found a haven at Columbia during the war, even though most of them could not quite accommodate their intellectual interests to the structure of an American university. On March 7, 1970, I learned from *The New York Times* and the *Columbia Spectator* that among the dead in the townhouse in Greenwich Village that had blown up the day before was one Ted Gold, Stuyvesant High School and Columbia College graduate and a denizen of Furnald Hall. The photographs made clear that this was the same person who had introduced me to the Frankfurt School in the Furnald Hall lounge sometime in the spring of 1968.

All this said, I much preferred SDS and its allies to the Majority Coalition, comprised of conservative students who were intent on blocking, perhaps even harming, the strikers. At this juncture, my earlier observation that a number of folks did not want to accompany me to the football game against Princeton re-emerged. I now understood that my pals who didn't want to go to the football game envisioned a different America from those that attended such games, let alone played in them.

Even though it would take me far afield to explain why, of the four culturally hegemonic team sports in the United States (baseball, football, basketball, and ice hockey), football is the most conservative, a few cursory remarks might be in order. Clearly, the martial nature of the sport and its close association with war and the military in terms of its institutional history, strategies, and terminology have something to do with this phenomenon. Moreover, its religion-like centrality in the South and Southwest of the country lend it a conservative bent, as opposed to basketball, which is anchored in the concrete playgrounds of large cities of the Northeast and rural Midwestern regions like Kentucky and Indiana. While I have long opposed any kind of characterological linkage between a sport's gestalt and that of its society—as in, the Germans play organized soccer because they are organized; the Brazilians play jogo bonito because they dance the samba; or Americans bombed Vietnam because they play football—each sport creates institutions that have their own language and traditions and project a certain image.

The code of American football, like the codes of Rugby League, Rugby Union, Australian Rules Football, and Association Football (soccer), emphasizes a certain physicality that has favored a machismo more prevalent in conservative circles than in liberal ones. But because in all societies hegemonic sports have been disproportionately the bailiwick of men, sports always have been disproportionately conservative, jingoistic, and, as in the case of European soccer, often downright fascist and Nazi.

These two Americas confronted each other across the lines surrounding four of the occupied buildings (with Hamilton Hall, occupied by African-American students, creating its own separate world). Inside the buildings was the new America, the America of freaks and critics who wanted an end to the America the outsiders congregating as the Majority Coalition represented: the America of the 1950s, the America still rejoicing in the values and codes of the Victorian era. Not having Robert Austerlitz's gumption and chutzpah, but also lacking his stature as a full professor and, above all, the safety of being an American citizen, I could not interject myself as a peacemaker between these two groups.

Perhaps this was all for the better. At least in the case of Fayerweather Hall—where Austerlitz took up his position as a peacemaker and where I said good-bye to him that night—most of the victims of the police raid were folks milling around outside the building, rather than its occupiers. Many of the occupiers avoided getting busted by exiting through underground passages. Thankfully, Austerlitz survived the police raid unharmed, and I saw him regularly for the next six years of my studies at

Columbia. He came to know my father well, and the two of them would gab for hours in Hungarian and Romanian as I looked on with pleasure.

Spring term 1968 was finished after April 30. The students decreed a university-wide strike in protest against the police raid and the brutality of its methods. This meant that entering any of the university's buildings—apart from its dormitories and libraries—amounted to breaking the strike. Under no circumstances was I going to do that. But I was also under no circumstances going to take incompletes in all five of my courses and worry about exams and grades over the summer and into the fall. My father would not have understood that his son returned home to Vienna not having completed his classes with the required exams. So I set out to contact all five of my professors to arrange to take my exams without doing so in a Columbia building. To my pleasant surprise, all were extremely accommodating, and we made alternate arrangements. I took two of the exams on two different mornings at one of my favorite eateries near Columbia, Tom's Restaurant, owned by a Greek-American family since the 1940s. This establishment on the northeast corner of 112th Street and Broadway became famous by dint of Suzanne Vega's wonderful song, "Tom's Diner," and—perhaps more important still—by having its exterior represent the fictionalist Monk's Café so central to the sitcom *Seinfeld* where the eponymous protagonist and his pals met for meals.

I took two more finals during two afternoons at the West End, a Columbia bar preferred by the freaks, with the jocks congregating at the Gold Rail. This was the only time I had ever entered the West End before 10 p.m. The last exam, the one for Dr. Guyot, I wrote in my dorm room and mailed to her on my way to Kennedy Airport to catch my flight to Vienna. The results of these exams and the ensuing course grades: two A's; one A-minus; and two B-pluses. I was on the mend after my disastrous first semester. My turbulent first year at Columbia College had come to its end.

My second year at Columbia, which became my de facto senior year, commenced very well in that shortly before arriving back on campus I received a letter from the dean's office that said the university was going to pay half my tuition. More comforting still was that I was again assigned Room 214 in Furnald Hall, a place I had come to feel comfortable in during my first year at the College. Other than having to take Humanities B, I was free to choose any course in the government department that fulfilled my major. The selection was beyond stellar in terms of the courses available, as well as the professors: Roger Hilsman, Mark Kesselman, Ira Katznelson, Lewis Edinger, Alexander Dallin, and Joseph Rothschild were not only sensational teachers, but also wonderful human beings I truly enjoyed meeting during their office hours and with whom, in the cases of Kesselman and Katznelson, I formed life-long friendships.

Via these encounters I came to learn the immense value of getting to know your professors on a closer level than is possible by watching them stand in front of a lectern pontificating about their expertise. In my nearly fifty-year professorial existence at many universities I have urged my students to avail themselves of this experience and get to know their teachers as human beings, not in order to earn better grades but to expand their horizons. But two year-long courses were especially life-shaping. The first was Eugene Santomasso's art history course, which fulfilled my Humanities B requirement. Even though the class met at the ungodly hour of nine in the morning three times a week, I never missed a lecture, because the man made every painting and sculpture he discussed come alive and shine. This course altered how I came to visit any art museum anywhere in the world, as well as how I came to understand, if not always appreciate, the artistic value of the most abstract painting.

The second such course was Allan Silver's political sociology, which, though listed in the Department of Sociology, counted towards my major in political science/government. Here I came to learn my Marx, my Weber, my Durkheim, my Tocqueville, and other authors who formed the core of my intellectual existence and shaped the theoretical contours of much of my scholarly work. Just like Kesselman and Katznelson, Silver became a lifelong friend. I have never met a man who embodied the category "intellectual" more fully and aptly than Allan Silver.

By the end of the first semester, I realized that I wanted to study political science on the graduate level. However, I couldn't decide whether that was to be for the Ph.D., and thus an academic career, or an M.A., with the possibility of valorizing that degree in the "real" world with a "real" job. Enter my father. Though he was immensely impressed with the courses I had taken and my professors, all of whom he had come to know during his now frequent visits to New York, where he always attended lectures with me, he could not imagine how one would make a living as a "political scientist." He wanted me to master a more concrete subject before departing the university, if only as a secure fallback if things went awry with my real preference, the less marketable abstract option. My father also reminded me that my blazing through Columbia College in two years and graduating at the age of twenty allowed me two extra years that, under normal circumstances, I would have had to "waste" getting a liberal arts education. Didn't Columbia have an excellent business school that offered a two-year MBA, perhaps the hottest American degree on the international scene, sought by companies all over the world? How about applying and seeing what would happen?

I did, and I was accepted. But I refused to attend the graduation ceremonies for my BA. Too bourgeois, too conventional; I had my diploma mailed to me. My father was beyond angry and heartbroken. He never understood this behavior and chided me about it for many years thereafter. Not until I became an assistant professor at Wesleyan University in 1977 and was asked to attend graduation ceremonies the following year did I realize the value and beauty of this concluding—but also commencing—ceremony. I purchased my very own Columbia University doctoral gown for oodles of dollars just so I would have it to wear in the many graduation ceremonies I hoped to attend in my academic career. Indeed, I have done so with great pleasure on many occasions, while I curse myself for not having attended my own commencement out of hubris and spite.

Intellectually speaking, my four semesters in business school were a waste of time. This is not to say I deem the study of political science and sociology intellectually, let alone morally, superior to the study of finance and marketing, as so many of my colleagues in the liberal arts do. I detest the fact that most intellectuals disdain everything related to money and commerce, which they find pedestrian at best and evil at worst. I cannot count the instances in which I heard dismissive remarks about the Harvard Business School on the Cambridge side of the

Charles River, how that river was deep and wide, with real knowledge of moral value and purpose only produced on its Cambridge shores and never the Boston ones. Quite the contrary! I was awed by the complexity of some of the subjects that confronted me at the Columbia Business School, none more so than operations research, statistics, and finance.

But business was not my language. It is not fashionable these days to speak of talents and proclivities, the assumption being that all of us are equally talented in all things, with a matter of access to resources determining the ones in which ones we excel. But I never developed the passion and interest for the subjects taught in the business school that I did for those taught in social science departments. I passed the necessary exams, but I never once found myself doing any reading apart from the required material in business school the way I constantly did in college and later in graduate school. I loved reading Weber and Durkheim; I never enjoyed studying marketing and finance.

However, several people made my two years at the Columbia Business School enjoyable, even memorable. First there was Yitzhak Weinstock from Israel, with whom I shared my love of basketball as I had with no one before, and perhaps no one since. He and I danced with joy, possibly in tears, when our beloved New York Knickerbockers clinched their first NBA title on May 8, 1970, in that legendary game seven at Madison Square Garden. Our captain, Willis Reed, came onto the court hobbling on one leg and, with his teammates, miraculously defeated the mighty Lakers of Wilt Chamberlain, Jerry West, and Elgin Baylor for the championship. Yitzhak and I were forced to listen to the game on radio because—incredibly—it was not televised in the New York area.

Acquiring Some Yiddish, Finally, and Thriving in Graduate School

Then there was Jerrold Katz, who was not one of my classmates but the teaching assistant for my section in our large statistics course. Jerry insisted on having his last name pronounced "Cates" as opposed to the conventional "Cats." He hailed from Winnipeg in the province of Manitoba in Canada and had entered the doctoral program in operations research at the Columbia Business School in the fall of 1969, just when I commenced my studies for the MBA. A heavyset man with a kind face, a full black beard, and a balding head, Jerry had a rabbinical look that his manner only accentuated.

Helping me with a problem set, Jerry began a conversation on general topics of interest to him and me, and for more than twenty years we never stopped talking. I became a North American Jew solely by dint of Jerry's influence. All the Yiddish I had never learned from my bourgeois Hungarian-speaking family with quasi-aristocratic aspirations in Timișoara and Vienna, all the mannerisms this milieu spurned as being "too Jewish," all the *Yiddishkeit* that has become so integral to my persona, came from Jerry Katz. When my friend Eileen Pollack expressed surprise that a bourgeois, secular, Hungarian-Viennese Jew like me knew and constantly used Yiddish words, I informed her that all of this hailed from my becoming fast friends with a Jew from the Canadian tundra. Ditto with learning to *bentsch*—that is, to say the blessings over a meal—and enjoying the food that has been commonly associated as being Jewish by American culture—brisket, gefilte fish, kugel, kishke, pastrami, corned beef, kreplach, hamentashen, and kneidlach, to name just a few!

Oddly but understandably, the most essential traits that Americans continue to associate with being Jewish hail from Eastern Europe writ large, the place where I grew up. Yet, the Jewish milieu of my youth and upbringing bore virtually none of the characteristics Americans identify as key markers for being Jewish, demonstrating the class-bound origins of these behavioral and cultural patterns. My Jewish Timișoara and Jewish Vienna had virtually nothing in common with the world of Delancey Street and the Lower East Side so brilliantly depicted in Irving Howe's *World of Our Fathers: The Journey of the East European Jews to America and the Life They Found and Made.* The attributes mainstream American culture construes as typically Jewish do not include the ways of the Germanized Jews of the *Bildungsbürgertum.* The constant peppering of my lectures with Yiddishisms—tellingly, only in America and never in Europe—hails completely from Jerry Katz's lasting influence, and has nothing to do with that of my parents. In a way, I became an East European Jew in New York City in my early twenties by way of Jerry Katz from

Winnipeg, Manitoba, not by dint of having lived the first nine years of my life in Romania.

Soon after we met, Jerry invited me for Friday evening dinner at his apartment. There I met his wife, Brenda, who worked for some company in town while Jerry pursued his doctoral studies at the business school. I became a regular every Friday evening, even after the Katzes moved uptown to Washington Heights and welcomed their first child, Rena, and I became the baby's godfather. Jerry and Brenda came to know my father during one of his visits to New York, and he became a regular at their home on Friday evenings whenever he was visiting me, be it in New York or later in Boston.

I met Brenda's parents and Jerry's mother (his father was killed by a bus when Jerry was nine) during a visit to Winnipeg in 1970. Jerry was not a music fan; he disliked sports; he had no interest in museums, art, or theater, nor in popular culture. We did share a mutual interest in politics, though often we found ourselves on opposite sides, he on the conservative and I on the liberal. Yet, we shared this deep bond based on Judaism, not at the cerebral level in terms of knowing texts or theology, but on an emotional level we never articulated, omnipresent in an ineffable yet powerful way.

After Jerry received his Ph.D. in 1974, he and Brenda and their daughter left New York for Cincinnati, where Jerry began a job at Procter & Gamble. Barely one year later, Jerry and Brenda's second daughter arrived, and shortly thereafter, Jerry received an offer for an assistant professorship in business studies at Simmons College in Boston. The family moved to Brookline pretty much at the same time I left New York to move to Cambridge. I resumed my presence at Friday evening dinners at their house and on the major Jewish holidays, though I preferred going to services at Harvard's Hillel as opposed to the Orthodox shuls the Katz family attended. I was the main speaker at the three Katz daughters' bat mitzvahs and a close and cherished member of the family, reveling in being so different from them on the one hand, but so like them on the other. Alas, a disagreement between Jerry and me over a loan I provided him ended our friendship. I consider this to be the greatest loss of my life, apart from losing my mother, father, and Aunt Manci.

The MBA curriculum allowed students to take a few credits in any of the university's other graduate programs. Naturally, my eyes drifted toward the offerings in the sociology and government departments, the latter of which was in the process of being renamed Political Science. And there it was: a year-long political sociology course offered by Robert Alford, a visiting professor from the University of Wisconsin, Madison. Together with the course taught by Allan Silver, this class amplified to me that my calling was to become a political sociologist teaching at an American university. Finish business school, I told myself, receive your MBA, then do what you really want to do: study how societies construct political systems and do so in a comparative manner.

In the last semester of my MBA, I found out the Department of Political Science had awarded me a President's Fellowship to begin my doctoral studies there in September 1971. My father was proud, but still worried about my receiving a doctorate in political science. "What can you do with this degree, especially outside the walls of the academy?" he often wondered aloud. But when I began getting offers from a number of top-notch firms on account of my MBA, his tune changed. With Andy receiving job offers from fine firms in the real world, the issue of material security had become resolved. If this political-science-academic-doctorate thing was not going to work out, all was fine with Andy having an MBA. He would survive! From that moment on, my father became my biggest booster in terms of my academic career, often imploring me not to rush, to take my time, to sit back, read, ponder, learn, and contemplate. "We have a clear division of labor in this tiny Markovits family of two!" he would say. "You think, read, and write; and I make money that is all yours. End of story!"

Thus did I commence my four years of doctoral studies in Columbia's Department of Political Science. My cohort comprised the first entrants to a fundamentally revised program that emphasized examinations and minimized required courses. The idea was to accelerate the pre-dissertation process to have students concentrate on the writing of a dissertation that was to propel them successfully into the increasingly competitive academic job market. I entered the program brimming with confidence. With total chutzpah, I scheduled the first of three so-called divisional examinations for December of my first term. Well-armed by my political sociology courses with Professors Silver and Alford, I was certain that, with some serious studying, I could master this task. To maximize my discipline, I formed a study group with three other students, making certain we would all read the texts we chose from week to week and then discuss the readings with each other, gaining insights and interpretations.

Passing my first exam with distinction, I hummed along, taking my second examination—in American politics—at the end of my first full year in the program with equal success on account of having prepared so well with another study group. Over the summer of 1972, I read extensively on student politics in the United States and western Europe, hoping to formulate a dissertation topic. At this juncture, I came to deepen my interest in the scholarship of Seymour Martin Lipset, whose phenomenal work on socialism, trade unions, class-based voting, and American society in a comparative context I had encountered in both of my political sociology courses.

Lipset and his collaborators wrote fascinating studies on student politics, which I devoured that summer in addition to studying for my third divisional exam and the so-called comprehensive exam each student had to undertake in her or his major field. In my case, that was comparative politics. I passed both exams with flying colors, with the latter's oral portion occurring on the very Friday morning—May 11, 1973—after my New York Knickerbockers had won their second NBA championship by beating—just as they had in 1970—the Los Angeles Lakers. One of my examiners, Ira Katznelson, could not contain his joy, smiling and winking at me as his two colleagues on the committee took turns asking me questions. When it was Ira's turn, he asked me to elaborate on an essay I had provided on the written portion of the examination. Satisfied with my response, he turned to his colleagues and said: "Enough! Andy passes with flying colors. Let us celebrate him and the Knicks for the few remaining minutes." And that we did!

One course in the program that had a profound impact on me was Seweryn Bialer's comparative sociology of political elites, with an emphasis on the Soviet Union and Eastern Europe. Here, too, the subject of the course mattered less than its professor. Bialer was a Berlin-born Polish Jew who had joined the anti-fascist Polish underground in Łódź in 1942. He was captured by the Nazis and imprisoned in Auschwitz from 1944 until the end of the war. He joined the Polish Communist Party and rose through its ranks, becoming a member of its Central Committee. He also became a professor of sociology at the Polish Academy of Sciences. But in 1956, Bialer defected to West Berlin and made his way to the United States where he received his Ph.D. from the government department at Columbia. Due to his brilliance, he became an assistant professor in the same department and, eventually, the holder of a named professorship, as well as the winner of a "genius" MacArthur Fellowship.

Bialer and I took to each other deeply, and I spent many an hour in his office discussing Marxism, communism, Soviet politics, and eastern European developments. In this context, we came to analyze extensively Stalin's "rootless cosmopolitan" campaign of the late 1940s and early 1950s and its ramifications for Soviet and Eastern European communism, particularly in Hungary and Czechoslovakia. As regards leftwing antisemitism and authoritarianism, Bialer enlightened me as to the infamous Moczar affair of the mid-to-late 1960s about which I had been woefully ignorant at this time.

As minister of the interior, Mieczysław Moczar became the leader of a powerful faction of the party that pursued ultranationalist, xenophobic and antisemitic policies against Polish Jews, particularly members of the party and other leftists and intellectuals. In 1968, this culminated in expulsions as Moczar used student protests in Poland to purge Jews from the party and the government using openly antisemitic language and exhortations. This campaign led to a serious emigration of Jews from Poland, including doctors, lawyers, and engineers who were far from active in the Communist Party.

I wrote a paper for Professor Bialer on the antisemitism of the left, based on a body of literature on which I have continued to draw during my decades-long disputes with many leftists on this contemptible ideology that remains alive and well among the left on both sides of the Atlantic. In researching this paper for Professor Bialer, I first encountered the phenomenon of National Bolshevism in the Weimar Republic. This represented a significant movement on the country's left that was deeply antisemitic, xenophobic, nationalistic, and authoritarian. Though never quite called this, the phenomenon of National Bolshevism existed in other countries apart from Germany—such as in Poland under Moczar's hatred of Jews as cosmopolitans. Most important, its characteristics have remained alive and well in our contemporary world.

Being a leftist does not automatically mean that one is tolerant, inclusive, understanding, and supportive of outsiders and the weak. I have found that identifying with the "left" has become *de rigueur* for any self-respecting academic in the social sciences and, even more so, in the humanities of any leading university of the West. It has often become a fashion statement of intellectual conformity, rather than of a deep commitment to compassion and empathy. Alas, a certain negativity towards Jews as ipso facto representatives of the powerful has often been part of this culture. I have spent a good deal of my intellectual energy fighting the common mantra that antisemitism can only exist on the right and never on the left.

The summer of 1973 became my time to explore America. From 1960, when my father and I first arrived in the United States, and 1967, when I commenced my studies at Columbia, I had seen virtually nothing of the country apart from the greater New York City metropolitan area. I had visited Bill Gillespie in Washington, D.C., in August 1965, when I stayed with him for one week and toured all the sites of our nation's capital. I had spent Thanksgiving 1967 with the Dreschers in Port Huron, Michigan, and Thanksgiving 1968 with the Gillespies in Annandale, Virginia. That was it!

Luckily, one of my father's friends in Westchester County had an extra VW Beetle that nobody in the family seemed to be using, so I asked whether I could borrow it for the summer, fully intending to pay for the use of the car. His affirmative answer was both generous and speedy. Even though I had an Austrian driver's license, accompanied by a document that validated it as an international certificate, I decided to obtain my first American license. With that document issued by the State of New York in my possession, I was on the road for my first cross-country trip by early June.

Many travelers have experienced such a journey as transformative. Count me among them. Of course, I had every predisposition to love the trip, because I loved driving and I loved America. From the first turn onto westbound I-90, I listened incessantly to my AM and FM car radio, learning more in two months about Americana of all kinds than years of college courses on American culture could have conveyed. I was Chicago bound for two reasons: first, because I wanted to see this important city and consume its unique architecture and blues, which I did at its famed Checkerboard Lounge on the South Side of town where one of its owners and founders, the legendary Buddy Guy, performed brilliantly on his guitar; and second, because Chicago was important as the beginning of Route 66, rendered world famous by the Bobby Troup song "Get your Kicks on Route 66." I came to know and love this song by listening to the Rolling Stones' stellar rendition on their first album back in the Vienna of the early 1960s. Even though much of the original U.S. Route 66 (the Will Rogers Highway; the Main Street of America; the Mother Road; the main artery of the Dust Bowl migrations out west; the road invoked in Steinbeck's *The Grapes of Wrath*) had been rendered obsolete by the superhighways of the Interstate Highway System; I still got to see and travel remnants of it in patches along the way.

Above all, I traveled through Illinois, Missouri, Kansas, Oklahoma, Texas, New Mexico, Arizona, and California, never mind the states I crossed on my way from New York to Chicago, getting to know America. Constantly having Simon and Garfunkel's brilliant song "America" in my ear (even though I had yet to travel the New Jersey Turnpike and/ or make it to Saginaw or Pittsburgh), this trip was a quasi-religious experience for me. Eating in rundown diners along the way and sleeping in cheap motels may not be everyone's bliss, but it surely was mine. After sightseeing in Los Angeles, I drove up the Pacific coast on California Highway 1 all the way to the Bay Area. Once there, I visited Berkeley and Stanford, where I went to the Center for Advanced Study in the Behavioral Sciences in search of Seymour Martin Lipset, who at this time was a fellow at this august institute. Alas, Lipset was not around on the day I visited, but I made the acquaintance of Hanan C. Selvin, the noted SUNY Stony Brook sociologist, who not only invited me to have lunch with him and all the fellows on the Center's stunningly beautiful sun-draped patio, but also spent the afternoon with me discussing my academic interests. I did not even dare dream that I, too, was to become a CASBS Fellow at Stanford exactly 35 years later.

I then drove to Oregon to spend time with my former Columbia pal Allen Drescher, who had just completed law school and begun his new life in Ashland, where he became a successful lawyer. After a detour to Nevada, where I wanted to visit Reno (was it perhaps on account of its mention in Johnny Cash's brilliant "Folsom Prison Blues" or in the Grateful Dead's classic "Friend of the Devil"?), I took a straight shot back home to New York City on I-80, the highway that connects two iconic bridges on opposite sides of this majestic continent: the Golden Gate and the George Washington. With my uncle and aunt having sold their candy store in 1972, before moving to Vienna to be closer to my father and hoping for a better life than they had in New York, I left dormitory life at Columbia and took up residence in my uncle's old apartment, 14J, at 215 West 92nd Street.

My last two years in the Department of Political Science at Columbia were consumed by working on my dissertation and, beginning in the fall of 1974, taking on teaching gigs at New York University and the John Jay College of Criminal Justice of the City University of New York. These were the only options for someone like me to get any teaching experience at the college level, clearly an important ingredient on any aspiring academic's resume. Because Columbia was the smallest of the Ivies, with only 2,800 undergraduates, and because of a certain educational culture, graduate students in the social sciences had few, if any, opportunities to teach Columbia undergraduates if they didn't write their dissertations in political and social theory or intellectual history, the disciplines most akin to the subjects comprising the CC curriculum. As I did not fit that bill, I had to look elsewhere to gain my teaching experience.

I adored teaching in both schools, particularly the opportunity to offer an introductory course in American politics at John Jay, where I had to deliver identical lectures to "regular" students in the morning and to New York City police officers in the evening. Receiving diametrically opposed interpretations of the same material from these two very different constituencies proved an excellent pedagogical experience for honing my teaching skills. By the end of the semester, I knew I genuinely enjoyed lecturing, talking, and listening to students. In my nearly fifty years as a professor, I have been by far the proudest of having been a fine teacher for thousands of students in many universities in the United States and abroad.

I spent the summer of 1975 locked away in my apartment frantically writing my dissertation which I wanted to defend by the end of October. Other than going to a movie on Saturday nights, I never left home, subsisting on TV dinners and lots of coffee. In fact, I swore that the last cup of this beverage would cross my lips on the morning of my dissertation defense and never thereafter.

On Friday morning, October 24, I took the 104 bus to Columbia and defended my doctoral dissertation. Thereafter, my adviser and, by this time, friend Mark Kesselman took me to lunch at—yes, Tom's! He wanted to take me someplace fancier, but I insisted that on this solemn day on which I closed my eight-year Columbia life I wanted to have one more omelet with American cheese and toast at Tom's. When the waitperson asked me whether I would like my coffee black, as I often did for lunch, or with milk, more dinner fare, I answered that I would like neither, a glass of water would do just fine. The festive dinner meal had to take place with Robert Austerlitz at Ideal. Both occasions were the last time I ate at these two establishments that were so important to me during my years at Columbia.

I had to make some minor corrections to my dissertation before I was to hand it in to receive my doctoral degree in May 1976. Unlike seven years before, when not having attended my college graduation caused me to feel disgust and anger with myself, this event simply never registered. Getting a BA is a communal experience, obtaining a Ph.D. a solitary and lonely one.

I will forever love Columbia for three reasons. First, the professors on its faculty fulfilled the most basic mission of a university, which is to enhance a student's knowledge. This is no mean feat, and I have never taken it for granted as a pedagogue. But an institution of learning also is obligated to provide its students with skills they can use in their professional lives. Columbia did this well on two levels and in two schools. The business school taught me skills I would never have learned anywhere else. True, I did not much enjoy acquiring those skills and then let them lie fallow. But providing someone with a skill set he is reluctant to acquire bespeaks a higher degree of pedagogical achievement than teaching only the most eager students.

As for Columbia's training me as an academic political scientist, the tally is superb. Again, it was not the department's fault that at some point in my career I decided to depart from the path of a conventional political scientist—or political sociologist, to be more precise—and study an amalgam of topics that necessitated my utilizing epistemologies and methodologies that conventional political scientists typically do not employ. On the most basic levels of conveying knowledge and providing skills and useful training, my eight years at Columbia must be gauged a success.

Second, there is the level of education that goes far beyond the accumulation of knowledge and skills. I do not want to engage in a discussion of what constitutes education, as opposed to training, because I find this a futile exercise in arbitrary definitions. Without doubt an education entails the ability to think critically, to be a moral person, to be a fine citizen, to have *Bildung*. If training pertains to tactics, education entails strategy. Rather, what I mean here is that Columbia offered a rich environment beyond the classes and classrooms in the form of the professors' willingness to engage with me and commit to my education, my advancement, my development as a person.

Beyond that, I happen to have been lucky to have benefitted from a zeitgeist that constituted a critical shift in pretty much everything that affected our lives. Whatever opinion one has of the student revolt—and mine was on balance supportive of its causes, though sometimes less so of its participants—it was clearly part of a larger movement that changed the world. I was fortunate to have been at a university of Columbia's intellectual excellence experiencing this event in real time.

Third, for me Columbia represented a real synthesis between Europe and the United States. On the most banal level, Columbia is an American university. Yet, from the get-go, I chose topics of study that involved Europe, many of these classes taught by European immigrants or their American disciples. Columbia permitted me to study Europe while safely ensconced in the United States. At Columbia, I truly came to know the writings of giants such as Marx, Weber, Durkheim, Tocqueville, Schumpeter, and Sombart, never mind literary figures such as Homer, Dante, Goethe, and Shakespeare. Given my personal history, I am convinced I would not have gotten to know any of these figures' thoughts as well as I did at Columbia had I studied them in Europe.

This sounds ludicrous but it is true. The difference would not have lain in the better pedagogy of Columbia compared to any European university, an iffy assumption. Rather, it would have depended on how receptive, how eager, I would have been to learn at these universities compared to Columbia. I know I would have failed at them for the simple reason that I would never have enjoyed the psychic and mental comfort I enjoyed at Columbia, despite the initial obstacles I faced such as my inability to type. Ultimately, Columbia represented the *Goldene Medine* to me, the Golden Land. I arrived at its gate an insecure and arrogant European boy. I departed as a well-trained and well-educated American man, fully confident of his skills and his knowledge of European thinkers, politics, and social movements.

Kiki:
Big Politics and Little Andy

During my first two-week break from Columbia, a few days before Christmas 1967, I traveled to Vienna to see my father. I did so as a proud student at one of the world's leading institutions of higher education, which I had long cherished and now touted by sporting its name on sweatshirts, hoodies, T-shirts, and decals.

As was the custom in the small Viennese Jewish community at the time, my father planned to spend a few days over the Christmas break at the Hotel Panhans in a small town called Semmering, one hour's drive south of Vienna. This offered the closest possibility for downhill skiing, sparing us the longer journey to Austria's vaunted ski meccas in Salzburg and Tyrol. My father and I knew this hotel well, having made day-trips there, especially on weekends, so that I could learn to ski. But in summers, too, the place was lovely, with green hills full of forests, its allure very much like the beauty of Vermont.

The Hotel Panhans and the town of Semmering were the equivalent of Grossinger's or Kutsher's and the Catskills to New York's Jews, but without the stellar humor and brilliant shtick of the Borscht Belt comedians. Unlike their New York counterparts, the Jews of Vienna were far too few in number, far too insecure and—above all—far too ill-equipped in any language (including Yiddish) to create a cultural expression akin to what the New York Jews achieved so impressively in the Catskills, which was to shape American comedy and humor to this day.

On New Year's Eve, we went to the Panhans' large ballroom to ring in 1968, and I spotted a gorgeous woman, petite, her skin dark brown, her short hair pitch-black, her eyes glowing. Dimples appeared on both cheeks as she exhibited a radiant smile. Her miniskirt was flirtatious but not trashy—I was struck! Somehow, I managed to meet her and she introduced herself as Kiki Feder. I could tell she was wearing Diorissimo, a wonderful throwback to the 1950s that was one of my favorite perfumes, perhaps because I continued to associate it with the women who had attended my mother's parties back in Timişoara. Kiki would become the love of my life and the partner who has enriched every minute of my existence since the fall of 1991.

What happened between 1968 and 1991? Attracted as I was to Kiki from the instant we met, why did I require 23 years to declare my love and marry her? Why, in all the years we were apart, didn't I commit to and marry someone else? To solve this mystery, I need to go back to the beginning and retrace not only the off-and-on nature of our romance but also the complex web of influences—historical, political, cultural, and familial—within which both Kiki and I grew up and achieved adulthood and middle age.

That night at the Hotel Panhans in Semmering, we danced to the band's lousy rendition of the Beatles' "Eight Days a Week," in which the singer, as was often the case before lyrics became readily accessible, mimicked the English words without having properly learned or understood them. I asked why I had never heard of her, let alone encountered her, before that evening. After all, the community of Viennese Jewish kids my age comprised fewer than one hundred, if that, and we all had congregated in three youth organizations that were rivals but also part of the same close-knit group. I had left for the United States for good only four months earlier, so I still knew most of my peers, or at least knew of them. But not Kiki Feder!

She responded that she and her mother had lived a secluded life, with virtually no relationship to the Jewish community, and the only reason she was at the Panhans that New Year's Eve was a friend had invited her. To my immense gratification, she gave me her telephone number, which I called immediately after my father and I returned to Vienna after two days of skiing in Semmering.

Luckily, Kiki agreed to a date with me two days before my return to New York to finish the fall semester at Columbia. As was only proper, I was to pick her up at her home, and we could then go to a movie or one of the lovely cafés near her apartment for a chat.

Neither of these possibilities took place. When I arrived at Kiki's apartment—on the fourth floor of a typical Viennese apartment building, thankfully with an elevator—I was greeted by three characters, none of whom were Kiki. First, a pretty middle-aged woman with reddish hair opened the door and, before introducing herself, asked me to rush inside lest Burli the lovebird escape the premises. Then, a cuddly Samoyed dog named Mischu came bouncing down the hallway, jumping on me and barking with joy. Lastly, the aforementioned woman extended her hand and said: "Welcome to our home. I am Kiki's mother, Erika!"

I detected a slight Hungarian accent in her German and responded in Hungarian that I was delighted to be here and happy to meet this menagerie. My speaking Hungarian to Kiki's mother was an instant icebreaker and furnished an immediate bond between the two of us.

"Oh, you speak Hungarian?" she asked, genuinely surprised. "How so? Aren't you a student at an American university?"

I told her that I had been born in Timișoara to Hungarian-speaking Jewish parents and that my father and I continued to speak Hungarian with each other. Erika walked me into the small living room where Kiki sat alongside a table full of Hungarian-style pastries.

"Sit down, have some," Erika said. "Would you like tea or coffee?"

We engaged in a wonderful conversation, having now switched to German since Kiki did not speak Hungarian, although, Erika told me proudly, Kiki understood the language well. So much for being alone with Kiki at a movie! To my slight annoyance, Erika, as was the case with a number of my girlfriends' mothers, seemed to like me more than did her daughter. Erika was loquacious, charming, stylish, a chainsmoker, and a bit of a flirt. She struck me as typical of a certain genre of Hungarian Jewish women that came to populate the beauty industry in places like Los Angeles and New York. I cannot describe them properly, but they were a type of which the Gábor sisters became a well-known caricature.

Kiki's mother, Frederika Talmud, was born in 1919 into a middle-class Jewish family in Budapest. Her father had died of natural causes when she was young, and her mother survived the war. Her brother was the only member of the Talmud family who was deported to Auschwitz, where he died. Erika spent the last two years of the war partly in hiding in the city, but also working for the famed Swedish diplomat Raoul Wallenberg.[5]

During the war years, Wallenberg found himself in Budapest, where he heroically issued Swedish certificates of protection to thousands of Budapest's Jews, saving them from certain death in Auschwitz (the conservative estimate is that Wallenberg saved 60,000 lives, but the number might be as high as 100,000). In this amazing undertaking, Wallenberg had much assistance from the locals, one of whom was Erika Talmud, Kiki's mother. The Nazi and Hungarian authorities never caught Wallenberg, but the Soviets did. In January 1945, they took him to the Soviet Union, where he died under secret circumstances; even today, we do not know where, when, or how. For his unique humanitarian deeds, Wallenberg was posthumously declared a citizen of the United States, an honor bestowed only on Sir Winston Churchill. He is honored by Yad Vashem in Jerusalem on the roll call of the Righteous Among the Nations.

In the winter of 1945, after the Red Army had liberated Pest but while it still had to conquer the northern district of Buda, which remained occupied by the Wehrmacht, Erika found herself working in a hospital. One of her patients was a young Russian Jew by the name of Isaac Julius Fedorov, who spoke excellent Yiddish as well as flawless German, which was, to say the least, quite odd. Erika never told Kiki how this man made his way to Budapest, whether he was a soldier (or officer)

---

5   Hailing from one of Sweden's most pedigreed aristocratic families, Wallenberg enrolled at the University of Michigan's School of Architecture in 1931 and was graduated in 1935. The American Institute of Architects bestowed on him the silver medal as Michigan's outstanding student that year. How he could have remained virtually invisible to the university community, at that time and for decades afterward, is beyond my comprehension. The University of Michigan established an annual lecture named after him held by a speaker honored by the Raoul Wallenberg medal for her or his valiant contributions to human rights causes. There also exists a modest sculpture in his honor at the entrance of the School of Architecture properly entitled "Köszönöm" meaning "Thank you" in Hungarian. Still, Wallenberg's presence at the University of Michigan is minimal at best and he remains virtually unknown to students and faculty alike.

in the Red Army, or whether, perhaps, he was one of the partisans who spent years in the forests of Belarus and other places fighting the Germans and joining up with the Red Army on its march westward.[6] Erika also never told Kiki what this man's profession was or even whether he was certifiably Jewish. After the war, the two married and made their way to Vienna, where they settled, fully intending, like so many other Jewish refugees, to continue their westward trek to North America.

By the time Kiki was born in November 1950, the family name had morphed into Feder. Kiki's official given name is Irina, which is as Russian as a name can be. She was so named for one of Julius's two daughters both of whom were murdered during the war (maybe in the forest depicted in "Defiance"?). However, Julek, as Julius came to be known, never called Kiki by that name but by Kiki, which stuck with her for the rest of her life and is her father's most vivid legacy. Julek died in 1956 when Kiki was not quite six. From then on, Erika raised Kiki alone, in a parallel situation to my father raising me alone after my mother passed away when I was nine.

To support the family, Erika worked as an office manager at the Austrian headquarters of the British pharmaceutical giant Glaxo Laboratories (GlaxoSmithKline as of 2000). Austria was meant to be a convenient waystation, and so remained temporary for decades—actually, for the rest of their lives, as was true for my father and so many other Jews in Austria and Germany in the postwar era. That first evening, Erika proudly showed me a valid Canadian tourist visa in her Austrian passport, emphasizing that this was "just for good measure, because one never knows."

---

6   Like millions all over the world, Kiki and I spent many an evening watching movies during the COVID-19 pandemic. On Friday evening, December 11, 2020, I chose the film "Defiance," an Edward Zwick directed movie hailing from 2008 depicting the true story about the four Jewish Bielski brothers who saved Jews by hiding them in the Naliboki Forest in Belarus and fighting the Germans from 1941 to 1943. Kiki, who is no fan of war movies, agreed to watch this film in good part because its topic spoke to her by virtue of what she knew from her mother in terms of her father's stories that seemed relevant to the film. When we encounter that typhoid causes the Jews in the forest major problems, Kiki exclaimed that her father contracted precisely this disease in some forest. Then, when, in the film, the Jews flee the forest from the approaching Germans and have to traverse a marshy swamp, Kiki became so agitated that we had to stop watching for a while because she recalled her mother telling her about a swamp through which her father had to wade. Who knew that this film would strike a chord so close to Kiki's story.

Kiki informed me that they always had a packed suitcase ready so they could depart at a second's notice, again "just for good measure." So did my father, as did my aunt and uncle, as well as many Jews in Vienna at the time. (Sadly, some Viennese and German Jews have resumed this custom, if they ever stopped it.) As one more marker of Erika's reticence to embrace Vienna and Austria as her real home, she had Kiki attend Vienna's Lycée Français, the secondary school preferred by many Viennese Jewish parents, as opposed to the regular German-speaking public schools.

I bade Erika and Kiki good-bye that evening, delighted to have met Erika, secure in her affection, but sad I never got the chance to spend time alone with Kiki. Back at Columbia, I commenced an intense correspondence with Kiki, which I maintained throughout the ensuing five months, even during exam time, when I should have been devoting all my energy to doing well in my courses. She replied as prolifically and affectionately as I did, so I was certain she really liked me. Occasionally I called her on the telephone, though we never spoke more than a few minutes since this was an expensive proposition at the time.

After what turned out to be a massively turbulent spring in 1968 at Columbia that I described in the previous chapter, I returned to Vienna for the summer, taking a physically demanding job as a stacker of items in one of my father's supermarkets. In my off hours, my romance with Kiki flourished. Her lovebird, Burli, keeled over one morning in June while Kiki and her mother were eating their breakfast; Kiki's visible sadness lasted for days, while her inner sadness—I am sure—lasted months. This was the first time I witnessed a person grieving over an animal. In my nine years in Timişoara, followed by my nine years in Vienna, I knew virtually nobody who owned a pet, and the few who did—like our landlady Frau Kohler—never exhibited any pain close to Kiki's when her pet died.

Making Kiki's and Erika's grief worse was the sudden death of Mischu, who somehow found himself in the basement of Kiki's apartment building where he ate rat poison. Poor Kiki and Erika! I must have displayed the appropriate compassion because I found Kiki becoming much closer to me. Indeed, many years later, Kiki confirmed that my empathy and genuine sadness about the death of those two animals, something that was not par for the course in the culture of the time (*hey, it's a bird, it's a dog; get over them and get yourself another one*) landed me many positive points in Kiki's evaluation of my emotional make-up.

In the middle of August, my father and his partner, Maria, booked a two-week vacation in Lido di Jesolo on the Adriatic Sea, a favorite seaside resort for the Viennese. They asked me to join them for the second week, then drive back with them to Vienna just in time for my flight to New York, where my second year of college awaited. I agreed, and then asked whether Kiki could accompany me. My father remembered Kiki from New Year's Eve and found her enchanting. Now all I had to do was ask Kiki and convince Erika to let Kiki come with us. (Again, this was the tail end of Victorian culture, in which the freedom and mobility of young women of a certain social station were strictly curtailed, to be transgressed only at the peril of their reputation.) I ran this by Kiki, who was certain her mother would not grant her permission to join us.

On our next date, I made a point of taking the elevator to the Feders' fourth-floor apartment to meet Kiki there, rather than wait for her to appear downstairs. Erika opened the door and invited me inside. My heart was racing, and out of nowhere I said to Erika in Hungarian, which we had stopped speaking after our first meeting seven months before, that I had an important request. Erika looked at me warmly and asked me what it was. I blurted out my wish to have Kiki accompany me to Italy to join my father and Maria.

By this time Kiki had joined us from her room, ready to go out with me for the evening. We stood there motionless awaiting Erika's reaction, which we couldn't anticipate. A decisive no? An angry no? An indignant no? We certainly did not expect a yes. But wonder of wonders, Erika agreed to my invitation, with the proviso that she have a lengthy telephone conversation with my father first.

They spoke. Apparently the conversation went according to Erika's wishes because she permitted her daughter to join me for a week's stay in Italy!

August 1968: Adriatic Bliss Cut Short by Czechoslovak Tragedy

Kiki and I had the time of our lives. We spent tons of time on the beach, doing all kinds of beachy things—playing volleyball, taking paddle boats out to the lagoon, going on long barefoot walks on the sand. We ate great fish, lots of pasta of various kinds, superb desserts, and we twice traveled with Maria and my father for a full day's stay in nearby Venice, where we took in all the sights.

Kiki stayed in a room with Maria, and I with my father. In addition to the need for propriety, Kiki insisted on calling her mother at least once a day, sometimes twice. At the time, one still had to call the hotel operator, who then called an operator in Italy, who then called the equivalent operator in Austria, who then put the call through to Kiki's mother. This was not only time-consuming but also fraught with technical glitches that made the success of such a call hardly a certainty. I seem to recall spending hours waiting for Kiki to have spoken with her mother!

And then at breakfast on Wednesday, August 21, my father and I overheard two of the Italian waiters saying something about a Soviet invasion of Czechoslovakia. Even though neither my father nor I spoke any Italian, it was a Romance language like Romanian and shared many similarities with French, which I spoke quite well and my father a bit, so we could understand the gist of conversations, the news on television, and even articles in the broadsheets. My father and I scurried to our transistor radios in the hope of getting some German- or English-language newscast to learn more. To no avail! So my father decided to call friends in Vienna, who were news junkies and would know more than we did.

We rushed to our room while Kiki and Maria stayed behind at the breakfast table. After a few calls which like Kiki's to her mother were cumbersome, we knew for certain that the Soviet Union and four of its allies invaded Czechoslovakia on August 20, one day earlier. My father turned to me and said: "We have to leave immediately and drive back to Vienna!" Informing my father that we still had two nights left on our prepaid stay did not sway him one bit. We informed Maria and Kiki of our decision and barely two hours later we were on the road back to Vienna.

To this day, I don't understand the reasons for my father's rash decision. His action was so panicky and precipitous that he seemed determined to singlehandedly stop the Red Army at the Czech-Austrian border were it to invade Austria. When asked about this later, he mentioned that he never trusted the Soviets or the communists and was convinced they would want to conquer all of Europe, an opinion widely shared by many East Europeans who detested and never trusted the Soviets. The speed of my father's actions betrayed a fear that the communists were about to expropriate him once again, as they had in Timişoara in 1948, and ruin everything he and his business partner had built up with their popular supermarkets in Vienna. My father was so nervous that he wasn't fit to get behind the wheel, so Maria and I shared the eight-hour drive back to Vienna.

I, too, was deeply upset by this invasion, but for different reasons. In this, I had a clear ally in Kiki, who all summer showed a deep interest in the developments in Prague, which formed the largest component of our many discussions about politics and international relations. Kiki was not as steeped as I was in the literature of the left, but she cared deeply about humane actions in all of political and social life. Her main concern wasn't how Alexander Dubček and his crew might reshape Marxism such that their reforms were compatible with the humane and inclusive and tolerant sides of this important movement and thereby also furnish real examples of its shining incarnations. Rather, she felt for the Czech reformers because she truly believed they wanted to improve the lives of the citizens of their country who, as she knew all too well, had suffered at the hands not only of Stalinists but also Nazis. Whereas my father was frightened by Soviet power, Kiki and I were frightened by the loss of Czech dignity.

All spring, I had followed the developments of the Prague Spring as closely as I could from my Columbia dorm. Dubček, the head of the Czechoslovak Communist Party, and his fascinating group of reformers had challenged the Soviet Union to allow Czechoslovakia to pursue something they beautifully termed "socialism with a human face." Kiki did the same from nearby Vienna, and we discussed the events in Czechoslovakia in the letters we exchanged. Now here we were together on a long car ride triggered by the wanton destruction of this fascinating experiment at the hands of the brutal Soviet Union, ruled by a boring and conservative gerontocracy.

In notable contrast to their counterparts in Hungary in 1956, Dubček and his reformers never wanted to jettison socialism and establish a capitalist system. Nor did any strains of reactionary nationalism emerge among the Prague reformers like they most certainly did in some circles in Hungary 12 years before. Rather, they hoped their reforms would permit a certain level of individual freedom in an environment in which any deviation from the party line was mercilessly repressed by the secret police. They also hoped their desired reforms would allow not only a plurality of opinions, but a new framework of economic life in which certain segments of the population were to have some autonomy from the rigidity of the central plan that dominated all Soviet-style systems. The reformers never challenged the existence of the Communist Party, nor were they keen on having the market and private property rule the economy unencumbered.

Whether these reforms would have worked will remain forever a mystery because the August invasion nixed all such endeavors. Dubček and his reformers were arrested, hundreds of Czechs and Slovaks were killed, and the genuine hopes of the Prague Spring became the victim of the unforgiving brutality and rigidity of what was then known as the Brezhnev Doctrine. This policy held that the Soviet Union and its Warsaw Pact allies would never tolerate any perceived challenge to the continued monopoly of the Communist Party's power. Were such challenges to occur—as they did in Czechoslovakia under the leadership of Dubček—they would be met by military force.

Only a decade later did I become fully conversant with the writings of such major players in Dubček's movement as Ota Šik and Zdeněk Mlynář (with whom I had wonderful chats when we were colleagues in the Department of Political Science at the University of Innsbruck, when I was a Fulbright professor there in 1996). I loved the core of their ideas about a "third way" between unbridled capitalism and dogmatic communism. In 1968, on our hurried drive back to Vienna, I knew only that Soviet-style communism was never going to permit any meaningful reform and the only way communism's transformation could take place would be if it crumbled from within, which is exactly what happened twenty years later.

Far from panicking like my father, I merely felt sorry for these reformers, as well as for the left in general, which had taken yet another hit in its attempt to wiggle free of the communist stranglehold it had endured since the Bolshevik Revolution. I was upset at how little Western leftists cared about the Prague reformers; to this day, the Germans talk about the *Achtundsechziger* and the French about the *soixante-huitards*—the Sixty-Eighters—yet remain parochial in thinking only about activists of their own nations in those momentous days. At best, they might share a mutual glance across the Rhine, but neither looks at the events in Prague. If anything, the mention of "1968," so epochal in both Germany and France to this day, might include a superficial mention of events in the United States, most notably the protests at Columbia and the assassinations of Dr. Martin Luther King Jr. and Bobby Kennedy. But it would never invoke the extensive reforms attempted in Czechoslovakia and certainly nothing about the struggle of Czech students at the Charles University in Prague.

In March of that fateful year, a group of German SDS members, led by their superstar, Rudi Dutschke, paid a visit to Prague to meet their Czech counterparts. The Germans behaved abominably. Rather than engage the Czechs and learn about their struggles in an honest and empathetic way, the Germans lectured their hosts with "Teutonic arrogance," as one commentator called it, and demonstrated "an ignorance fostered by their seminar-style Marxism." Inevitably, the two groups talked past each other. The Germans put forth all their views, comprising the Western New Left's core: anti-authoritarianism; anti-imperialism; opposition to the United States, most notably as regarded the war in Vietnam; hatred of the German establishment, which they labeled fascist; extolling of Third World liberation movements such as the Viet Cong and, increasingly, Palestinian groups such as El Fatah. The Czechs pleaded for liberal values such as freedom of speech, autonomy from the Soviet Union, and pluralism within the Communist Party. The Germans dismissed these wishes as nothing but slow accommodations to capitalism and a betrayal of the socialist revolution.

In a way, the Czechs hoped to attain everything the Germans already had, but disdained and rejected. What made this event so problematic was the Germans' disregard for the legitimacy of the Czechs' views and their open contempt for the Czechs themselves, whose demands the Germans saw as evidence of bourgeois liberalism, the opposition to which provided their own reason for existence. Never did the Germans express empathy for the Czechs' predicament, operating under a stringent dictatorship that punished people for any dissent with serious prison terms or worse. The German student left maintained this view even after the Soviets and their allies crushed the Prague Spring. While condemning this action in a tepid pro forma manner with virtually no compassion, the SDS and its milieu decried the Dubček-led reforms as nothing more than "social democratism" (*Sozialdemokratismus*), to use the neologism of Hans-Jürgen Krahl, one of the SDS's prominent members; in this view, social democratism was not one iota better than American imperialism.

What always bothered me about this was the contemptuous tone of the Germans' dealings with the Czechs, rather than any substantive disagreements they might have had with the Czech reformers, which, given the different histories of these groups, made sense. That disdainful tone reminded me of the old imperial German haughtiness, dating to the Second German Reich's formation in 1871, when Germany saw only Russia when it looked eastward and ignored the peoples in between. This arrogance towards an eastern European neighbor reappeared in the German left in the late 1970s and early 1980s when *Solidarność* commenced its epochal revolution in Poland. In that case, too, many members of the West German radical left, and not only the established and then governing middle-of-the-road mainstream leftist Social Democratic Party (SPD), disdained the Poles, just as they had disdained the Czechs roughly a decade before, chiding them for their supposedly reactionary behavior and attitudes. When German leftists spotted pictures of the Madonna on the walls of some of the Polish workers, their contempt for this movement required no further substantiation.

I had encountered equal ignorance about and intolerance toward the Czech struggle for democratic reforms whenever I mentioned it to my radical friends at Columbia. The American SDS, like its German counterpart, had no patience for any opposition to communist dictatorships. The association of anti-communism with the repressive conservatism of the 1950s and the first half of the 1960s in the United States and in the Federal Republic of Germany was so fraught that any criticism of communism appeared tantamount to a valorization of conservative forces. This led to a virtual silence on the part of much of the Western student left regarding events in the Soviet bloc, most notably the Prague Spring. That is not to say that either of these leftist movements admired the Soviets. Rather, they regarded the Soviet Union as a bumbling, irrelevant gerontocracy that was clearly a lesser evil than capitalism and its leader, enemy number one, the United States of America! It was the Western student left's ignorance of and contempt for developments in Eastern Europe that always tempered my associations with it. Above all, it upset me that the left, too, practiced the Markovits theory of intra-European relations: you dislike all your neighbors but those to the east you disdain!

And so, when we heard on our car radio that the Soviet Union was not alone in its invasion of Czechoslovakia, that it was aided and abetted by troops from four of its Warsaw Pact allies—Poland, Bulgaria, Hungary, and East Germany—I was not only sad and disappointed, but angry. That East Germany would participate enraged me because Czech citizens would need to endure yet again, as they had endured thirty years earlier, the ignominy of German troops goose-stepping down the streets of Prague in uniforms and helmets eerily similar to the ones worn by the Wehrmacht in 1938. This aspect of the invasion had nothing to do with crushing a threatening movement or ideology. It was, rather, an act of outright humiliation of the Czechs by the Soviets. In the 1990s and beyond, I met a number of East German intellectuals who still were ashamed of what their country had done in August 1968.

Back in Vienna, Kiki and I saw each other a few times before I needed to fly back to Columbia for my second year of university. Once in New York, carrying an extra load in order to finish school in four instead of five semesters, I became overwhelmed by my classes. I was required to write a long paper for my seminar in comparative politics, tantamount to a senior honors thesis; this meant that for the first time in my life I had to engage in serious research involving primary materials, something

I had never done nor envisioned doing. My relationship to Kiki cooled considerably. I wrote letters less frequently, as did she, and by November or so, our correspondence petered out. We never officially broke up; neither of us made a scene; the relationship simply ended.

Over the years, my father would tell me that he had run into Kiki in downtown Vienna and she looked wonderful, that she was her sweet self and he had been as happy to see her as was she to see him. I also knew Kiki had started working in Austria's leading bank and was on track to a successful career there. Sometime in the mid-1970s, I heard she had married Alex Friedmann, a prominent young man in Vienna's Jewish community by reason of his impressive oratorical skills and sharp wit. Alex became one of Vienna's leading psychiatrists, specializing in treating marginalized groups and refugees. But after our break-up in the fall of 1968, Kiki and I had no contact with each other.

Twenty-Three Years without Kiki

On the other side of the Atlantic, I led the life of a bachelor consumed by his work. I had many girlfriends but no home. My beautiful condominium in Cambridge was sparsely furnished, and the refrigerator was empty with the exception of lots of diet soda and yogurt. I never used the stove and used the burners only to heat water for tea. I never cooked dinner for my girlfriends, but rather took them out to restaurants. I hired a reliable service that not only cleaned my apartment but also did my laundry, changed my bedsheets, and bought the yogurt and diet soda. I never went to grocery stores other than to pick up a copy of *The New York Times* in case the one that had been delivered to the downstairs mailroom was stolen. Because a number of my girlfriends lived far from Boston—in Montreal, Toronto, Philadelphia, New York City, Albany, Washington, Miami, London, and Frankfurt—I rarely spent more than one weekend a month in my apartment. On weekdays, I never arrived home until 11 p.m., or even later, spending all my time in my warehouse of an office near the Center for European Studies, in an old barracks from WWII, a place called "Vanserg Building" best denoting its marginal existence on the Harvard campus by not being officially labeled "Hall" on the marker outside.[7]

This place, Room 213 to be precise, became legendary among my friends and colleagues as "Andy's Abode" a.k.a. "the Bunker." (An elderly Asian man actually lived in Vanserg, doing his dishes in the men's room and brushing his teeth there. I spent a number of Christmas and Thanksgiving days at my office and—without fail—I ran into this man in the bathroom, with the two of us being the only living beings in this building, maybe all of Harvard. I have no idea where and when he showered, but I figured he did so in one of the Harvard gyms nearby. I referred to him as the Phantom of Vanserg.) I came to love Vanserg and will forever associate it with some of the most productive but also fun-filled years of my life. It so perfectly represented my institutional marginality at Harvard coupled with that university's centrality for my intellectual development and academic career.

Living this life was satisfying on one level. I traveled a lot, spent time with many beautiful women, took them to movies and plays, and treated them to fine meals, all of which fed my male ego and allowed me to pride myself on being a successful ladies' man. In my defense, this satisfaction was completely internal: true to my father's dictum that a gentleman never talks about his private life and most certainly does not brag about his love life, I never shared any information about these relationships with my male friends. In fact, I delighted in some of those friends getting irritated by my silence as I never revealed the names of any of the women I was seeing. Whenever a girlfriend came to visit me in Cambridge, I made sure we spent the weekend by ourselves and did not run into any of my friends or colleagues.

Of course, one need not have an advanced degree in psychoanalysis to realize that with all this womanizing, I was in direct competition

---

7 An article in *The Harvard Crimson* of October 14, 1982, introducing Vanserg to a student body that was completely ignorant of it, bore the telling title "Harvard's Craziest Building." Hastily built in 1943, Vanserg became the repository of a motley array of completely unrelated entities like Harvard's piano tuning service, a day care center, the Project for Kibbutz Studies and an assortment of rooms used primarily for language classes featuring Czech, Polish, Hebrew, Chinese, and Tech Writing. Most office doors had handwritten words scrawled on them instead of plaques that are normally quite common at institutions such as universities, Harvard included. The name is an acronym for its early Harvard tenants: Veterans Affairs, Naval Science, Electronic Research, Graduate dining hall.

with my father. He had two girlfriends in Vienna? Fine, I would show him who was the real Casanova. I would have six girlfriends in towns all over the United States, even the world. Have some of that, Dad! Not by chance was I constantly humming Ricky Nelson's "Travelin' Man." However, I also knew that deep down my father approved of my behavior, perhaps even delighted in it—his son was collecting women just as he did degrees. A chip off the old block!

I realize this all sounds dreadful to current sensibilities about how a decent man treats women. But these were different times. I admired my father for juggling two women—possibly more. Certainly, in the macho world of Central Europe, and I am sure in the United States as well, boys were brought up to see women as trophies, the more the merrier. As long as I treated each of these women with respect, did not lie to them about having other relationships, bought them meals and movie tickets and—most important, per my father's dictum—never talked about them to anybody, most assuredly not to my male friends, all was fine. What made this *omertà* concerning these relatively casual relationships with women so odd was that the silence, of course, also pertained to my never mentioning anything to my father meaning that I had to celebrate my triumphs over him in total silence. No bragging, no gloating, no trash talking. I never shared any of these exploits with anybody but my own ego thus establishing my bona fides not by including my real father in my exploits but somehow defeating my imagined father in a weird macho game of father-son competition.

While feminism had already entered my world, and while I had read and wholeheartedly supported the work of Simone de Beauvoir, Betty Friedan, Kate Millett, Germaine Greer, Alice Schwarzer, and Carol Hanisch, their writings were distant politics, fine for the ideological basis of a movement, but hardly relevant to the conduct of my own life. I even became a kind of hero to the German feminist movement with the publication of an article in the December 1979 issue of *Gewerkschaftliche Monatshefte*, the leading academic and intellectual periodical of the German Trade Union Federation, the Deutscher Gewerkschaftsbund (DGB). In this piece, I complained about the sexism I had observed among the German trade unions which I had researched for eight months in 1979. I still have the many letters from women thanking me for this exposé as well as the vile denunciations by many German leftists, women included, who found my attack on one of the main pillars of German progressive politics downright blasphemous. But all that was "big" politics, and then there was little Andy.

This behavior continued through most of the 1970s. Beginning in 1979, however, and all throughout the 1980s, instead of juggling multiple women at the same time, I entered into a series of monogamous relationships of great importance to me. I loved all four of these women and respected them as intellectuals, as people of integrity and compassion, of real *Menschlichkeit*. I introduced all four of them to my father and my aunts—real, as in the case of Manci; acquired, as in the case of Frau Kohler—and had them meet my father whenever he came to see me in Cambridge. I also had the honor and privilege to meet each of these women's families and visit their respective homes. In the first instance, the woman left me while I was in Germany doing research. I was devastated! In the next three cases, the relationship began to fray when the inevitable "next step" appeared on the agenda: living together, possibly even discussing marriage.

In one case, the woman moved all her belongings into my Cambridge condominium, and as soon as she started living there, I basically moved out and lived in my office at Vanserg, sometimes even sleeping on a lousy couch that had been left there decades earlier. I would appear in my condominium at 4 a.m., knowing my girlfriend had to leave by seven to start teaching at the secondary school where she had a job. After a month of this, we decided she needed to leave, which she did.

In another case, my girlfriend and I actually drove to a city hall in a small Vermont town to pick up application forms for a marriage certificate. When we arrived in the city hall parking lot, I refused to get out of the car, broke out in a sweat and hives, and was about to vomit. This relationship, as well, did not survive. And yet, I am happy to say I remain friends with all four women. In most cases, I got to meet their new partners, attend their children's bar and bat mitzvahs, and stay knowledgeable about their lives. None of the women ever gave me the feeling she thought ill of me. They simply realized I wasn't ready or willing to commit to a longtime relationship, be it an official marriage or another form of cohabitation.

Kiki Re-enters My Life

Then, on a Saturday in early October 1991, I returned to my apartment on Harvard Street near Central Square in Cambridge, having played tennis as I always did on Saturday mornings. As usual, I checked my mailbox before taking the elevator to my condominium on the seventh floor. This time I saw an airmail envelope with Austrian stamps and an Irina Friedmann as the sender. Oh well, another request for a letter of recommendation from a student I had long forgotten!

I opened the letter, which commenced, in German: "Dear Andy, I am sure you have no idea who Irina Friedman is, but I hope that you, perhaps, will still remember who Kiki Feder was." The letter proceeded to tell me that Kiki had become a big shot at the bank in which she worked and was now tasked with creating staffs for the new offices of her Viennese bank in Warsaw, Prague, Budapest, Zagreb, and Ljubljana, among other cities that were about to join Western-style capitalist economies after four decades of Soviet communism. Kiki went on to tell me that her mother had passed away in 1990 and she had heard my father died the same year. She hastened to add that she always had liked my father and never forgot the great time we enjoyed with him in Italy in August 1968, and how much she had appreciated running into him on the street over the past two-plus decades.

She concluded by telling me that she and one of her girlfriends were about to take a one-week vacation in New York during the last week of October, which was to be Kiki's first trip to the United States. The PS was particularly poignant: "I know that you have come to Vienna very rarely over the last few years, which will be truer with your father gone. But I do know that you still have an aunt living in town and should you come see her at some point in the future and would like to have a cup of coffee with me, here is my telephone number."

I called her immediately, and we spent more than two hours on the phone. She told me how and when her mother had died; explained she had been married to Alex for ten years but got divorced in 1985; described how much she loved traveling all over eastern Europe for her job. She ended our conversation by telling me the details of her forthcoming trip to

New York and asked whether I could pop by for a day or two and meet her friend Gaby, with whom she would be traveling. I responded this was impossible because I had a heavy teaching-load at Boston University that term and needed to finish a paper for a forthcoming conference in early November. Also, I did not have a proper dog-sitter for my darling golden retriever, Dovi.

"What?" Kiki said. "Did I hear correctly? You have a dog? No, this is impossible."

I am sure this was the crucial information that made Kiki receptive to my suggestion that she rebook her return trip from New York to Vienna by flying to Boston, spend a day with me in town, and then depart from Boston across the Atlantic.

And this is exactly what happened. Kiki and Gaby made plans to arrive in Boston, stay with me two nights, and then depart for Vienna on Sunday. I thought: What can go wrong here? Under the best of circumstances, our attraction for each other might rekindle, and we could restart a relationship that abated 23 years ago. Under the worst of circumstances, I would have a boring or even contentious weekend with two women I would then never see again.

I set out to meet Kiki and Gaby at the baggage carousel of their arriving flight at Logan Airport. I was nervous and hopeful, but clearly not nervous and hopeful enough to wear something decent in lieu of my ragged Yankees hoodie and a pair of baggy chinos. (This reminds me of a bell hooks essay in which she writes so brilliantly that one aspect of male power is that many male professors blithely wear the same unshapely clothes all semester long with zero repercussions, while female professors rarely enjoy this kind of freedom.) What would Kiki look like after 23 years? Would I recognize her? What if I didn't because she had aged so much or gained so much weight?

And then there she was—this slim, attractive, immensely stylish woman with jet-black hair and a radiant smile, just as when I first met her that New Year's Eve, ushering in 1968 at the Hotel Panhans in Semmering, and just as when I had last seen her in early September 1968 in Vienna. We hugged for a long time, as one does after meeting someone dear and close after not having seen them in decades, more akin to friends than lovers. Kiki introduced me to Gaby. We picked up their bags, hopped into my Camry, and off we drove to my Cambridge condominium.

When we entered the apartment, we were greeted by my Dovi, this broadly smiling and tail-wagging golden retriever. Kiki knelt and hugged the dog. "I assume that your father never got to meet this darling creature?" she said. And I replied that three weeks before his death, when he last visited me in the United States in March 1990, and when the Immigration and Naturalization Service took away his treasured green card, he spent one week with Dovi, whom he at first tolerated reluctantly, but whom he patted before leaving for the airport, never to return.

Kiki and I had a wonderful weekend. I showed her and Gaby the sights of Boston and its environs, and we took Dovi on many walks along the Charles River. I invited them both to two fancy dinners, and we talked and talked about the previous 23 years, in which Kiki and I had no contact whatsoever. Kiki told me about her marriage to and divorce from Alex, with whom she maintained cordial relations to the point that Kiki became best friends with Alex's second wife, and later de facto aunt to his three children.

Knowing my great interest in the Jews' fate in postwar Europe, Kiki told me about her volunteer work for the legendary Simon Wiesenthal, a fascinating Jewish personality mostly reviled in Austria by dint of his restless uncovering of Nazi criminals hiding all over the world. While hating the sobriquet "Nazi Hunter" bestowed on him by the media, Wiesenthal compiled a set of archives on the Nazis that became legendary. Unworried by his heavy Polish and Yiddish accents when he spoke German, blithely oblivious to his "typical" Jewish looks, Wiesenthal plowed ahead in his quest never to forget the Shoah and make at least some of its perpetrators pay by putting them behind bars. He also needed round-the-clock police protection. But even that did not prevent a number of attempts on his life.

Kiki began as a translator of Wiesenthal's French correspondence, and then became one of his confidants. She knew Wiesenthal and his family well and regaled me with amazing stories about his life, some of which were classified due to their sensitive nature involving the governments of a number of countries in Europe and beyond. In turn, I told Kiki about my life during the preceding 23 years: how I had completed my degrees at Columbia; how I had become an academic, a profession I now cherished; how I had moved from New York to Boston; how I had taught at Wesleyan University and now at Boston University but considered my spiritual home to be the Center for European Studies at Harvard; how I had become an expert on German politics and society; and how all this took me to Europe on a regular basis.

I also told her that, unlike her, I had never gotten married. Asked about such opportunities, which Kiki assumed must have been plentiful, I told her that I most certainly had serious girlfriends whom I loved and who, I think, loved me back, but with whom things just did not work out in the end. I added that much of the blame lay in my fear of committing to a woman, not least because I always dreaded their leaving me alone at some point, just as my mother had. That's when Kiki smiled her amazing smile and told me that her mother had always adored me, but warned Kiki to stay clear of letting our relationship become serious because she—Erika—knew the kind of man Andy was: a charmer, generous and kind, but absolutely not marriage material.

On some level, I was flattered: being judged this way by a woman of Erika's style and panache bespoke a certain worldly masculinity on my part, close to how I saw my father and wanted to be seen by him. In other words, Andy, like his father, was a seductive charmer, fun to go out with, a wonderful guy, but not to be married. On another level, I was irritated because Erika never knew my father's marriage to my mother in Timişoara, and only gauged him based on the rumors that swirled around his life in Vienna. Then again, what about my father's sleeping in my room all these years, and not in the bedroom with my mother? Might there have been some truths to the distant hints from my aunt and my mother's closest friend regarding my father's possible affairs at the bank? I also thought Erika's characterization of me as an unreliable sort might have been self-serving, in that she wanted to have Kiki tied to her and not even think about her only child leaving Vienna for distant America.

Before I drove Kiki and Gaby to Logan Airport on Sunday evening for their flight to Frankfurt and then onward to Vienna, Kiki said the most loving good-bye to Dovi. She sat on the floor next to him and held him for a long time, all the while kissing his head. I was moved beyond words. At the airport, Kiki and I hugged again warmly and lovingly, but neither of us said one word about ever seeing each other again.

I remember driving back home on Storrow Drive, the Boston side of the Charles River, with tears welling in my eyes. *Andy*, I thought, *what is wrong with you? How can you let this wonderful woman slip through your fingers as you did so many others? You cannot let this happen!* (To this day, I never know in what language I talk to myself. When the subject is American sports, the language is most definitely in English. When my internal conversation is about Continental European soccer, it is in Viennese dialect. When it is about Manchester United and English football, back to English. All matters professional and academic harness the English language. On the rare occasions I speak to myself about my parents, I definitely use Hungarian.

But what about personal matters like relationships? I just don't know, although I suspect it depends on the language I used when speaking with the relevant person. Since most of my serious relationships happened with English-speaking women, I think I spoke in English to myself about anything relating to any of them. But what about Kiki? Back to German? If German, proper high-German? Viennese dialect? I am sure, though, on my drive home from Logan that night, I spoke in English to myself because I really could hear myself asking me: *What is wrong with you?*)

This was the time when my expertise about political parties, trade unions, social movements, and other crucial ingredients known as "civil society" created a high demand. Normal and natural in liberal democracies, these institutions did not exist in the countries that had just emerged from forty years of Soviet domination. Everything was new, everything had to be constructed de novo, experiments abounded. The Friedrich-Ebert-Foundation, a quintessential German institution in that it was one of the four foundations closely associated with a political party—the Social Democrats, in this case—though also independent of it, asked me to deliver lectures on social democratic parties and related trade unions all over Eastern Europe. The Ebert Foundation asked me to speak in Prague to the Czechs and then in Bratislava to the Slovaks, sometime in late November. This was fortuitous because the invitation coincided with our Thanksgiving break and I would not have to miss classes or reschedule them. I accepted, and off I went!

Remembering that Kiki's birthday was on November 30, which fell on a Saturday that year, I called her from Bratislava and told her that I was in the neighborhood—barely an hour's train ride to Vienna—and if she had no plans for her birthday, I would love to take her out to her favorite restaurant in Vienna. I remember Kiki being speechless. Then she said she had to rearrange something with some of her girlfriends, but this was going to work and I should make my way to Vienna, which I did on Friday night after my last lecture. I got to Kiki's fabulous penthouse apartment in one of Vienna's poshest districts, and so began a magical weekend that restarted the relationship we had severed so unceremoniously in 1968.

That Saturday evening, over dinner at a fabulous restaurant near Kiki's place, she told me the story of how, after 23 years apart, she had thought to get in touch with me. After Erika died in November 1990, Kiki and her friend Gaby cleared the apartment of Erika's belongings. In one of Erika's drawers, they found an opened envelope that clearly came from overseas because it had the distinct red-and-blue margins that were so particular to air mail at the time. They also noticed the United States stamps. The letter turned out to be one of the last I wrote to Kiki that fall after our trip to Italy. Erika hadn't intercepted Kiki's mail—Kiki recognized the letter and remembered reading it. Now, for reasons that will forever remain a mystery, Erika kept this letter and stored it in this drawer. Why this letter and no others? That will also remain a mystery.

The two women got a chuckle out of finding the letter in Erika's drawer, and Kiki told Gaby about our relationship. Then, in May of the next year, Gaby noticed several inexpensive opportunities to visit New York that fall. She suggested they travel there, since this would be Kiki's first trip to the United States and Gaby was an old hand, having traveled there many times. Kiki agreed, whereupon Gaby reminded her of the letter and encouraged Kiki to get in touch with me, assuming I still lived in New York City. Kiki chided Gaby that she would do no such thing. After all, I was probably married, had four kids, and lived in the suburbs. She knew nothing about me and was not eager to find out more.

And then, in late September, four weeks before her planned trip with Gaby to New York City, Kiki found herself at a big Jewish event in town, seated at a dinner table with one of her pals from Lycée Français days, Ariel Muzicant, who in the meantime had become the president of the Jewish Community in Vienna. Somehow, Ari mentioned "his former partner, Dr. Markovits," who had died more than one year earlier. Kiki froze. Was this the Dr. Markovits who was Andy Markovits's father? "Yes" came the answer. Kiki asked Ari whether he knew anything about me, where I was and what had happened to me.

Ari told Kiki that he did not know much about me because I rarely came to Vienna, but he was quite sure I lived in Cambridge, Massachusetts, and was some kind of academic involved with Harvard University. As far as he knew, I had never married and lived by myself. Kiki asked Ari whether she could get my address so she could send her belated condolences on my father's death. And that evening, Kiki sat down to write the letter I received six days later at my apartment in Cambridge.

The day after Kiki's birthday dinner, a Sunday, she insisted on taking me to the airport so I could return home and resume teaching at Boston University on Monday. As we sat in the back of the taxi, Kiki turned to me and said she knew that for our relationship to blossom and become more than a fling—which, she added, was totally fine with her—she must come to the United States to live because I was never going to return to Austria, or even Europe, regardless of the job I might be offered. I asked her how she knew this, because we had never discussed my feelings toward the United States or Europe. She just smiled warmly, as she often does, and said: "I know this because I feel it."

And so began our six years of commuting between Cambridge and Europe, and later between Santa Cruz and Europe. I crossed the Atlantic 26 times, Kiki 23 times. (We know this because we had to document every trip with the Immigration and Naturalization Service, to which we applied for a fiancé visa so Kiki could come to the United States permanently.) Whenever I traveled to Europe for any lecture or meeting, Kiki flew in from Vienna. We met in Hamburg, Cologne, Frankfurt,

Berlin, Bonn, London, and Paris. Kiki popped over to Cambridge for weekends and even flew all the way to the West Coast for three-day sojourns on several occasions.

Twice we indulged in lengthier stays with each other, which were immensely helpful in ascertaining that we weren't just wowed by the excitement of these short visits to exotic places. In January 1993, Kiki kindly took a three-month sabbatical from her job at the bank to help me move to Santa Cruz and get settled there, no matter how tentatively. I, in turn, agreed to move into her beautiful condominium in Vienna for five months during my Fulbright professorship at the University of Innsbruck; thanks to the wonders of the Austrian train system, Innsbruck was an easy commute from Vienna.

But how to get Dovi to Vienna? Having flown Dovi twice a year across the United States from Boston to San Francisco and back, I had seen how taxing it was on him to be flown in the cargo hold of a jet for five hours; I wouldn't submit him to this torture for even longer. I researched all the possibilities for flying a seventy-pound golden retriever across the Atlantic in the cabin and came up with only one: the supersonic Concorde, which permitted one dog of such size per cabin, seated in a window seat, with the guardian next to the dog on the aisle seat. I purchased two such roundtrip tickets at a cost of nearly three months of my salary. (The Evian water and wonderful croissants that the flight attendants brought Dovi almost compensated for my expense. And on the way back from Paris to New York we got to meet Liza Minelli, who went crazy for Dovi.)

We applied for Kiki's K1 visa in August 1997. I initiated the process at the INS's New England office in New Hampshire. The application then made it to the United States Embassy in Vienna where, we were told, the wait might take up to six months or even longer. We set the date for our wedding for Memorial Day 1998 and reserved the largest hall on the second floor of the Harvard Faculty Club, expecting 150 guests. But for unknown reasons, Kiki received a call from the embassy in late September asking her to come for her interview two days later. She passed with flying colors and was now the holder of a fiancé visa with which she could enter the United States. However, once here, she was to get married within ninety days or be subject to being deported and not readmitted to the United States for up to ten years.

Kiki arrived just in time to celebrate my birthday on October 6, and we set Friday, November 7, as our official wedding date. That is how we ended up with two wedding ceremonies: the official secular one in November 1997 and the Jewish one in late May 1998. Some of my Cantabrigian friends found out about our stealthy plans to get married at Cambridge City Hall and convinced Kiki and me to organize a small celebration with 15 people in one of the upstairs dining rooms of the Harvard Faculty Club. The justice of the peace performed her duties with charm and efficiency, and Kiki and I were officially married. The dinner was lovely and lasted until the staff asked us to leave at around 11 p.m.

Then, the following year, in May, Kiki and I celebrated the Jewish version of our wedding, to which we invited 150 people from all over the world. Nearly thirty of Kiki's friends joined us from Vienna which made the event truly special. Tellingly for Kiki's marginal relationship to the Viennese Jewish community throughout her and Erika's lives, most of these people were Gentiles. Kiki and I had a beautiful chuppah which four of our close friends held for us.

For our rabbi we chose one of my dearest friends, David Karen, professor of sociology at Bryn Mawr. Rather than pick a rabbi whom neither Kiki nor I knew, and who would have delivered a boilerplate sermon, we wanted somebody who knew one of us very well and the other at least to some degree. Though Brooklyn-born, David hailed from a working-class Jewish family in Queens in which he was the first to go to college. This made him unique to me as I had rarely met any working-class Jews.

What rendered him more special still was his Orthodox upbringing, in which he attended yeshivas where he acquired not only a deep knowledge of Jewish texts but also a fine mastery of Hebrew. Lastly, David looked the part of a rabbi: on the portly side, he sported a wonderful beard that framed his kind face, enhanced by a perennial smile. To epitomize the rabbinic presence, David wore a stunning tallis draped over his Harvard University doctoral gown. David's warm words and his wonderful *neshume*—Yiddish for soul—made this wedding celebration truly special for Kiki and me.

Kiki and I spent the ensuing academic year at the Wissenschafts-kolleg zu Berlin—the Institute for Advanced Study, Berlin—along with our new golden retriever, Kelly, who was our mutual wedding gift following the loss of Dovi. While at this heavenly place, I received an offer to join the faculty of the University of Michigan. It was time to let go of my Cambridge life and begin anew in Ann Arbor—with Kiki, with Kelly, with a new house, with a new job at a fine university. Kiki and I purchased the first house we were shown during our three-day house-hunting visit; as urban, apartment-dwelling people, it was the first house for both of us in our lives.

At first, I was worried about Kiki's moving to a small college town in the American Midwest after having spent her life in a large metropolis like Vienna. And what a life Kiki had there: a stunningly beautiful penthouse condominium that was fully paid for; a fulfilling job at a company where she had worked all her adult life, a job that was expanding into new venues in Eastern Europe, helping to create a whole new world there; a coterie of dear friends, some of whom were like family; and Vienna itself, the clear number one among cities in the world in terms of the quality of life it offered—or, at the very least, in the top ten on all such lists.

Kiki's English, though serviceable, was nowhere close to the quality of her French. Indeed, attending the Lycée Français channeled her into a Francophone cultural orbit that stymied her acquiring the full appreciation of Anglo-American popular culture she would have attained had she gone to an Austrian secondary school. Kiki knew and enjoyed the music of Gilbert Bécaud, Charles Aznavour, and Juliette Gréco rather than the Animals, the Kinks, or the Spencer Davis Group. She knew French films better than American ones, and among the latter, only the ones dubbed into German. As social scientists know, cultural differences acquired at an early age accompany us all our lives. Kiki has come to appreciate some of Bob Dylan's lyrics, but she will never swoon over them as I always have and will.

However, to Kiki's immense credit, she quickly made Ann Arbor her home. She has come to cherish three sets of friends: from the Jewish community, from the dog-rescue community, and five women from Europe with whom she has met on a weekly basis for many years. Vienna continues to play a central role in Kiki's life, in that she visits the city at least twice a year for a fortnight stay and regularly has a number of her Viennese friends visit us in Ann Arbor. Over the years, Kiki's English has become not only excellent, but even elegant. Her spoken English is full of colloquialisms and bespeaks a complete comfort with the language in terms of expressing everything from daily events to complex thoughts. To Kiki's amusement, her accented English receives nothing but rave reviews in a town like Ann Arbor, where people ask her to say something just so they can enjoy her sophisticated, exotic, authentic, so-European way of speaking!

Kiki has always been amazed that people find everything "European" better. Many Americans of the middle and upper classes (that is, consumers of elite culture) perceive "European" to connote higher quality, whether with respect to European makeup, European education, European flair, or European sophistication. Judging from the way our circle of friends extols everything British as refined, sophisticated, and cultured, Kiki surmises that the British won the War of Independence.

In fact, Kiki has come to prefer reading books in English rather than in German. She consumes the news in English and rarely consults German-language websites. She will always have difficulties understanding certain British accents, such as Cockney, never mind Scottish pronunciations, but that has never detained her from voraciously watching all kinds of BBC series, as well as television programs as varied as *Friends* and *Shameless*. To keep our relationship intact, we had to buy two television sets and put them in separate rooms so Kiki could watch her shows and I my sports!

Kiki's English became good enough for her to author a book in which she highlights a method of movement meant to aid everyday activities. The idea is that everything in the body is interconnected and every physical aspect of human activity, such as putting on a hat, may have salutary effects on one's body and health if properly harnessed and deployed. Enjoying a modest success with the book and her website, Kiki then wrote a German version specifically for brides. Both books led to friendships for Kiki she would not have otherwise made.

The two of us love each other's company, even as we maintain our separate interests. I once persuaded Kiki to accompany me to a football game in Michigan Stadium (a.k.a. The Big House) when it was 100 degrees, and—promptly, as if on cue—a drunken fan vomited on Kiki's shoulder. No more Big House for Kiki since then. She would never step anywhere near a European soccer match, not even onto the subway line running in the venue's direction, because she detests the vile racism, antisemitism, and latent violence accompanying all such events. Still, Kiki has never criticized my sports mania. She tolerates it generously with a smile like the one adults have for children's pastimes.

Kiki also told me she would never have left her life in Vienna had I been anything but a university professor, meaning I control my time almost completely and am able to work from home and spend time, not only with Kiki but with our dogs, the love of whom binds Kiki and me both tightly and affectionately.

As we were walking with our golden retriever Cody along the Huron River in Ann Arbor's beautiful Arboretum on a stellar spring evening about ten years ago, Kiki suddenly turned to me and said: "I hope you realize that our relationship and marriage would never have happened had both or either of our parents been alive. On my part, I know that I would never, ever have left Vienna to be with you with my mother still there. Remember how I spent considerable time in Lido di Jesolo calling my mother? Well, I did that every day of my life until she died, not only when I was a 16-year old girl as I was back then in Italy. I called her for ten years from our home in Vienna while being married to Alex, as well as on our trips to Italy and Israel. Rightly or wrongly, this was the bottom line: had my mother been alive, I would never have been able to leave Vienna and start a new life with you in America. And I am sure that this pertains to your relationship with your father as well."

Did it ever! Clearly, there were fascinating parallels between Kiki's childhood and upbringing and my own: both of us were only children; both of us had lost a parent early in our lives; Kiki and her mother lived in a totally female world, my father and I in a male one. Even though Tante Trude's presence in my father's and my life was beyond significant, somehow—to my eternal shame—her contributions remained psychically marginal by virtue of her not being family and "only" our landlady/servant. Just as Kiki's relationship to her mother was entangled with a history that made a lasting relationship with anyone else impossible, mine to my father was also fraught. For all those years before Kiki visited me in Boston, I did not come close to marriage even though I was involved in serious monogamous relationships with a number of wonderful women.

Kiki's assertion was spot-on: had my father been alive when I re-met Kiki, I would not have been able to marry her. I knew how brutally difficult it was for him to emigrate with a ten-year old child, first to Vienna and then to New York, all within two years of losing his wife. Finding schools for me, finding himself a job in a culture not his own—these were immensely difficult tasks. Soon after our arrival in Vienna, and in our sublet in Frau Kohler's apartment, my father commenced to build a kind of shrine to my mother—a corner of our living room decorated with many of her photographs. This shrine later included all my diplomas and awards, video cassettes of all my television appearances, and audio cassettes of all my radio interviews.

My mother had somehow become a saint. When my father wanted to express his approval of something I had done—receiving a fine grade on an examination, obtaining a degree, winning an award—he would say, without fail, "Your mother would be so proud of you!" Rarely did he say, "I am so proud of you," and when he did, the praise was of a lesser degree than when he invoked my mother. He constantly mentioned that he would never remarry, because any stepmother would be a burden for me, and his job in life was to unburden me as best he could, to run interference for me, be my blocker. While I think he truly believed this, the conviction became a handy excuse for him never to marry and to remain uncommitted to any woman.

Sure enough, at some point in the early 1960s, after he was certain Vienna and not New York would be the place where he would spend the rest of his life, he got involved with two women, both of whom stayed with him until the day he died in 1990. Neither of them was Jewish, one was widowed, the other married; these two women fulfilled different needs in his life. Maria, the widow, became his official partner, with whom he travelled all over the world and whom he took to concerts, operas, the theater, receptions, and parties. Maria became his wife in everything but name. Helga, the married one, was his mistress. I cannot recall her ever appearing with my father in public. When he first introduced her to me, he seemed ashamed and wanted to shoo her away as fast as he could. And yet, this triangle served all three parties well. Maria got to travel and live a life of comfort bordering on luxury that she otherwise could not have experienced. Helga enjoyed regular moments of affection and kindness she never received from her abusive husband whom, for reasons I didn't understand, she would never leave. My father had the constant company of two attractive women with few emotional strings attached.

From the time I started dating my first girlfriend, Daphne Scheer, my father tried to caution me about getting too seriously involved with women. He always warned me of the danger women posed to me, as if I were a gullible and helpless being whose generosity they would abuse and take advantage of. On the way to the Vienna Airport just before I was to board my flight to New York to commence my first year at Columbia, my father did not warn me of getting a woman pregnant. No, he told me that he had to bear a heavy emotional burden by remaining in Vienna alone, but my departure was worth the reward. The *Goldene Medine*—the Golden Land of America—was going to provide me with a sense of belonging and security that nothing in Europe ever would.

Even though all his friends and his sister, as well as Maria and Helga, beseeched him to keep me with him in Vienna and train me to take over his flourishing supermarket business, he knew the only plan that would make him and me happy was my succeeding in America. However, I had better not succumb to silly diversions that could derail my future. His last words to me at the gate were something like this: "Remember, my burden will all be worth it and will all turn into pride and joy if you get good grades and if you succeed in your studies at Columbia. You surely will if you do not fall prey to some emotional involvement with a woman that will then detain you from studying and will lead to your failure. Don't let your emotional attachment to women torpedo your career!" He then added one more sentence that came to scare me in many ways for the rest of my life: "And remember, women will leave you, your achievements never will!" What he failed to add but must have been thinking was: "Women will leave you, as your mother and my wife left us!"

No wonder that during all my years at Columbia, I never ever dated a young woman from Barnard or anybody living on the Upper West Side, lest this person be geographically too close to me, meaning that she and I might spend too much time together having fun which would interfere with my studying. No wonder that my first serious girlfriend after Kiki and I had broken up lived near Pelham Parkway in the Bronx and was a student at Lehman College's Bronx campus, meaning we would see each other every Saturday night and, under the rarest of circumstances, once during the week.

But then, beginning with the completion of my Ph.D. and continuing with my successful integration into the Center for European Studies at Harvard and my attainment of an assistant professorship at Wesleyan, my father began changing his tune. "It's really not so great to remain alone," he said. "Don't get me wrong, you have plenty of time and many years ahead of you. But at some point, try to think about settling down, about being with one person. Because if you don't, you will end up alone, and that is not good for anybody, but particularly bad for somebody like you who so hates to be alone." For the first time, I had come to hear my father's feelings about his own mortality. Tellingly with regard to his love for me, the only thing that he seemed to fear about his own death was that I might end up alone.

I never could fulfill my father's expectation of being a ladies' man while also realizing his hope of seeing me settle down in a safe relationship. Not being able to solve this conundrum would have never allowed me the inner peace, the psychic authority, the solid security to settle with Kiki with my father being alive. Only his death abated the torrent of the sea for me. After that, it was smooth sailing into Kiki's arms!

CHAPTER NINE

The Grateful Dead:
My American Family

I acquired the Beatles' *Sgt. Pepper's Lonely Hearts Club Band* album in the middle of June 1967 (just two weeks after its official release) and played it so often that by the middle of August, the disc was scarred with scratches. I went to my trusted Viennese record store Drei Viertel to purchase another copy of this masterpiece which was to be the sole album that was to accompany me during my first semester at Columbia University in a few weeks. As was always the case, the resident music guru, Edek Bartz, who had introduced me to so many great artists and recordings, tried to persuade me to buy something new instead.

"I know you love Dave Van Ronk," he said. "You may even have seen and heard him live in the Village during one of your many New York summer trips. Listen to this record by a new group called the Grateful Dead. Even though these guys are totally different and play electric music in contrast to Van Ronk's acoustic work, you will encounter passages in which you will hear the Dead's guitarist, Jerry Garcia, play patterns that have reminded me of Van Ronk."

I listened carefully and, truth be told, could not quite hear those patterns. I chalked up this failure to my shortcomings, rather than to Bartz's possibly eccentric interpretation. I found the record, called simply *The Grateful Dead*, appealing and interesting. However, one song, "Morning Dew," written by the Canadian folk musician Bonnie Dobson, moved me deeply. Not only was the song haunting but Garcia's solo was exquisite, his guitar bell-like but also weeping, just the way George Harrison was to sing and play in his unforgettable "While My Guitar Gently Weeps" on the Beatles' *White Album* (officially called *The Beatles*), released one year later, in 1968.

In New York, my connection to the Grateful Dead took the form of the already mentioned disc jockey named Alison Steele, who became my female conduit to the heavily male world of rock 'n roll. As is common for students, I stayed up late into the night doing homework. This is how I came to listen to a wonderful music station called WNEW-FM. And there she was: the Nightbird, with whom I fell instantly in love upon hearing her sultry, soft, immensely seductive voice, though I seem to recall having heard her earlier on rare occasions in the afternoons, prior to her being rewarded with the graveyard shift that allowed her so much freedom in her programming. Her gravelly voice was beyond sexy: only much later did I find out its timbre was partly due to her smoking small cigars, making her belatedly even sexier.

Steele always began her show by reciting poetry over the sound of an Andean flute. She would always end her introduction with "Come fly with me. Alison Steele, the Nightbird, at WNEW-FM, until dawn." Adding to this seductive perfection was the fact that Steele often hosted her show with her poodle, Genya, lending another extraordinary aspect to her gig. Lastly, it bears remembering that Alison Steele may have been the only female DJ at a serious rock station in New York, maybe even the country, at that time.

The Nightbird loved the Grateful Dead and gave them a lot of airtime. Through her, I came to know and love their music, and I remained a loyal and passionate listener to "the Grande Dame of New York Night" until fall 1975, when I left New York for Cambridge. But even then—and throughout the ensuing fifty-plus years—rock has always had a strong female ring to it for me. I did not have a more loyal and steady companion throughout my eight years at Columbia than this woman's voice. Her death in 1995 saddened me deeply.

Still, I might never have become a Deadhead if the New York Police Department had not, in the middle of the night on Tuesday, April 30, 1968, initiated an attack on five Columbia buildings occupied by students. The occupying students, especially in Mathematics Hall, were evicted with much brutality. In response to the violence with which this was accomplished, the student body issued a call for a strike, shutting down virtually all activities for the semester. Friends of my father's in Forest Hills asked me to come spend the following weekend with them, in part to protect me from the mayhem that engulfed the campus. I had heard rumors that a rock band—possibly the Grateful Dead—was to show up on campus to play for the students in order to declare their solidarity and offer a few hours of levity. But the plan didn't seem definite, so I took the subway from Morningside Heights to Queens.

And sure enough, on Friday afternoon, May 3, the Dead did show up at Columbia. They set up their equipment in front of Ferris Booth Hall, which was the de facto student union, and played for two hours. They did so free of charge and as spontaneously as possible, given the preparation entailed in setting up electric instruments with all the necessary gear in a place not designed for a concert. Even though the band was already in New York and did not fly in from its West Coast home to play this free gig, it gained moral brownie-points with me and many other Columbia students. The quality of their musical performance, which I did not hear until the advent of YouTube, was mediocre at best, but I will never forgive myself for missing the Dead playing a concert literally fifty feet from the entrance of Furnald Hall, my dormitory during my two undergraduate years at Columbia.

Even though the music was hardly stellar, the band wanted to demonstrate their solidarity with the striking students. They didn't say a word about the students' causes—the Dead almost never revealed any of their political preferences at their shows, something that endeared them to me, since I have always hated when artists bask in their alleged moral virtues to the audience's delight—but instead they let their music do the talking.

The following year, I purchased two tickets to see the Dead at the famed Fillmore East in Manhattan's East Village. Though not as legendary as its West Coast progenitor in San Francisco, by September 1969 the Fillmore East had become the venue for all the big rock acts of the time. Jimi Hendrix, the Kinks, Eric Burdon and the Animals,

Creedence Clearwater Revival, the Allman Brothers, and Pink Floyd appeared there, often more than once. (Only the two unrivaled giants, the Rolling Stones and the Beatles, never played at the Fillmore East, with the latter ceasing to perform in public as a band in August 1966.)

The Dead shared the bill with Country Joe and the Fish, as well as with Sha Na Na, an a cappella group comprised of former and current Columbia students sporting Elvis Presley hairdos with lots of grease, dressed in gold lamé outfits, and singing classic 1950s rock. (One of the band members, Alan Cooper, graduated from Columbia in 1971 and later became provost of the Jewish Theological Seminary of America.) All three of these bands had performed at Woodstock, two to much acclaim, while the Dead put on an abysmal show, as the band was wont to do at showcase events.

I asked a Viennese friend who happened to be in New York to accompany me to the Fillmore, which she gladly did. This was only my second live rock concert, the first having taken place almost exactly four years earlier to the day at Vienna's Stadthalle where, as I already mentioned, I saw the Rolling Stones. I could hardly contain myself as my friend and I entered the hallowed halls of this rock mecca. First up, Country Joe and the Fish! I must say I was disappointed. They indulged in far too many antics on the stage, screaming instead of singing, talking to the audience way too much, and uttering obscenities merely for their own sake.

Then, after a break, the announcer shouted: "And now, ladies and gentlemen, straight from San Francisco, California, the Grateful Dead!" Huge applause and hollering . . . but no band appeared on the stage. Nothing. Finally, we saw a few obscure figures, some with cigarettes in their hands or in their mouths, enter and take their places next to their instruments, ignoring the audience. A meticulously precise tuning process, which seemed endless, began. But once out of this tuning ritual, the band transitioned seamlessly into the first chords of—you guessed it—Bonnie Dobson's "Morning Dew."

By the time Jerry Garcia completed his haunting guitar solo, I was hooked. As with love at first sight, explanations go only so far. I loved the fact that the Dead came onstage not with an upbeat, fast-paced tune, as most rock bands do with their opening number, but took their sweet time tuning their instruments and then proceeded into a slow ballad. Unlike Country Joe and the Fish, the Dead spoke not a word to the audience for the duration of their gig, a custom they more or less held onto for the 2,318 shows they performed in their decades-long career.

The Dead behaved like classical music performers who only have one mission: to play their music and exhibit their artistry in the medium in which they are masters, and not chatter away with the audience or pander to it with cheap talk. I also came to love the fact that the Dead refrained from pontificating about political causes. They played a number of important benefits for worthy causes over their illustrious career, but never bothered the audience with their views. I loved their modesty, but also their intelligence that instructed them not to share their own values with the audience in anything outside the purview of their expertise: music. From that very first concert, I came to love the fact that the Dead were musicians who eschewed ego trips and megalomania, both ample characteristics of the rock scene and much of public life beyond music.

How can anyone explain why they fall in love, with a person or a band? Such truly charismatic moments have been described by the great Max Weber in his comparative study of religions: the event and its reception defy explanation and thus replication by other agents. In my case, even though the event took place in front of thousands of people, I experienced it as intensely intimate and private. That Garcia attained a certain sound by using a particular guitar; that he used a certain fretting technique with his left hand and a particular picking technique with his right hand; that Phil Lesh's bass assumed a solo-like quality, on occasions harmonizing with Garcia's lead guitar, all these observations may have been true, but essentially were beside the point in terms of my falling in love with the band's music. The sound just spoke to me like few others ever had!

Of course, the musicians' virtuosity had something to do with my appreciation of their art. But I have always been offended when I encountered yet another ranking of rock guitarists or bass players on some Top Fifty list. Really? By what measure? How demeaning to their art to have So-and-So at number 17 and some other musician at 26! Thankfully, classical music has not been victimized by this ranking mania. At least in my experience, I have never seen one pianist ranked over another; nor have I seen a rank order of singers or orchestras like it has been commonplace in the world of rock music.

I do not think it a coincidence that "Morning Dew" has remained one of my favorite Dead tunes. A slow ballad, the song offers Garcia plenty of possibilities, not only to demonstrate his virtuosity as a guitar player, but also to highlight his compassion, his empathy, his sadness, which, in turn, enhance the listener's quasi-religious experience of the music. Indeed, I was often reminded of the Yiddish word "kavone" when I watched Garcia play over the decades of my following the band. From the Hebrew "kavanah," it means literally "intention," though it actually bespeaks a merger of the creator's, the producer's heart and mind in her or his activity. It evokes the intellectual and skill-based just as it does the emotive and passionate. On one level, one can definitely discern a brilliance in expertise and skill in the artist's performance, while on another one observes and experiences a deep devotion and emotional absorption that the artist clearly experiences while performing. As a listener and viewer, one seems to share in the performer's supplication to a higher power that her or his playing clearly entails. Besides "Morning Dew," Garcia's playing other Dead ballads such as "Loser," "Sugaree," "Black Peter," "Brokedown Palace," "Althea," "Peggy-O," "Stella Blue," "Wharf Rat," "Black Muddy River" and "Jack-A-Roe," among others often invoked "kavone" for me. Some of these songs are written in a minor key, and many of them involve death or loss. All allow Garcia to offer us solos full of "kavone" that make us cry.

I was so taken by the Dead's performance that I did not wait to see Sha Na Na, but walked into the beautiful fall New York night feeling that I had experienced something immensely meaningful. My Viennese friend enjoyed the concert (she loved the Dead), but to her, Garcia's solos were just that: great runs by a masterful guitarist deserving of much respect. They held no transcendent meaning for her, inspired no moments of awe, no "kavone." I walked her home to the Murray Hill neighborhood of Manhattan where she was staying with friends, never to see her again.

Thus began my attachment to the Dead. From the early 1970s until Jerry Garcia's death on August 9, 1995, I attended well over one hundred Dead shows. In New York State, I saw the Dead in New York City, Albany, Utica, Syracuse, Buffalo, and Uniondale; in Massachusetts: Boston, Worcester, Foxborough, Springfield, and South Yarmouth; in Maine: Portland and Lewiston; in Connecticut: Hartford and New Haven; in Rhode Island: Providence; in Pennsylvania: Pittsburgh and Philadelphia; in New Jersey: Passaic and East Rutherford; in Maryland: Landover; in Illinois: Chicago; in California: San Francisco, Berkeley, Oakland, Stanford, Mountainview, and Los Angeles; and in Florida: Lakeland. As my only venue outside the United States, I also saw the Dead in Essen, Germany. Typically, I would catch them twice a year on their fall and spring East Coast tours. I would see about four or five shows per tour, bringing the total to about ten shows per year.

Whenever I tried to explain to an uninitiated person why I loved the band, my words sounded contrived. I could not convey why a rational professor my age took the trouble and expense to drive from Boston to New Haven and back in the course of one afternoon and a very late evening to hear a rock band he might well have heard the night before in Boston.

One of the justifications I have given friends is that seeing the Dead five times in ten days made musical sense because, unlike any other band, they rarely repeated any song for an entire tour, and even if they did repeat one out of hundreds, they played it differently each time. One never knew which songs one might get on a given night. Sometimes, the quality of the music was mediocre for the entire performance, only to explode into a moment of genius that made the trip worthwhile. Other times, the music was excellent from start to finish, putting smiles on thousands of faces.

The band saw these concerts as expressions of their musical desires on that particular night, which might be diametrically opposed to what they exhibited the following night. They never went on stage with a clear set-list. Songs were cued to the band members by the elaborate tuning of the instruments and by certain chord patterns and tones that emerged spontaneously and unplanned. A knowing wink and a barely discernable nod signaled what the next song would be. This cuing included not only the band members but also the immensely knowledgeable and attentive audience. To the initiated, this all provided further reason to love the band. At a Dead show, the band and the audience were often one entity. The band did not play for the audience; it played with the audience. It was all like an evening's conversation among a large group of friends.

I attended most of these concerts on my own, occasionally with a male friend or colleague, but almost never with a woman. No particular reason, it just emerged that way. Going to Dead shows was in many ways akin to my attending sporting events that I also did mostly alone or with men. I did not mind traveling by myself because I always found a real community at these concerts. Not that I knew anyone formally. As is true of a religious experience, everyone came for the same purpose: to delight in the sound this band produced, and derive succor that few other experiences could offer with such gentle conviction.

Here, among the Deadheads, I was as rootless and as much of an outlier as I was elsewhere in my life, yet I felt very much at home and included, often even loved. Most nights, I was the only person in a crowd of thousands who had not consumed any drugs—I have remained a teetotaler all my life—yet I felt completely accepted in the family of Deadheads. Unlike to most, the Dead to me were never about drugs—which they started using prolifically with the Acid Tests of the mid 1960s—but solely about their music. For me, Jerry Garcia was not "Captain Trips" but an ingenious and encyclopedic musician. I loved the fact that an anarchic democracy governed the band's relationship with its devoted followers. People smiled at each other; people helped each other. Following the Dead, one felt genuine friendliness rather than the aggression that often accompanied concerts by other bands. Nothing bespoke the democratic persona and mellow nature of Deadheads better than their complete tolerance of my never accepting the joints that were passed around prolifically throughout all the shows. Unlike at a Paul McCartney concert of all things, when some patrons around me gave me contemptuous looks for not wanting to partake in this pleasure, Deadheads never judged me for this breach of etiquette. If anything, they found it endearing.

Deadheads were almost totally white with virtually no African Americans or Latinos among them. But this was true of most rock audiences at the time. And at least Deadheads were fairly evenly divided between women and men. A fascinating shift in age occurred over the decades I followed the band. Throughout the 1970s, most of the audiences were comprised of baby boomers the same age as the band's musicians. But by the 1980s, when the band's popularity began to soar and it played in huge football stadiums to packed audiences, the age and social class of the fans became more varied.

By the 1990s, it was not uncommon to see entire families attending these concerts, with the children carrying the tradition of fandom on into adulthood. Bespeaking the band's origins in time and space, the hippie element predominated. Women wore wide, flowery skirts, very little makeup, and lots of jewelry, and sported flowers in their hair (though not always scarlet begonias, as the Dead's eponymous tune might indicate). Men wore jeans and T-shirts. The haberdashery of both genders exhibited Grateful Dead symbols that have since become iconic in American popular culture, none more so than the ubiquitous tie-dye. As a bear lover since my childhood in Timişoara, nothing pleased me more than the famed Dancing Bears (also known as Jerry Bears) that symbolized the Dead—obviously *bashert*, the Yiddish word for "fated."

I also observed a fascinating phenomenon among the Deadheads on the East Coast and in Los Angeles: the large presence of Jewish men (though not Jewish women). While the Internet is full of articles trying to explain the curious affinity between the Dead and their Jewish fans via various arcane links between the band's music as well as lyrics and various aspects of Judaism, I have remained stumped for a plausible explanation and must resort to a meek sociological one. The Dead have always been disproportionately popular in college towns and on university campuses, as their many appearances in Ann Arbor, Madison, Bloomington, Berkeley, Ithaca, Urbana, Palo Alto, Eugene, New Haven, Iowa City, Durham, Williamsburg and even Missoula attest. Jewish men are denizens of such places, as well as larger metropolitan areas such as Boston, New York, Philadelphia, and Washington, D.C., to which the Dead frequently returned on their tours often playing multiple shows at a time. This, however, hardly explains the relative paucity of Jewish women among the Deadheads when compared to men.

Indeed, a quasi-anarchic but deeply democratic ethos permeated the band throughout its existence. Though Garcia was touted as the Dead's leader by virtue of his musical genius, this was actually never the case in terms of the band's daily existence and operations. Everything was decided collectively, not only by the six or seven band members, but also their families, roadies, and others in the Dead's circle. Had the band been run more authoritatively, it might have attained much greater commercial success than it did with this disjointed operation. But that is part of what made the Dead so simpatico to me—and to millions of other Deadheads: they flaunted conventional success and the necessary modalities that led to such. They exuded a kind of mellow anarchy that soothed me immensely or, as Garcia so poignantly once put it, "we are pathologically non-confrontational." Being a time-obsessed person who always seems to be rushed, Dead shows rendered time totally irrelevant to me.

Finding the recording studio far too confining, the Dead spurned this space of metronomic regimentation and opted for three-to-four-hour concerts defined by open-endedness and improvisation. The band barely had any real top-fifty hits in their half-century career; their music was underrepresented on conventional rock radio—except for shows hosted by rare folks like the Nightbird. They knowingly dismissed commercial success. Nothing made this clearer than the Dead's permitting—even fostering—the taping of their concerts by hundreds of Tapeheads seated in the best sections on the floor with exquisitely expensive equipment yielding studio-quality tapes. Every other rock band forbade the taping or filming of its live performances. Not the Grateful Dead! They were fine with their fans availing themselves of their music, making the Dead far and away the most recorded band of all time, with every one of its notes played in its 2,318 concerts available for all to hear, anytime, anyplace. Another aspect of the Dead's deeply democratic, as well as anarchic, penchant and convictions.

The strictness of this egalitarian ethos of non-monetized exchange became clear to me in 1981, when I placed an ad in Boston's two alternative papers, the *Phoenix* and the *Real Paper*, seeking a tape of a concert the Jerry Garcia Band (not the Dead) had performed the night before at the Beacon Theater. (Perhaps the most rewarding reason to follow Garcia's work outside and apart from the Dead's was his superb covering of many artists, ranging from Irving Berlin to Paul McCartney, from Jimmy Cliff to J.J. Cale. My favorite of all of Garcia's covers were his prolific interpretations of Bob Dylan's songs.) A young man responded to the ad, but when I asked how much he wanted for a duplicate of his tape, he was taken aback and informed me that he would make me a copy only if I procured for him some tapes from specific concerts he did not have. Under no circumstances was he going to accept money for this transaction. When I told him that I owned none of the concert tapes he wanted, our contact ended abruptly without my getting the cassette of the Beacon Theater concert.

The Dead were never rock stars; rather, they were musicians. In an interview, one of Garcia's four daughters—he did not have sons—said that when she was in high school, she was embarrassed by the goofy Earth Shoes her famous father wore onstage, and by his portly body, which never moved. She wanted a rock star as a dad, and Jerry Garcia clearly did not fill the bill!

And then the tragedy came to pass. Kiki and I were staying at a bed and breakfast in a beautiful little village near Lake Constance in Germany where, in August 1995, I taught a seminar on sports at a summer school held at Schloss Salem, a stunning chateau. Kiki and I had just returned to our B&B, having enjoyed dinner at the chateau with all twenty of my sprightly students. Before going to bed, I decided to call my answering machine back in Cambridge. When I pressed the code to get the messages, a torrent of beeps greeted me. It was the middle of the summer; why were so many people calling me? And then the messages commenced: "Oh Andy, I am so very sorry, this is awful!" "Can you believe this? I don't know what to say, I am in such pain, *sob, sob sob?*" What made this even eerier was that I barely recognized these people's voices. The callers were not my close friends but rather acquaintances who lived various distances from my home. Finally, caller number eight or nine, my friend Jim Steiker from Philadelphia, said something like: "Andy, with Jerry's death, a major era has come to an end. May he rest in peace."

I hung up in shock. Now I understood what the common denominator of all the previous disparate callers was. I must have looked awful because Kiki hurried to my side and asked what had happened back home. My eyes welled with tears, and I said simply: "Jerry Garcia died!" I walked out of our hotel room and into the street, where I ambled around aimlessly, sobbing into the quiet German night. When I got hold of myself, I went back to our room. Kiki said: "I only have a vague idea as to who this Jerry Garcia is, but it is evident that he was immensely close to you. He must have been a very dear friend of yours whom you knew very well and with whom you shared and did much. I am so sorry for your loss!" When I responded that the closest I had ever been to Jerry was 50 feet, though most often 500 feet away, with binoculars in my hand, she looked at me, stunned.

I called friends in the United States pretty much all night long to find out what had happened. I also watched the late-evening news on German television, where Garcia's death received a mention but not nearly the emphasis and attention it received back home, with public mourning reaching levels on both coasts not seen since John Lennon's murder in 1980. San Francisco mayor Frank Jordan ordered the city's flags to be flown at half-staff, with Republican Governor William Weld wanting to do the same at the Massachusetts State House in Boston, only to be persuaded by veterans' groups to desist. Condolences and eulogies poured in from all over the art world, none more meaningful or empathetic than Bob Dylan's. I will quote the text because no one has better captured the essence of Jerry Garcia, and the words emanated from someone who not only knew Garcia, but has been a life-long connoisseur of American music and culture:

> There's no way to measure his [Garcia's] greatness or magnitude as a person or as a player. I don't think any eulogizing will do him justice. He was that great, much more than a superb musician, with an uncanny ear and dexterity. ... He really had no equal. To me he wasn't only a musician and friend, he was more like a big brother who taught and showed me more than he'll ever know. There's a lot of spaces and advances between The Carter Family, Buddy Holly and, say, Ornette Coleman, a lot of universes, but he filled them all without being a member of any school. His playing was moody, awesome, sophisticated, hypnotic, and subtle. There's no way to convey the loss. It just digs down really deep...

With these words, Dylan captured the essence of Garcia and the Dead as quintessential icons of Americana. Many have described the Dead as the most American of rock bands and not merely because of its musicians' birth certificates. Rather, their themes—the open road, trucks, railroads, card games, cowboys, outlaws, the rain, the sun, the search for success and happiness that often remains unfulfilled—and the catholicity of their styles, ranging from jazz to blues, from country to rock, from Buddy Holly to Ornette Coleman, made the Dead truly an American treasure. Not by chance did this most American of bands become Andy Markovits's all-time favorite.

In my grief, Kiki was wonderfully warm and supportive, but deep down she never understood that I had lost a major figure in my life. I still love the band's music. Even without Garcia—his avuncular smile from the stage, his bearlike comfort and warmth—the Dead's music lives on as vibrantly as ever. I still attend concerts when the band, in its various post-Garcia guises, visits my area. However, I travel a good deal less than I did in the 1970s and 1980s, and not only because I have gotten so much older. I respect John Mayer, who has become the lead guitarist for Dead & Company. I enjoy his riffs, and I appreciate his musicality and virtuosity on the guitar. He is a most worthy successor to Jerry Garcia, as a musician and a guitarist, as were Warren Haynes and Trey Anastasio, who also played for the Dead in Jerry's former capacity. I simply experience their musicality as not having any of the "kavone" that Garcia's did which merely goes to show that the actual "kavone" has much more to do with the reception of the artist's work than its creation.

None of these immensely accomplished musicians are Jerry Garcia, at least not for me. With his portly persona, his flowing gray hair and beard, his profoundly rabbinic—dare I say Chassidic—presence, Garcia projected a certain comfort, a certain succor, that rendered him—and thus the Dead—as family. To make the band and Garcia even more simpatico for me, one of the Dead's iconic symbols were the aforementioned "Dancing Bear" cartoon characters which, unlike the real bears back in Timișoara that were made to dance by being tortured, warmed my heart with their beaming faces and bright colors every time I saw them.

Garcia's presence on the stage made Dead concerts a safe place for me, a real community, even though the performances occurred in huge football stadia or drafty concrete arenas to which I traveled by myself. Garcia-led Dead concerts helped to solve the contradiction between my love of rootlessness and my desire to belong and feel at home. As such, the band's concerts, their music and lyrics—written by the invisible but omnipresent Robert Hunter—represented what I perceived to be the essence of America. My love for Garcia and his musical genius never ignored the other band members' fine skills and artistry, so essential to what constituted The Grateful Dead. But it was the inimitable sound emanating from Garcia's fingers on the guitar that embodied the charisma that captivated me for all these decades.

I am not sorry I never got to meet the real Jerry Garcia, even though I wrote him numerous letters inviting him to address various study groups on comparative culture at the Center for European Studies at Harvard during one of his many visits to Boston, either with his own band or the Dead. I read interviews with Garcia and heard him speak on many radio and TV shows, and he always displayed a remarkable eloquence and erudition about music and art, way beyond the world of rock 'n roll and the Dead. Garcia was a learned man despite his never having gone to college. But had I met him in real life, my image of Jerry Garcia would have been shattered, because Andy's Garcia was a larger-than-life figure who embodied many of the hopes and dreams and comforts that Andy enjoyed or wanted, some of which he attained, but many of which he did not.

When I was flying from Boston to Vienna, the night my father passed away, I had only the Garcia ballads previously mentioned on my Walkman. Those tunes in their minor keys soothed my soul that night crossing the Atlantic. And I played the very same songs in my car, driving to Schloss Salem to teach my German students on August 10, the morning after I found out about Jerry's death.

CHAPTER TEN

Harvard's Center for European Studies: The Interloper Finds a Home

In the summer of 1975, when I was frantically writing my dissertation in my Upper West Side apartment, I realized how deeply Seymour Martin Lipset's wide-ranging and prolific scholarship, especially his fine publications on student politics all over the world, had influenced me. Since it was much too late to go on the academic job market that fall for a position beginning in the 1975 school year, I came up with the idea of creating my own private postdoc. I had some savings, and my father was more than happy to supplement my income with his funds. Equipped with the Markovits Postdoc Fellowship, I decided I would go to Harvard for an academic year and work with three professors whose writings I had devoured in my studies at Columbia.

That my plan was an act of supreme chutzpah is beyond question, as is my conclusion, looking back, that such confidence is almost a prerequisite for success in academia and perhaps any endeavor. Where did my own dose of courage come from? First and foremost, from my father's absolute belief that if I were properly unleashed, I could go places. He was a very controlling person and yet oddly democratic and never repressive. He delighted in my expressing myself apart from him.

Second, from the cultural capital I had accrued growing up in Timişoara and Vienna, steeped in so many languages and infused with so many markers of the *Bildungsbürgertum*, all of which I knew status-insecure Europhile Americans lapped up with delight, a fact I used to my advantage even though the morality of doing so has always bothered me. Why are American academics so servile to European mores and cultures and so ashamed of and insecure about their own? Third, from the excellent education and training I received at Columbia, both as an undergraduate and a graduate student. This even includes the business school, which accorded me an ability to work with numbers I otherwise would not have had.

And yet, the success of my self-funded fellowship at Harvard was also the result of the generosity of most of the mentors I chose and our shared sense of dislocation, of being refugees, exiles, within the larger institution in which we worked and studied. Why did the Center for European Studies, where I found such a welcoming home, foster my development as a scholar as well as the careers of the talented women and men I met there? As I will explain later, the Center's outsized influence was a result of the particularly fertile zeitgeist of the immediate post-1968 world, which valued interdisciplinarity and innovation in a way that was unique in the postwar era, coupled with Stanley Hoffmann's rare and prescient tolerance for interests and opinions not his own.

The first professor whose counsel I sought was Lipset, the reason being that I had used his work extensively in my dissertation and wanted to learn more. But there were two other giants I wanted to contact: Barrington Moore Jr. and Karl W. Deutsch. I was deeply impressed by both scholars' research, and featured them extensively in my responses to the prompts that comprised the written portion of my comprehensive exam at Columbia. Neither man's work had yet influenced my writings. Still, I wanted to learn more. A preliminary inquiry made clear that all three professors were going to be at Harvard during the 1975–76 academic year. So all was clear for me to contact them with my unorthodox request that I essentially be their groupie for at least two semesters with no official academic standing.

As this was the beginning of September, with Harvard's classes scheduled to start in three weeks, I thought it a good idea to take one day away from my dissertation and fly to Boston to find lodging for the coming year and possibly meet these three heroes of mine. I hopped on an early Eastern Airlines shuttle at LaGuardia and landed at Logan before 9 a.m. on a gorgeous fall morning. I had only been to Boston once before, in the early 1970s, and had found the city lovely and hospitable, even though I was there on a dreary February weekend. The simpatico nature of the city was made even clearer by my being able to take public transportation from my terminal at Logan Airport all the way to Harvard Square. A friend had mentioned that he had seen a sign that apartments were available at 2 Ware Street, an ideal location across from the Broadway supermarket and a five-minute walk from Harvard Square. He furnished me with a phone number that I called upon my arrival, and, miraculously, a real person responded. Yes, he could show me the place now. So off I went to 2 Ware Street, saw the one-bedroom apartment on the first floor in the back of the building, liked it, paid him the September rent plus a one-month deposit, and just like that I had acquired a place to live in Cambridge.

It was mid-morning by now, and I found my way to William James Hall where, on its fifth floor, the Department of Sociology resided. I asked the person at the desk where I might find Professor Lipset, and with that information went off on the first leg of my big adventure. I knocked on the door and a friendly voice beckoned me to enter. I could barely open the door against all the boxes that were stacked on the floor, obviously full of books because the large bookshelves were empty. Before I sat down, I asked Lipset what these boxes were all about, whether he might be changing offices.

"No," he said, "I am changing universities: off to Stanford in 48 hours!"

I was devastated. Lipset saw the air go out of my body and invited me to sit for a few minutes and tell him what had brought me to him and to Harvard. I informed him about my dissertation, my station in life, how his work had influenced me ever since Allan Silver and Robert Alford introduced me to it. I also conveyed my cockamamie idea of wanting to hang around him for an academic year, learning from the master.

While I was mentioning all this, I saw Lipset grab a piece of paper and begin writing with a Montblanc fountain pen. When I was done, he looked up and asked: "Have you ever heard of the Center for European Studies here at Harvard?," to which I replied sheepishly that I thought

I must have, but couldn't place it. "Have you heard of Guido Goldman?" he asked, to which I replied: "Any relation to Nahum?," to which Lipset responded, "His son." He handed me the piece of paper. "Here is a letter to him at the Center. Show it to Guido and he will take good care of you. The Center is just around the corner. Take a left when you walk out of William James Hall; then make another left at the very first cross street—that will be Francis Avenue—and then hang a right at the very first possibility. That will be Bryant Street where Number 5 will be the second small house on the left." End of meeting!

In later years, I saw Lipset repeatedly at the annual meetings of the American Political Science Association in cities all over the country, almost invariably in the huge exhibit hall featuring all the fancy university presses with their recent wares, engrossed in a new publication. But I never felt comfortable disturbing him at such moments, so I left him reading. I also was immensely honored when, in 2001, Princeton University Press persuaded him to blurb my book *Offside: Soccer and American Exceptionalism*. But I never got to have a proper conversation with the man whose scribbled note changed my life.

The Center for European Studies

So off I went to the Center for European Studies. Walking along Francis Avenue, I saw a towering, lanky figure leave his parked car in the driveway and walk towards the house. He took a while to find his keys, long enough for me to recognize him as John Kenneth Galbraith, the famed liberal economist, former US ambassador to India, Kennedy confidant, general savant, and public intellectual. Welcome to Harvard! As I entered Bryant Street, the first house on the left—right next to the Center—had a sign that said "Harvard-Radcliffe Hillel." This organization, led by rabbi Ben-Zion Gold, who hailed from Radom, Poland, and was the only Shoah-surviving member of his family, became my host for all the major Jewish holidays during my 24-year stay in Cambridge.

And then, walking through a wide-open door, I stepped into the Center with Lipset's letter in my hand.

"Yes, can I help you?" said this woman with a kind face and welcoming smile who, it appeared to me, was not a receptionist but simply found herself sitting at the reception desk, which did not look like your typical reception desk by virtue of the adjoining couch and all the posters, fliers, and books surrounding it in close quarters.

"I am here to see Dr. Guido Goldman," I replied. "I have a letter of introduction for him written by Professor Lipset."

The woman informed me that Dr. Goldman was not in and asked if I minded waiting; in so doing, maybe I would meet some of the Center's members who were bound to come in at some point. She then took me to the adjacent room which looked like the large living room of a messy and funky but warm family. Newspapers were strewn about, not only *The New York Times* and the *Boston Globe* but also *Le Monde*, *Le Figaro*, *Frankfurter Allgemeine Zeitung*, *Corriere della Sera*, and magazines such as *Der Spiegel*, *Stern*, *Le Point*, and other European publications. Wonderful posters replicating the art of Toulouse-Lautrec and similar fin-de-siècle French and German artists graced the wall. The back door opened into a well-worn kitchen. What was this, a stately Harvard center for higher learning, or some hippie pad inhabited by cosmopolitan intellectuals?

The woman sat next to me on the sofa and introduced herself as Abby Collins, the Center's assistant director. She looked at me warmly but also quizzically, as if to ask: What's with these love beads hanging down your blue Oxford button-down shirt and the wild, curly hair hanging below your shoulders? Tell me about yourself. What are you doing here, who are you, what do you want?

I told her about finishing my doctoral dissertation at Columbia and wanting to come to Harvard on my own money to work with Professors Lipset, Moore, and Deutsch for this coming academic year. And then, perhaps because I had mentioned that my dissertation dealt with Austrian students, Abby asked whether I knew a Heinz Fischer, rising star of the Austrian Socialist Party, who had spent the summer of 1964 at Harvard in a program for promising international leaders run by Henry Kissinger, Abby's boss at the time.

Not only did I know Fischer, but he had played a crucial role in my doctoral thesis as the person who had taken and published stenographic notes of lectures that one of the Austrian professoriate's most outspoken right-wingers, a man with clear Nazi sympathies, had delivered. Indeed, Abby and her boyfriend visited me in Vienna during the mid-1980s, when we all spent an evening as Heinz Fischer's guests at his vacation home near Semmering. This was the same Heinz Fischer who served as Austria's president from 2004 until 2016! Over the years, Abby became one of my dearest friends. We celebrated each other's birthdays and shared many joyful and sad moments with each other in many locations, from Cambridge to Berlin, from New York to Washington.

A born and bred New Englander, Abby had become an assistant to Henry Kissinger at Harvard. In that position, she came to know one of Dr. Kissinger's star doctoral students, Guido Goldman, who, in 1969, joined forces with Stanley Hoffmann to found Harvard's West European Studies program, which, in 1974, was to mutate into the Center for European Studies. The Center was thus the product of the troika of Hoffmann as its chair, Goldman as its executive director, and Abby Collins as its assistant director; Abby was an integral part of this endeavor's leadership from its inception and remained so for decades.

Soon, Abby and I were joined by Leoni and Rick Gordon, a delightful Australian couple. Both had graduated from Monash University in Melbourne and come to Harvard so Rick could pursue his doctoral studies under the guidance of Barrington Moore, while Leoni became the Center's librarian. Somehow, the conversation turned to baseball, and the couple revealed themselves to be ardent Red Sox fans who listened to every game on their radios in addition to making a number of forays to Fenway Park. They both adored the Sox's eccentric pitcher, Bill "Spaceman" Lee, which I took as their only saving grace for being such ardent Red Sox fans since I, too, found this player's individuality immensely refreshing in the cookie-cutter world of Major League Baseball. My informing them that I was a huge Yankees' fan commenced an exchange of good-natured ribbing.

But what stopped the conversation was when I mentioned I was in town partly because I wanted to meet Barrington Moore to see whether he would be interested in accommodating my academic interests. Rick's demeanor changed from joyful to pensive, and he chose his words carefully in his response. However, his body language amplified what he said, making amply clear he believed my endeavor would fail. "Dr. Moore is a complex man," Rick said. "Let's just leave it at that!"

Rick and Leoni also remained my friends for life, even after they divorced, with Leoni remaining at Harvard running its extension school and Rick becoming a professor of politics at the University of California, Santa Cruz where, in January 1992, I became chair of that department. Tragically, four years later, Rick died of cancer at the age of 51.

Before long, two Peters joined us: Peter Lange, then assistant professor of government at Harvard, an eminent Europeanist specializing in Italian politics; and Peter Gourevitch, an associate professor in the Department of Government, an expert in comparative politics and international relations with mastery of many fields. Both were warm, welcoming, and encouraging, with Lange regaling me with wonderful stories about Karl Deutsch's teaching escapades. Lange later became provost at Duke University where I visited him in 2013. Before escorting me to a fabulous restaurant for dinner, he honored me by taking me to see a Duke basketball game (against rival University of Miami) at Cameron Indoor Stadium, arguably the venue with the best atmosphere in all of North American sports.

Gourevitch became a towering figure at the University of California, San Diego, regarded as one of the world's foremost experts in comparative political economy. In this stellar capacity, Gourevitch has been joined by two other Peters whose lifelong work has represented the core of the Center's intellectual being: Katzenstein, eminent professor at Cornell; and Hall, who spent his entire academic career at Harvard's Department of Government and its Center for European Studies.

By noontime, we were joined by two graduate students: John Keeler, who was to become my officemate at the Center and with whom, in 1978, I published one of my first scholarly articles; and Stephen Bornstein, an immensely cultured Canadian Europhile. Both went on to distinguished academic careers. In two gestures that proved characteristic of the Center's soul, this collective declined to send me out to find lunch in distant Harvard Square and simply accorded me a bite from this sandwich and that salad. Then Abby asked me to write down my full name and a few words about my academic interests because, for the first time, the Center was going to publish a mimeographed sheet with all its affiliated faculty, graduate students, and visitors for academic year 1975–1976. To my bafflement, Abby wanted me included, but with the unforgettable admonition: "You had better pass your dissertation defense at Columbia because we only have Harvard and MIT doctoral students on this list. All others must be postdocs!" I was beyond flattered and immensely pleased.

Then, finally, in came a tall, handsome figure who clearly was not an academic but also not a businessman or a politician or a doctor or a lawyer. He did not fit the group assembled in the room for lunch, yet he fit this building's inchoate gestalt. He was sui generis: Guido Goldman! Abby introduced me and told Guido that I had been waiting some time for him, I had a letter from Lipset, and she hoped Guido would have a few minutes to spare for me.

"Of course," Guido said with a huge smile. "Let's go to my office, shall we?"

We walked up the narrow stairs to the second floor. Right next to the copy room, we entered a small, cluttered office where I could barely find a chair. When we both sat down, Guido once again confirmed my initial impression of him as being askew to the world of the academy and not fully of it: he lit a cigar! I had never seen that at any university. Businessmen did that or union bosses or sports promoters, but no academics who, of course, smoked pipes clad in their tweed jackets with suede elbow patches on their sleeves or rolled their own cigarettes with Dutch tobacco. (Then there was also Austerlitz who, as already mentioned, chainsmoked Chesterfields.) So began my lifelong friendship with Guido Goldman, with whom I shared so much, not least an unparalleled rootlessness, his possibly even more pronounced than mine.

"So you are the son of the legendary Nahum Goldmann," I said even before he had a chance to look at Lipset's letter.

"Wow," he said. "Few, if any, have ever commenced a conversation with me here at Harvard by mentioning my father. Do you know him?"

"Not personally," I said, "but sometime in the middle 1960s, my father took me to the Grand Ballroom of the Vienna Intercontinental

Hotel where your father addressed the Vienna Jewish Community. You must surely know that to diaspora Jews, perhaps apart from those in North America, your father is as close to a saint as one can come. After all, your father is responsible for having negotiated with Chancellor Konrad Adenauer the reparation moneys that the Federal Republic of Germany has been paying to the victims of the Holocaust. Your father is a hero to my family!"

Based on this initial expression of admiration, Guido later invited me to meet his father. Apparently, his father was about to fly to Boston to spend the day at Harvard and MIT talking to these two illustrious universities' presidents, boards of trustees, and other potentates. He, Guido, did not have the time to spend the entire day with his father, but he would rent a comfortable limousine for me to use to pick up his father at Logan Airport and be his chaperone all day before the elder Goldmann returned to Logan to fly back to New York. Guido wanted to pay me some outrageous sum that I rejected because I owed Guido this favor; because I regarded Guido as a friend; and because I knew the day with Nahum Goldmann could be one of the most interesting days of my life in terms of listening to stories about world leaders from across the globe.

What a day it turned out to be! Dr. Goldmann regaled me with stories about Adenauer and other German politicians such as Willy Brandt and Helmut Schmidt; about key European leaders like Josip Broz, better known as Tito, and Charles de Gaulle; and pretty much every Israeli political figure of note from David Ben-Gurion to Moshe Sharett, from Golda Meir to Moshe Dayan, from Abba Eban to Yitzhak Rabin. I was actually annoyed when at some point he said something like, "So what do you do? And who are you?" I mumbled a few words and immediately redirected this segue from the order of the day, which was for me to ask questions of the great man about his interactions with this and that leader, and for Nahum Goldmann to provide detailed responses. Andy Markovits being a non-person here did not bother me one bit. In the rare presence of a great man, mere mortals don't count!

In 1980 and 1981, Guido invited me to private lunches with his father at his home in Concord. The last time, we had an amazing talk about antisemitism out on Guido's deck, with Nahum covered in blankets to ward off the chilly fall winds. I taped the conversation because I thought I might need it for a project on antisemitism I never implemented. I gave one copy of the cassette to Guido, who had it digitized and placed in the Nahum Goldmann archives at Brandeis University; I gave the other copy to my father, who treasured it until his dying day. Obviously, Nahum reminded me of my father pretty much every minute that I spent with him on all three of these occasions.

At our first meeting in his office, Guido was so impressed with my knowing about his father that he almost forgot to open Lipset's letter. I had no idea of its contents, but it must have been laudatory because Guido said something to the effect that I was precisely the kind of young scholar they wanted at the Center. In our nearly fifty-year relationship, I never dared ask Guido what Lipset actually said about me.

Guido Goldman (only one "n" as opposed to his father's two) was born in 1938 in Zurich, from which his parents and his brother Michael left for the United States in 1940. They settled in New York City where Guido lived until he entered Harvard in 1955. There he studied with Stanley Hoffmann and Zbigniew Brzezinski, whom Guido liked and I did not when he was my professor at Columbia more than ten years later. After receiving his bachelor's degree in 1959, Guido began spending time in the Federal Republic of Germany, where he perfected the already excellent German he had learned from his Berlin-born mother. He continued his involvement with Germany on an intellectual level by writing an award-winning doctoral dissertation on the interaction between heavy industry and foreign policy in the Weimar Republic.

Guido could easily have become a superb academic in the field of comparative politics and international relations, but his interests drove him towards the real world. In 1967, he became an advisor to the John F. Kennedy Memorial Fellowship, which the Federal Republic of Germany set up to honor President Kennedy, a beloved figure, particularly in Berlin's western sectors. Two or three German social scientists at a time were to spend one academic year at Harvard to perfect their doctoral dissertations for publication. Guido asked me to be of assistance to these Kennedy Fellows, providing me with invaluable connections and deep friendships with many German academics.

In honor of the twenty-fifth anniversary of the establishment of one of the United States' most significant foreign policy measures—the European Recovery Program, better known as the Marshall Plan—in 1947, Guido Goldman convinced the West German government to set up a reciprocal program that became the German Marshall Fund of the United States. To inaugurate this major program, headquartered in Washington, D.C., Guido had the chancellor of the Federal Republic, Willy Brandt, give the commencement speech at the 1972 Harvard graduation, exactly 25 years after Secretary of State George Marshall established the original plan as Harvard's commencement speaker in 1947. Guido's charisma, panache, and gravitas assured that Brandt was not going to be the last German chancellor to speak at a Harvard commencement. Rather, this gig became kind of a requirement for the job since Helmut Schmidt, Helmut Kohl, and Angela Merkel fulfilled the expectation as well, with Guido serving as master of ceremonies for all of them.

Guido remained deeply involved in the German Marshall Fund as one of its leading board members. His reach beyond Germany's government and into its corporate establishment led to the founding of the Werner Otto Museum at Harvard, which came to house Harvard's unique holdings of German Expressionist art. Guido's friendship with Werner Otto, the founder of Germany's largest mail-order group, provided the basis for this massive donation to Harvard. (Completing the circle, Alexander Otto, Werner's youngest child, wrote his senior honors thesis, for which he garnered a rare *summa cum laude*, under my mentorship at Harvard's Committee on Degrees in Social Studies. We also co-authored and published an article in *Comparative Politics* in 1992 based on Alex's thesis.)

These expressionist gems by the likes of Max Beckmann and Otto Dix formerly resided at Harvard's Busch-Reisinger Museum, located in Adolphus Busch Hall. Now empty, in 1989—that *annus mirabilis* in European politics—this space became the stately new location for the Center for European Studies, which departed its funky little home on Bryant Street and became the Minda de Gunzburg Center for European Studies at Harvard University.

Hailing from one of Canada's best-known and richest families, Minda Bronfman married Baron Alain de Gunzburg, had two children, and became deeply involved in many philanthropic endeavors before dying in 1985 at the age of sixty. Guido was one of her dearest friends, and by dint of that connection, her children donated $10 million to the Center for European Studies which henceforth has borne their mother's name. Making matters still more interesting, one of Minda's younger brothers, Edgar, became a prominent president of the World Jewish Congress, whose co-founder and first president was none other than Nahum Goldmann.

There cannot be a more fitting monument to Guido's life than this Center with its accompanying museum a few yards away: a building named after a German-American beer magnate housing a center that bears the name of a prominent Canadian-American-European Jewish family in a location that formerly exhibited cutting-edge German art. Guido, too, had long been involved in philanthropy and the arts, notably as a major benefactor of the Alvin Ailey dance company. However, among the many roles Guido played, none was more important than his towering presence in the postwar German-American relationship where his contribution was immeasurable.

This relationship also formed a key pillar of my friendship with Guido. Even though he and I differed as to which part of Germany was our interlocutor—his always being elite Germany at the highest level; mine the world of trade unions and new social movements—we respected each other's views and positions. No question that the "Jewish thing" played a crucial role in our differing relationships to Germany. Guido understood fully that his uniquely prominent position in postwar German life owed much to his father. And no one embodied the complexity of post-Shoah German-Jewish relations more starkly than Nahum Goldmann. He was the principal figure who made the Germans pay billions in reparations for their heinous acts which remain singular in human history.

I always felt that this key issue made Guido uneasy on two levels: first, that he owed his unique access to everything German, particularly the country's business and political elites, to his father's standing with Adenauer and German reparations to the Jews and Israel; and, second, that Guido somehow felt guilty about his father's overt Jewishness and his capitalizing on the Germans' guilt. In an odd way, I thought Guido found me to be too Jewish as well. Even though we discussed virtually every aspect of German politics in our half-century-long friendship, I cannot remember discussing the Holocaust even once. He felt uneasy raising this subject and mentioned to me several times that we Jews needed to move on.

In this category, I also place Guido's profoundly uneasy relationship to Israel. Guido, for whom a trip to Europe for a one-day meeting was never a burden, and who traveled long distances with ease, did not journey to Israel for decades. This, in spite of his father's prominent resting place on Mount Herzl among the great leaders of twentieth-century Jewry, and in spite of one of the country's great museums bearing his father's name. Then again, I often noticed that, when addressing German audiences, Guido delighted in making a Jewish joke. Though always apropos and poignant, the joke's presence mainly performed the function of letting his audience know that a Jew was speaking and they had better never forget it.

I also found it odd that for years every December Guido arranged for me to receive a sensationally good *Weihnachtsstollen*, an authentic German Christmas cake in the form of a log, straight from one of Germany's foremost bakers in Munich, packed in a gorgeous wooden box and sent by special delivery. I know I was not the only one receiving such a lavish gift, and possibly not even the only one of his Jewish friends to do so. Still, this Christmas gift seemed a bit strange since I never heard Guido mention Hanukkah or any other Jewish holiday.

Though we never talked about the Holocaust, Guido and I shared two topics that provided us nothing but pleasure: dogs and sports. Guido adored his Welsh springer spaniels (most notably Tara and Sherman), whom he pampered as lavishly as I did my golden retrievers. I never can remember Guido not wishing my dogs well when we departed from each other, or not asking how the dogs were doing and what they were up to at the beginning of every single one of our many meetings. He deeply cared about their well-being, and when my darling Dovi died, Guido made a most generous contribution in his name to the Yankee Golden Retriever Rescue Society from which I adopted him.

We also were both huge NBA fans and connoisseurs, even though I hated Guido's Boston Celtics and rooted against them regardless of their opponents. This antipathy was most pronounced when the Celtics played my New York Knickerbockers, the Philadelphia 76-ers, or the Los Angeles Lakers. I had the good fortune to spend the entire 1980s in Boston when the Celtics–Lakers rivalry, fueled by the duels between the two teams' superstars of Larry Bird and Earvin "Magic" Johnson, saved the NBA and catapulted the game and the league to a national and global prominence never seen before. Even though Guido never invited me to join him in his courtside seats for any of the memorable play-off battles between these two NBA giants, he asked me to accompany him to many regular season games. I am certain we were the only fans in attendance who not only discussed a particular point guard's assist percentage, but also the problems confronting Germany's coalition government.

After that first meeting in his office, Guido and I shook hands warmly, and we parted by saying we would see each other often in the coming academic year, which we did. To my great sadness, Guido died on November 30, 2020, just as I concluded the writing of this manuscript. I will forever remain deeply grateful for his salutary and unparalleled influence on my life.

Before leaving the Center, I knocked on Abby Collins's office door because I wanted to thank her for everything she had done for me that morning.

"Great that you came," she said, "because I want you to take this letter to Holyoke Center in Harvard Square, where they will issue you a Harvard ID, which you will need to access the libraries and enter pretty much any Harvard building." What? How did all this happen? I thanked Abby profusely and promised she would see me a number of times before my doctoral defense, which I confidently claimed I would pass, because I fully intended to commute between Cambridge and New York before moving to the former for good having completed my defense at Columbia.

Here, a word might be in order as to my relationship to the third member of the Center's founders, Stanley Hoffmann, whom I did not meet that first day. Hoffmann was born in Vienna in 1928 to an American father and an Austrian mother. He fled with the latter to Paris during Austria's turbulent 1930s. When the Nazis occupied Paris in 1940,

Hoffmann and his mother fled to the French countryside. He received his education in France and became its citizen in 1947. In his two decades of living in France, Hoffmann became totally assimilated to that country's powerful intellectual milieu and culture in which he grew to be a central figure. This remained the case even when Hoffmann became an instructor at Harvard in 1955 and then rose to the highest peak of the Harvard professoriate.

In my lifelong contact with European immigrants to the United States, I discerned two distinct categories: those who continued to live in Europe despite their physical presence in the United States, and those who embraced America and its culture and wanted nothing more than to identify with and be identified by their new homeland. Stanley Hoffmann represented the prototype of the former. Examples of the latter: Karl Deutsch and Andy Markovits! Maybe due to this difference, or the cutting wit and powerful cynicism Hoffmann brought to bear in his many brilliant essays and criticisms of policies, politicians, and ideas, I never warmed to him. I never liked cynics and Hoffmann clearly was one. The feeling of distance and coolness was mutual, I am sure, at least until one event and its amazing aftermath. When I appeared one morning with my golden retriever Dovi at the Center in its brand new Minda de Gunzburg incarnation in the fall of 1989, I ran into Stanley in the corridor. He beamed from ear to ear, bent down, petted Dovi, and said in Viennese-accented German: *"Das ist ja so ein süßer Kerl!,"* this is such a sweet fellow! This was the first and only time I heard Stanley speak German. The cool, distant, brilliant French intellectual had mutated to a warm, cuddly, and fuzzy friend to Dovi, though not to me.

Three years later, I was summoned to Abby's office and informed that I was not allowed to take Dovi to the office any longer. New Harvard regulations permitted only service dogs to appear in Harvard offices. I was crushed. Well, no Dovi at the Center, no Andy! I started to work at home and only attended meetings and seminars at the Center. A few days later, I was told by reliable sources that Stanley Hoffmann vehemently defended Dovi's continued presence and was truly upset when he and one of his allies on the Center's governing committee lost their battle to allow my dog to accompany me to my office. In December 1996, when Dovi died in Santa Cruz, I received a wonderful handwritten condolence card from Stanley informing me how Dovi's death had saddened him. Whereas I could never soften Stanley's steely shell, Dovi did so in a second and to lasting effect. Stanley Hoffmann was a mensch after all!

In addition to his intellectual brilliance and scholarly credentials, Stanley's tolerance and magnanimity singularly equipped him to be a leader. He was the Center's chairman; he could have made it his institution, gathering only scholars who pursued his particular interests and research. Instead, Hoffmann "let a hundred flowers bloom," to use Mao Zedong's ill-fated slogan, by allowing scholars to pursue their own inclinations. At one of the Center's celebrations—maybe in 1999, at the thirtieth anniversary of its founding—the celebrant praised the unique intellectual and academic standing of the Center's seminar on the State and Capitalism since 1800. Stanley, in his thank-you response, gleefully admitted that, in all his years as the Center's chairman, he never once attended this seminar and really had no idea of its existence and activities let alone the reason for its being so highly regarded by scholars around the globe.

Back to my first day in Cambridge. After getting my Harvard ID at Holyoke Center, I crossed Harvard Yard and climbed to the second floor of Littauer Hall, where Karl Deutsch had his office. I was greeted by a friendly woman who introduced herself as Evelyn Neumark, Professor Deutsch's personal secretary. Professor Deutsch, she told me, was not around; she expected him in late September, though only to hold his two classes before setting off again to Brazil, after which he would fly back to Cambridge for his teaching duties, before then heading out again to Ann Arbor, Michigan. Meeting Deutsch during his office hours was difficult, because he often was out of town or getting waylaid by students and colleagues with whom he would chat with no regard to time. Seeing my disappointment, Deutsch's secretary asked if I would like to have a cup of tea with her. I accepted, and Evelyn became part of my Harvard family. She remained Deutsch's secretary until he retired from Harvard in 1985, after which she became secretary to Guido Goldman, of all people, remaining in that position until her retirement.

I ran out of time to make it to Barrington Moore's office that day. When I took my seat on the Eastern Airlines shuttle at Logan Airport,

I pinched myself. I had arrived that morning with nothing but a vague hope to work with Seymour Martin Lipset. By the time I returned to New York in the evening, I had rented an apartment in Cambridge and found an institutional home full of wonderful people who embraced me warmly despite being under no obligation to do so. Oh, and I had a Harvard University ID!

Upon becoming a fulltime member of the Center that fall, I quickly came to learn what that place actually was. First and foremost, the Center provided an informal and welcoming atmosphere for scholars working on modern Europe, which included the nineteenth century. Historians such as Charles Maier were as prominent and vital to the Center's mission as were its political scientists and sociologists. At a time when words like "interdisciplinary" and "cross-disciplinary" were not as common as they are today, the Center was a profoundly interdisciplinary place, not so much by design as by default. Folks working on various aspects of European politics and society from different disciplinary angles just happened to congregate at this place.

To be sure, the Center was also very much a product of its zeitgeist. This was an era in which a critical approach to the establishment and capitalism was *de rigueur* if one was to be considered a cutting-edge social scientist. While not everyone at the Center desired a socialist transformation of capitalism, a severely critical view of capitalism was clearly hegemonic. Being bourgeois or in favor of capitalism simply did not cut it with this group. As such, the Center was very much a creation of "1968," both in terms of the age of its main protagonists, most of whom became politicized in the late 1960s as students, some perhaps even as junior faculty, and in terms of the values "1968" created and embodied.

The Center's most prominent intellectual axis consisted of an amalgam of the works of Max Weber, Alexis de Tocqueville, Sigmund Freud, Karl Marx, and a bevy of post- or neo-Marxist writers such as Louis Althusser, Nicos Poulantzas, Ralph Miliband, Perry Anderson, Immanuel Wallerstein, Karl Polanyi, E.P. Thompson, and prominent authors of *New Left Review*. The Center's scholars tended to focus on the study of the modern state and its relation to capitalist economies and societies across European countries, predominantly Britain, France, Germany, and Italy. Not by chance, then, a study group called State and Capitalism since 1800 ("State and Cap," as it was known) became by far the Center's most prestigious seminar. This study group, which saw itself as giving voice to the best scholarship looking at "left institutionalism" in a comparative context, defined the Center's very being, within its own confines and vis-à-vis the outside world. Being invited to present a paper at this forum was an honor few, if any, declined.

I was accorded this honor only once, but it was a decisive event in my life. Given my background and interests, I spent virtually all my time comparing Europe and America from the micro level, such as how people use their cutlery or why they use different fingers when they count, to the macro, as in why no large socialist or social democratic labor party has played an important role in shaping American politics. The latter question preoccupied many great thinkers, perhaps none more than Lipset, who wrote crucial books and articles on precisely this topic, which falls within the larger complex of "American exceptionalism." To Lipset and me, this was never a normative question about American superiority, but rather a purely empirical one as to why America differs from a norm that has always been massively Eurocentric.

Being a huge soccer fan, I always wondered why Americans never took to this sport. Having a few weeks in the summer of 1986, I decided to pursue this question with serious research. The result was my paper "The Other 'American Exceptionalism': Why Is There No Soccer in the United States?" Everyone at the Center knew I had spent a good deal of the summer working on this topic. Somehow, the finished paper made the rounds among the Center's heavies, and one day, Peter Hall asked if I would be interested in presenting this paper at the State and Cap seminar in early October, leading the year's series.

I was ecstatic to be invited to present my work at this distinguished forum, particularly on such an unorthodox topic. But I feared that due to the topic's unconventional nature, this would be the first time a State and Cap event would attract no audience at all. Was I wrong! It was precisely the paper's unorthodox topic that drew a record number of attendees to the Center that Friday. We had to bring in extra chairs to accommodate the crowd which reached all the way into the reception area. The discussion following my presentation was so lively and on such a high level that Charles Maier's criticisms were co-published with my paper in one of the scholarly journals that accepted it. The Center also published my article in its Working Paper series where it became one of the most acquired items of all time. All told, this paper appeared in 15 languages, making it the most successful published article of my academic career.

Allowing me to present this particular work in this particular venue initiated a whole new academic life for me that simply would not have existed were it not for Harvard University's Center for European Studies. By its standing, this institution gave me legitimacy and permission to pursue research on comparative sports cultures in Europe and North America that was quite rare then. Sports, at this time, were studied mainly within schools of kinesiology and centered on micro-level issues such as the injury rate of softball players or the different concentration mechanisms of free-throw shooters; serious macro-level scholarship on sports that millions played and followed barely existed in the social sciences.

Because of elitism and the disdain for commercial pursuits comprising so much of academic culture, particularly at so-called elite institutions, the study of sports was regarded as too frivolous and commercial. To work on the rural precursors of badminton in eighteenth-century Lancashire was acceptable, but to write a monograph on Manchester United or the New York Yankees was *verboten*: the latter topics were a journalist's domain, never a serious scholar's.

This began to change in Britain in the 1970s and 1980s, but not in the United States. The study of sports remains taboo in departments of political science to this day. Despite my paper's tremendous global success, I will never forget the smirks on people's faces when they saw piles of a subsequent version in the American Political Science Association's paper room at its annual meeting at the Palmer House in Chicago. Soccer? Sports? As a topic of political science? Most certainly not! Even though I had a fine idea as to how to expand this work, I desisted until another institution of the Center's stature urged me to do just that a dozen years later. At the behest of the Rector of the *Wissenschaftskolleg zu Berlin*—the Institute for Advanced Study, Berlin—I used my fellowship at the *Kolleg* to resume work on this topic. This eventually led to a book published by Princeton University Press in 2001 that has remained a mini classic in the field. Since then, I have published three more books on sports-centered topics, as well as many articles and reviews in academic journals all over the world. Moreover, I developed a course called Sports, Politics, and Society that has become one of the most successful and popular offerings of the University of Michigan's undergraduate curriculum.

And most important to me in this endeavor has been my conscious attempt to include women in the world of sports, which, as I have often maintained, is the single most powerful male firewall keeping women at bay and away from men's safe spaces and thus their privilege. In my book *Sportistas: Female Fandom in the United States*, coauthored with Emily Albertson, one of my star undergraduate students, we show that nothing divides the daily conversations of Michigan undergraduates more than sports talk. Knowledge of sports is one of the only remaining domains in which men genuinely feel threatened by women knowing their stuff. "What, you know Mariano Rivera's ERA? Well, what about Derek Jeter's OPS?" Male Michigan undergraduates got defensive, even angry, when their female partners or friends knew sports trivia in ways the same men never did when women displayed a greater familiarity with European politics, international relations, world history, American movies, or anything else.

Sports was a male language and domain in which women were bothersome intruders never to be taken seriously. Above all, women were always marked as interlopers. As I have written elsewhere, in the world of sports fandom, women are like green-card holders—resident aliens but not fully accepted citizens. (Interestingly enough, this exclusion occurs much less often among male athletes than among male fans.) I made it my mission to dismantle this last bastion of unbridled masculinity by attending women's sporting events, including three women's World Cup soccer tournaments, and writing extensively about women's athletics, encouraging women to become sports fans if they so choose.

It is perfectly fine for men to have their own spaces. But if the exclusion of women becomes cemented, with sports talk—guy talk—

forming a major part of the wall that defines such spaces, I think it is incumbent upon male fans to change our demeanor and approach to the world of sports. It was solely the Center for European Studies that unleashed this strain of my academic pursuit, for which I will always remain most grateful.

Meeting on Friday afternoons at 2 p.m. after the wonderful Friday lunches that became a Center institution, the State and Cap seminars assumed a legendary status beyond Harvard. (So were the Friday lunches provided by Merry White, then a doctoral student or assistant professor, now a full professor in sociology, specializing in Japan. The collected recipes from those lunches led to a cookbook called *Cooking for Crowds* that, according to Amazon, is currently in its fortieth edition, making this book by far the most successful publication ever to emerge from the hallowed halls of Harvard's Center for European Studies.)

In addition to State and Cap, the Center hosted the Labor Study Group, the Women's Study Group, and, as of 1978, the Jews in Modern Europe Study Group, which I co-chaired with my friends and colleagues Dennis Klein and Phyllis Albert. Then there were the Iberian, British, French, and Italian study groups, with Guido and I chairing the German Study Group. Typically, each of these groups had a yearly budget of $1,000, which is laughably low but, this being Harvard, everybody wanted to present their work, so we got pretty much every speaker in whose scholarship we were interested, paying them a hundred-dollar honorarium and taking them to a mediocre dinner.

The Center also published a fine Working Paper Series and two scholarly quarterlies: *French Politics and Society*, later renamed *French Politics, Culture and Society*, and *German Politics and Society*, which Guido and I co-edited when it was first called the *German Studies Newsletter*. I remained this journal's editor until 2003, when it found its lasting home at Georgetown University, continuing to flourish as one of the leading scholarly periodicals on modern Germany in the English language. Additionally, the Center organized two or three major colloquia per academic year on topics of great importance in Europe at the time. These were elaborate affairs for which the Center applied for funds to house and feed out-of-town speakers and bring them to Cambridge from anywhere, including Europe. Some of these colloquia led to edited volumes published by prestigious academic houses. I remember one of these colloquia held in late September 1985 in the midst of Hurricane Gloria, which hit the Boston area with particular ferocity with some of the late afternoon sessions held by candlelight since we had no electric power.

During 1976 and 1977, a group of us began talking about organized labor's predicament in relation to European capitalism, which had experienced new challenges imposed by the oil crisis of 1973 and its ensuing ramifications. We began to meet regularly over brown-bag lunches, discussing labor's strategies and options in Britain, France, Italy, Sweden, and Germany and noticing how vastly the situation differed from country to country. At some point, we divided the work among five of us with proven competence with respect to organized labor's existence in a particular country: Peter Gourevitch on Britain; George Ross on France; Peter Lange on Italy; Andrew Martin on Sweden; and Andy Markovits on Germany.

Though immensely flattered to be asked to take on this role, I knew the honor had been accorded purely on my potential and my command of the German language; unlike the others, I had never researched anything on German labor and hadn't published a single word on the topic. I had a lot of catching up to do, particularly if the Ford Foundation was going to grant us the funds to spend nine months in the field. I ensconced myself in the basement of Littauer Hall where something called the Manpower and Industrial Relations Library then existed. This being Harvard, I was sure its resources on Germany would be superb, as was the case. I came to learn a huge amount about German unions, so that when we received the approval of our project from the Ford Foundation in 1978, I felt prepared to start my fieldwork in Germany the following year.

Thus began my 15-year commitment to the study of German labor, which yielded not only a fine chapter in one of the two volumes that emanated from the Center's Ford Foundation project, but also led to a monograph of my own, published by Cambridge University Press, which helped me earn tenure in 1986. A number of other articles and books in

German and in English established me as a prolific and respected expert on German (and even Austrian) labor in the ensuing years.

Four individuals who became my students and co-authors on this project and its successors deserve mention here because they have remained very important to me to this day. First was Stephen Silvia, now a professor at American University, who, though a doctoral student at Yale at the time, sought me out for guidance on his dissertation on German labor. We published quite a few scholarly articles together on various aspects of German industrial relations and politics in English and German. I have continued to delight in Steve's friendship and the catholicity of his interests and expertise, ranging from sports to politics, music to television.

Then there was Philip Gorski, now professor at Yale University. I co-authored with him the book *The German Left: Red, Green and Beyond* that enjoyed success in its English original but much more so in its German translation. The German edition appeared with the title *"Grün schlägt Rot: Die deutsche Linke seit 1945,"* which translates into "Green defeats or beats Red: The German Left since 1945." Derided at the time for the bold claim that the Greens were in the process of surpassing the Reds as the main voice of the German—indeed, the European and global—Left, the book has been celebrated in recent years as a particularly prescient prediction of the German Left's current state.

Next came the late Christopher Allen, who was a professor at the University of Georgia when he died in 2011. We co-authored a number of pieces on German labor, including the chapter that became part of the two-volume Center for European Studies book on European labor, which commenced my long journey into German labor and the Left. But much more significantly, we shared strong interest in American music, jazz and rock in particular, with Chris also being a fan of the Grateful Dead. Indeed, it was by my attending a Dead concert in Portland, Maine in 1980, that I came to know Chris' immediate and extended family, all of whom lived in Maine, where Chris was born and is now buried. Our interest in and love for sports formed a deep bond between us. We traveled to Lake Placid together to attend three days of the winter Olympics in 1980, seeing Eric Hayden win two of his record five gold medals in addition to the four-man bobsled and other events.

I will forever remain proud that it was through our acquaintance and friendship that Chris not only became a genuine soccer fan and connoisseur, but a pioneering figure in the early days of American soccer's institutional growth. Thus, for example, he became one of the driving forces in the creation of Sam's Army which formed the first real fan group—the first "ultras"—of the United States Men's National Team. I dedicated my book *Women in American Soccer and European Football: Different Roads to Shared Glory* to Chris' crucial contribution to the game's growth in the United States.

Lastly, Thomas Ertman deserves strong mention. Currently a professor at New York University, I hired Tom in 1979 to be my research assistant with the task of reading tons of German newspapers for me in connection with my work on trade unions and Social Democracy. When I interviewed Tom for the job, I was floored by the flawless qualities of his spoken German, which were only rivaled, as I found out in due course, by his equally perfect written command of that language. Just as with Chris, music and sports became the glue to our deep friendship. Rather than jazz and rock, it was classical music, mostly opera, which bound me to Tom, though it was patently obvious from the very beginning that Tom's mastery of operatic music far surpassed mine. We discussed and listened to arias for hours interrupting our work on German trade unions repeatedly. But then, just as with Chris, there was soccer!

Here, too, Tom's knowledge and expertise were beyond impressive. Opera and soccer also informed Tom's deep affection for and friendship with my father. When I first introduced the two to each other in early 1980, their mutual admiration was obvious. Tom reveled in talking to my father in German and touching on all kinds of subjects in addition to opera and soccer, such as my father's history in an area of the world about which—not surprisingly—Tom knew pretty much everything. (It is rare for young American men to know minute details about Habsburg Hungary's history or Romania's ethnic conflicts.)

I also came to know Tom's family in 1981 when they all traveled to Cambridge to attend their son's graduation from Harvard College. It is on that day that I delighted in meeting Tom's mother, Marianne, and his father, Charles, who was the pastor of the Our Savior Lutheran Church in Centereach, New York. Speaking German, knowing Hebrew, laughing all the time, exhibiting a gregarious, sunny, and warm disposition to accompany his obvious erudition, the man exuded a charisma I found utterly moving and unique. My father and I invited Tom to accompany us to the soccer World Cup in Spain in 1982. Spending time with Tom before and after the matches will forever remain one of my fondest memories as they were for my father who often talked to me about them in the remaining years of his life.

The bond between Tom and my father was so deep that when my father died, Tom immediately told me he was going to fly to Vienna to be there for the funeral. Other than Miriam Shuchman, my partner at the time, Tom was the only person from the United States who stood by my side at the gravesite and during the ensuing difficult days in Vienna. Upon my return home to Cambridge, I organized two evenings in lieu of the conventional seven days of morning—the Shiva—when friends could come by my apartment and spend time with me. Many came. Indeed, pretty much everybody from the Center for European Studies paid their respects and expressed their condolences. Only one person came for both evenings and stayed the entire time for both: Thomas Ertman!

All of this was the legacy of Lipset's note to Guido Goldman on that September day in 1975 when I traveled to Harvard in hope of working with Lipset. But, as will be recalled, I also wanted to meet Barrington Moore and Karl Deutsch. It is to those stories I now turn.

During the first week of Harvard classes, when I began my commute between the Upper West Side and Cambridge, I noticed that Barrington Moore offered a small colloquium on cruelty, a fascinating topic in anyone's hands, let alone Barrington Moore's. I found my way to a classroom that, I am virtually certain, was in a basement. Only two other students awaited Moore's arrival. Then in walked a tall, austere, elderly gentleman who seemed almost annoyed at being there. He handed us the syllabus, which was massive in its reading requirements, mentioned something about a paper as the course requirement, and then adjourned the class. I walked up to him after his presentation and asked if

I could audit the class since I was not a student but a postdoc fellow at the Center for European Studies. He agreed to my request though with zero warmth or interest. This was my first disappointment in a string of wonderful events that greeted me at Harvard. Still, I was determined to take Moore's colloquium by virtue of my interest in this unusual topic, his reputation, and the influence that his book *Social Origins of Dictatorship and Democracy* had exerted on my intellectual development.

Sadly, at the end of the week, I was informed that Moore had cancelled all his teaching for the rest of the academic year due to severe back problems. Other than seeing the man bicycling the streets of Cambridge frequently in the ensuing years, I never interacted with Moore again. I never even dared to re-introduce myself on one of the rare occasions he joined us for Friday lunches at the Center for European Studies.

However, even at Columbia I already had heard of one of Moore's students, who was about to finish her doctorate and whose comparative sociology of the French, Russian, and Chinese revolutions was, well, revolutionary in its scope and originality. This person was Theda Skocpol, who was to become my generation's leading political sociologist, in a league with Moore, Lipset, and all the greats of their discipline. She also became one of the leading scholars of American politics and society, while holding professorships in the Department of Government and the Department of Sociology at Harvard. In the fall of 1975, Skocpol offered a seminar entitled "The Sociology of Polities." I visited her during her office hours and asked if I could audit the course as a postdoc. She graciously gave her permission, but asked me to be an active participant by doing all the readings and engaging in class discussions, just as if I were a regular doctoral student, not a passive consumer.

I agreed, to my benefit, because the class readings vastly augmented my scholarly repertoire. More important still were the friendships I forged with a number of students, at least seven of whom went on to distinguished academic careers, in this exceptional seminar. Among these friends was David Karen, who, as will be recalled, officiated as the rabbi at Kiki's and my wedding in May 1998. The Yankees and the Grateful Dead provided additional material with which to bond our friendship.

Karl Deutsch: Teacher, Mentor, Friend, Sunny Genius

Then there was Karl Deutsch! Having read and studied his work at Columbia, I assumed the author of *The Nerves of Government* and *Nationalism and Social Communication* must be, if not a genius, then close to it. Was I ever right! Ten minutes before Deutsch was to commence his doctoral seminar on nationalism, I ran up the stairs to the second floor of Littauer Hall to connect with Evelyn Neumark. Evelyn wanted to introduce me to Deutsch so we could chat while walking to the classroom together.

The door to Deutsch's office was ajar, and I glimpsed a tall man with thick glasses wearing a dark three-piece suit with a white shirt and an elegant, dark tie. He was conversing on the phone in perfect English with a heavy German accent discussing how the Bariloche Model proved an important improvement over the Club of Rome Model that he, Deutsch, deemed too economistic, at least in the context of what I could glean from the telephone conversation. Seminar time arrived and Deutsch did not show any signs of ending his telephone conversation. At one point, Evelyn stepped into Deutsch's office, grabbed him gently by his arm, and subtly urged him to end the conversation since he was late for class. About ten minutes later, Deutsch ended the call and turned to Evelyn with the kindest of faces and a big smile and said: "Mrs. Neumark [he never called her Evelyn], what class do I have now?"

To which Evelyn dutifully replied: "Your nationalism class, Professor Deutsch."

"Oh yes, of course. Where does the class meet? It's the first time this semester, can you walk me to it, please?"

Evelyn obliged and out they came from his room, straight towards me. "Oh, Professor Deutsch. I want you to meet Andy Markovits, who is about to defend his doctoral thesis at Columbia and will be a fellow for the year at the Center for European Studies."

Deutsch came to me, grabbed my hand warmly and with enthusiasm, and said: "Welcome to Harvard. Do you know my former Yale students Douglas Chalmers and Donald Puchala, both teaching at Columbia now?"

"Not only do I know them," I replied, "but I took Chalmers' course on political parties, which was one of my favorites at Columbia."

"Yes," Deutsch said, "his doctoral thesis under my supervision on German Social Democracy was excellent, though his interpretation of Schumacher was too conciliatory for me in terms of Schumacher's neutralist tendencies. What do you think?"

To my luck, I knew a bit about this and replied that the SPD's anti-Western tradition lay deep and was understandable at the time.

"Which tradition do you mean?" Deutsch asked. "I am interested in hearing this!"

At which Evelyn gently intervened. "Professor Deutsch, you are really late for class, maybe you and Andy can talk about this after your seminar. Please, let us go to the room."

We walked into a packed seminar room, where I sat in the outer circle since I was not a student taking this class. And then the show began. Without one note, Deutsch proceeded to give a brilliant two-hour presentation on nationalism—its essence, its development, its differing histories in eastern and western Europe, its manifestations via religion as opposed to language. He summarized the works of all the major theorists of nationalism. Examples kept flying through the room, from contemporary Nigeria to Mughal India, from fifteenth-century Switzerland to contemporary Brazil. I had never seen a presentation so dazzling in scope and depth all delivered completely by heart.

The class ran well over the allotted time. The students began leaving quietly because they had other commitments. The whole performance reminded me of Joseph Haydn's famous Symphony No. 45—the so-called "Farewell" Symphony—where, in the final adagio, the musicians quietly leave their seats in the orchestra one by one, with only two remaining.

Deutsch seemed oblivious to this slow but steady student exodus until one student dared ask him what the assignment was for the next class. Stumped, Deutsch asked for a syllabus which another student gave him. He perused the extensive reading list and began rattling off a number of authors and their work. Asked by another student what parts of these works had to be read, Deutsch just smiled and said: "All parts!" The students' reaction was telling. They did not express any animosity towards the man; they just accepted his response with respect and admiration, as if to say, "What did you expect to hear from such a great man?"

This was a man with zero pretenses when he could have had so many. In one of the essays I published on Deutsch over the years, one passage seems most appropriate in capturing this aspect of his persona:

> What seems incredible, almost frightening, is the fact that Karl Deutsch embodied all this brilliance, erudition, learnedness, combinatorial and integrative ability without ever striking anybody as pretentious, boastful, intimidating, or arrogant. I had never seen Deutsch be mean to anybody when he trumped everybody in the room with his encyclopedic knowledge and his incredible mental abilities. His audience simply reacted with astonishment and admiration—it was an occasion for taking pleasure along with him, smiling joyfully and rejoicing in a man's obvious delight. Karl Deutsch had an unadulterated socialist disposition that knew nothing of hierarchy and status. He was only interested in focusing on material and content, knowledge and learning, never on status, station, or prestige.[8]

Also evident that first day I attended Deutsch's seminar was his genius. I have had the luck and honor of studying with some incredibly smart people, but this man's intelligence was of a different magnitude. Deutsch was a pioneering political scientist. He introduced quantitative methods to the discipline that were unique and revolutionary at the time, and have become par for the course today. But Deutsch's work reached way beyond the confines of political science, even broadly defined. The breadth and scope of his influence is apparent in his joint publications with dozens of scholars from all over the world from French mathematicians to Indian anthropologists, from German political scientists to Brazilian ethnologists, from Nobel Prize-winning economists to psycho-

---

8   Andrei S. Markovits, "From Prague to America: Karl W. Deutsch between Experience and Knowledge" in Dan Diner and Moshe Zimmermann, eds., *Disseminating German Tradition: The Thyssen Lectures* (Leipzig: Leipziger Universitätsverlag, 2009), 120, 121. As the author of this piece, I have taken the liberty to provide here the language of my original manuscript that I submitted to the editors and not their edited text that appeared in the book and is slightly different.

linguists, from historians of the Middle Ages to biophysicists and game theoreticians.

Deutsch's works appeared in the best political science journals on both sides of the Atlantic. But they also were published in journals of econometrics, orthopsychiatry, psychiatry, philosophy, and phenomenology. He wrote essays on philosophical treatises about teleology and ontology, as well as on the psychology of personality development; he composed statistical models for analyzing transaction flows, as well as articles on game theory. He wrote important studies about the military preservation of the Swiss Confederation in the fourteenth century, as well as about the perfect bilingualism of the Swiss canton of Wallis.

Making matters even more impressive was that I never saw Deutsch prepare for a lecture. At most, on rare occasions, he jotted a few words on a yellow legal notepad to prompt him (a fine product of a central European *Gymnasium*, Deutsch, like me, could not type, but unlike me, never seems to have had to pick up the skill), and off he would go, delivering a rousing lecture in front of 10 people or 300. At Yale, he won the Political Union's coveted William Benton Prize for delivering the most captivating lectures on global politics. Tellingly, this was the only award among the many Deutsch received (seven honorary doctorates alone) that was prominently displayed in his office at his house in Cambridge. I was in awe when I went to listen to Deutsch deliver lectures to Harvard undergraduates on the rise of the Nazis. So were they. One could hear a pin drop in this ninety-minute class, and at the end the kids all stood and gave Deutsch a standing ovation. They just loved this guy!

The seminar that first day was supposed to start at 4 p.m. and end at 6 p.m. Well, it started closer to 4:25 p.m. and ended at 6:25 p.m. Deutsch and I walked back to his office, from which Evelyn had already left for the evening. We sat there and started talking about Hungarian nationalism's emergence under the Habsburg rule. (Alas, we never came to discuss the SPD's neutralist tendencies of the 1950s, which we raised while walking to the classroom together, until years later sitting in a café in Berlin.) Deutsch seemed to be impressed with something I said and asked me: "Why do you know all this?" When I replied that I was born in that part of the world and spent my *Gymnasium* years in Vienna, his already warm demeanor turned almost paternal. "When I was in *Gymnasium* in Prague throughout the 1920s, I would spend many a summer in Vienna with my uncle Julius, who, as you might know, was the commander of the Social Democratic Party's paramilitary organization, Schutzbund."

I said I knew that, of course, having been a keen reader of the *Arbeiter-Zeitung* and also a student of Austro-Marxism. Deutsch became more and more animated and began regaling me with how his mother was from Hernals, Vienna's seventeenth district, and how she became the first female representative of the Social Democratic Party—of any party, for that matter—to be seated in Czechoslovakia's parliament. By now, it must have been well past 7 p.m. but Deutsch made no gesture to leave; in fact, he was getting more comfortable talking to me by the minute.

Suddenly, a small, elegant, Jewish-looking woman came bounding into the office, saying almost in exasperation: "Karl, it is well past seven! Where are you? We have dinner plans at 7:30, and you were supposed to come home before we went out. What is this?"

Deutsch took this in stride. "I am so sorry, Ruth, my darling. But I met this fine young man here who went to *Gymnasium* in Vienna, speaks Hungarian and Romanian, and is now finishing his doctorate at Columbia but is already a visitor at Guido's Center for European Studies over on Bryant Street."

Mrs. Deutsch shook my hand, and I could see the Vienna thing struck her deeply. "Vienna, listen, what are you doing this Saturday evening? Are you free to come to dinner at our house? We will have a fine young Austrian political scientist over. Come, 7:30 p.m., at 25 Lakeview Avenue! Just to the right off Brattle Street as you are driving towards Watertown. And now, Karl, we have got to go, end of story!"

Apparently, as Evelyn informed me the next day, and Mary Deutsch Edsall, the Deutsches' elder daughter, later corroborated, Ruth's picking up Karl in his office that evening was not the exception but the rule. In addition to Karl's socialist soul and kindness, as well as his genius, he exhibited a third trait: perpetual lateness. Once again, I am quoting from one of my publications:

Perhaps the very encapsulation of Deutsch's essential nature was pro-vided by a group of world-renowned political scientists, Deutsch's Harvard colleagues all, who ended the memorial minute in honor of Karl W. Deutsch that was officially adopted by the Faculty of Arts and Science at Harvard University on February 14, 1995, in the fol-lowing poignant manner: "Karl Deutsch, the eternal optimist, was never punctual but always ahead of his time."[9]

Both Karl and Ruth were born in 1912 into the homes of German-speaking bourgeois families in Prague. Karl's father, Martin, was an op-tician. His mother, Maria (née Scharf), was Viennese and not Jewish. By the racial concept of the Nuremberg Laws, Karl was Jewish. But by Jew-ish law, and by his self-understanding, Karl was not Jewish. He went to a German *Gymnasium*, from which he graduated in 1931. He then en-rolled in Prague's German University, receiving his diploma in 1934. An inveterate foe of National Socialism, which became increasingly popu-lar among many of the German speakers in Czechoslovakia at the time, Deutsch left the university and went to England to train as an ophthal-mic optician, which might come in handy if he wanted to follow in his father's footsteps. He always told me that his love of science, of num-bers, of angles, of broken lines, of transparency, of short- and near-sight-edness, of the human anatomy, all of which he used so prolifically in his work, not least in his brilliant book *The Nerves of Government*, hailed from his training in England to become an optician.

Upon his return to Prague, Deutsch enrolled in the Czech-speak-ing Charles University, from which he received a doctorate in 1938. Typ-ically, a man of his station in Prague at the time would have disdained speaking Czech and stuck to German, which he would have viewed as superior in every respect. Karl, who spoke good Czech when he enrolled at this institution, spoke perfect Czech by the time he graduated. Lat-er, he used this phenomenon in his study of the social character of learn-ing languages, noting that one typically learns a new language "up" not

---

9   Markovits, "From Prague to America," 121.

"down," i.e., the subordinate social group has to learn the language of the dominant group, not vice versa.

Karl and I discussed this idea prolifically during a trip to Montreal, where we noticed that all the Francophones spoke English, whereas the Anglophones spoke no French. Karl was fascinated by my telling him how my mother—and even Juliska, my mother's peasant helper—never learned Romanian, which they disdained as profoundly inferior to Hungarian, let alone German. When Karl returned to Prague in 1988 to deliver a lecture at the Charles University, he did so in perfect Czech, for which his huge audience gave him a lengthy standing ovation.

In 1936, Karl married his childhood sweetheart, Ruth Slonitz, and in 1938, the two embarked on a trip to the United States, not as refugees, but as holders of a fellowship, fully intending to return home to Prague. But their plan was rendered moot by Great Britain's and France's infamous capitulation to Hitler in Munich, which led to the Nazi occupation of the Sudetenland and the elimination of Czechoslovakia. Overnight, Karl and Ruth became homeless refugees. In 1939, Karl obtained a fellowship to begin his doctoral studies in government at Harvard. And so commenced his stellar academic career.

I went to the Deutsches' for dinner that first Saturday evening. My arrival with a big bouquet of flowers was all Ruth needed to begin loving me. (One of the good habits I learned from my father was always to come with a gift when one is invited, never to go empty-handed.) As I entered the gorgeous house on Lakeview Avenue, I immediately recognized the young Austrian political scientist who was the Deutsches' guest. He was Anton Pelinka, whom I had met in late 1973 or early 1974 in Vienna's wonderful Café Landmann, Anton's and my favorite among the city's fabulous such establishments. We bonded instantly, not only over our love of politics and our similar normative orientations, but also because Anton was that very rare European at the time who not only loved basketball but really knew his stuff. Anton was a Schumpeter Fellow at the Center for European Studies during the academic year 1990–1991; five years later, I spent four months at his Department of Political Science at the University of Innsbruck as a Fulbright scholar. Lastly, I invited him to the University of Michigan for an entire academic year, which he spent, pursuant to my affiliations, half in the German department and half in Political Science. Anton and I developed a life-long friendship. By Thanksgiving 1975, I had become a member of the Deutsch household.

At the office, Karl asked me whether I would be interested in assisting him on a project on global modeling that was to lead not only to a major conference but also a published anthology. The conference was to occur at Harvard in April 1976, and Karl was in need of some organizational help since Evelyn alone could not handle events of this magnitude. He wanted to hire a Harvard graduate student for this purpose, but hoped I could help instead. I accepted with glee for lots of reasons: working with Karl Deutsch; learning about this strange thing called global modeling, about which I barely had glimpsed the vaguest of contours; becoming the co-editor of my first bona fide book; and earning money by joining the Harvard payroll. This meant the Markovits Foundation only had to pay me for one semester instead of the planned two.

Beginning in January 1976, I basically became Karl's intellectual and academic gofer: getting him books from Widener Library, reading early drafts of articles as they existed on the yellow legal pads, but also driving him around town, especially to Logan Airport on Thursday afternoons when, with some regularity, he boarded a flight to Detroit's Metropolitan Airport for visits to the University of Michigan in Ann Arbor. At Michigan, Karl collaborated closely with J. David Singer from the Department of Political Science on the famous Correlates of War project. He also worked closely with Russian-born mathematical psychologist Anatol Rapoport and Vienna-born mathematician Manfred Kochen on various aspects of game theory. I would get to meet all three of these scholars at the modeling conference we organized at Harvard in April 1976.

In order to work full blast on preparations for this global modeling conference, Karl believed I would be much better off having my own office space and not sharing a tiny alcove masquerading as an office at the Center for European Studies. He offered me an office that he called the "warehouse" located on the outskirts of the Harvard campus and in which he had not set foot for more than five years. When I entered the room, it showed. Still, I fell in love with the place from the get go. This was the beginning of my 15-year long wondrous life in room 213 of the aforementioned Vanserg Building, a.k.a. the "Bunker."

The conference in April was a rousing success. Not only did I acquire considerable knowledge about the most varied of fields and meet fascinating people, but under Karl's tutelage I also learned that I had better approach all the speakers and ask for their papers so we might start producing the edited volume immediately. For a *Luftmensch* like Karl, who always seemed lost in his ideas, he conveyed a surprising organizational savvy and practicality. After all, he was the former head of the New England Political Science Association and the gigantic American Political Science Association, and, in 1976, became president of the International Political Science Association, all, to be sure, by dint of his towering intellect and his colleagues' immense awe for his scholarly work. Still, such positions also require a sense of practicality and organizational skills, no matter how fine the staff that handles daily matters. Surprisingly, Deutsch possessed both skills galore. In the summer of 1977, we published the conference volume *Problems of World Modeling: Political and Social Implications*. It was the first instance of seeing my own name on the cover of a book.

Perhaps a word of explanation of global modeling is appropriate here. Starting with the Harvard economist Wassily Leontief's famous input-output analysis of the interdependence of economic sectors and the resulting effect on social life, for which he won the Nobel Prize in 1973, an increasing number of social scientists came to use the newly available power of computers to analyze big data in pursuit of understanding human problems. However, not until the Club of Rome published *The Limits to Growth* in 1972 did global modeling assume enough of a popular presence to change human behavior and the content of politics.

Written by Dennis Meadows, Donella Meadows, Jørgen Randers, and William Behrens III, *The Limits to Growth* demonstrated the use of the World3 Model to simulate the consequences of the interactions between the earth's physical resources and human systems. The book's conclusion was anything but optimistic. Together with Rachel Carson's *Silent Spring*, which had been published exactly one decade earlier, the Club of Rome's work became the burgeoning ecology movement's guidebook and bible. As I was to argue often in my own work, this moment changed how we came to define progress, and altered what it meant to be left and progressive from its former color, red, to its subsequent and current green. Whereas progress until then had meant taming nature by building big dams, progress now came to mean defending the snail darter from the adverse consequences of precisely such dams and similar mega construction projects, i.e. the preservation and restoration of nature, not mastery over it.

Even though Karl liked many of the ideas expounded by adherents of this new green movement, he distrusted their profound pessimism and rejection of science, technology, and the essence of the Enlightenment. Eternal optimist that he was, Karl believed that science, technology, data, and learning always led to improvements in social conditions and a better life. He often told me that he believed knowledge always led to happiness. Of course, there would be setbacks such as the Nazis' and fascists' abuse of science, but ultimately virtue would triumph over evil, facilitated by the properly cognitive and ethical deployment of knowledge. I was not at all surprised when, in one of our myriad discussions, I learned Karl really disliked the Frankfurt School. He believed that Max Horkheimer and Theodor W. Adorno's *Dialectic of the Enlightenment*, arguably that eclectic school's signature work, was a deeply flawed and erroneous reading of the Enlightenment that could easily lead to an equally flawed and erroneous interpretation of politics.

I will never forget how we were walking back to Karl's institute in West Berlin after lunch on a bright sunny day in the early 1980s when we ran into a demonstration against the deployment of American missiles in Germany. Such demonstrations were part of German public life at the time, and nothing was particularly unique to this one. Karl was troubled, not by the demonstrators' demand that these missiles not be deployed in Germany and Europe (a wish he and I fully shared), but by their mystical signs, their invocation of the sanctity of nature, their anti-technological bent, all harkening back to a certain blood-and-soil texture Karl and I both dreaded.

Karl had nothing against the protection of nature. However, such action had to be the result of rational thinking and scientific planning based on knowledge and expertise, not on extolling the mythical past of an allegedly harmonious and blissful world. As an optimist, Karl's interest in global modeling centered on countering the Club of Rome's deep pessimism. He saw its model and interpretation as much too deterministic and argued emphatically that none of the adverse outcomes its authors envisioned was preordained. Rather, those outcomes were subject to human action, public choice, political will, and implementation, all of which depended on the enhancement of learning and knowledge and not its denial and replacement by vague emotions and fears.

My work with Karl created quite a backlash in some circles of the Center for European Studies. This was a time when being leftist and progressive entailed a deep skepticism of empiricism and a total rejection of positivism. For this academic milieu and intellectual orientation, the crunching of numbers, no matter how sophisticated the methods, was definitely not acceptable, and was spurned by the dreaded sobriquets of "positivism" or "empiricism" often accompanied by the adjective "mindless." While no one at the Center traveled down the road of deconstruction and postmodernism, which became the hegemonic epistemology dominating the discourse in so many of the humanities departments at this time, Deutschian modeling was decidedly not cool at the Center for European Studies.

Let us not forget that, for some time, parts of the Western left regarded science, facts, and empirical work as reactionary confirmations of the extant power structure, while critique and oppositional activism were accorded pride of place. Once, at a lecture in the 1980s—about the Holocaust of all things—an audience member admonished me to depart from all my *facts, facts, facts,* because they were merely different forms of interpretation, different readings, different texts, but not the truth since, in any case, truths do not exist. Only with the Republican Party's drift to the far right in the course of the 1990s and early 2000s did the rejection of facts become emblematic of the right, with the left becoming stalwart advocates of science, facts, data, and empirical reality. This would not be the only spot in which complete flips in position and character had come to inform the landscape of American politics over the past decades.

Karl and I discussed many of these matters not only in Cambridge, but also in Berlin, where, in 1977, Karl became one of the directors of the prestigious Wissenschaftszentrum Berlin (WZB)—Social Science Center Berlin—in charge of a large group of international scholars working on many aspects of global modeling. From then until 1985, when Karl retired from his professorship at Harvard, he divided his time between these two institutions, teaching the fall semester at Harvard and then spending January to August in Berlin; from 1985 until 1987, he was one of the WZB's full-time directors, though he often was not in Berlin, just as he often had not been in Cambridge. Karl loved to travel because he loved to interact with people constantly and everywhere and because he loved learning from others, regardless of their status or station. He loved learning from a freshman as much as from a Nobel laureate. Rarely did I see Karl's already sunny face become even sunnier than when he liked something I said, invariably exclaiming: "Excellent! I have to remember this!" Frighteningly, he always did.

Karl loved his experience at *Gymnasium* and thought a *Gymnasium*-style education was excellent; needless to say, I dissented vehemently. Out of such discussions arose a project: organizing a large conference on the trust in and fear of science. Held at the Aspen Institute in Berlin and co-organized with the WZB, the conference produced yet another volume that Karl and I co-edited. The book, *Fear of Science—Trust in Science: Conditions for Change in the Climate of Opinion*, highlighted the state of the debate on this crucial topic in the late 1970s. I remain proud of my work with Karl Deutsch and will never be able to express how much I learned by being part of these collaborations.

At one of my meetings with Karl at his office on Lakeview Avenue, Ruth asked me to housesit for the entire summer of 1976, when she and Karl were going to spend four months in Europe. Other than taking care of their cat—appropriately called *Katze*—I had no responsibilities apart from keeping the marvelous house intact. I already knew my father was going to visit me for longer than usual so he could experience the United States's bicentennial celebration and join me in attending the summer Olympics in Montreal. Now I knew my father would have a stately place to spend our weeks together in Cambridge.

It was one of the highlights of my father's life to find his son so welcomed by this family of Central European refugees, headed by Karl, this towering genius who had earned the world's respect. I loved seeing my father engrossed in talking theater and literature with both Deutsches, Bertolt Brecht being one of Karl's favorite authors, and my father being a huge fan of *The Threepenny Opera*. My father and the Deutsches just felt deeply comfortable with each other: same generation, same cultural background, same interests. That evening, when the Deutsches returned to their house for one brief weekend during their time in Europe, will forever bring tears to my eyes because I could tell my father knew for sure I had arrived, in terms of being safe, as well as respected by the best. When my father died in April 1990, both Karl and Ruth wrote condolence letters memorable not only for the warmth of their content, but also the style in which they were conveyed: Ruth's note on a beautiful card that, I am sure, she took great pains to find; Karl's on three legal-sized pages in the huge and distinctive handwriting whose familiarity warmed my heart.

Karl died on November 1, 1992, at his home on Lakeview Avenue, surrounded by his family. Ruth organized a testimonial for him at Harvard's Memorial Church. I was deeply touched when she asked me to be one of the four eulogists. I have since published on Karl's life and work in various encyclopedias and anthologies. I was also one of the speakers at Charles University when we dedicated a Karl W. Deutsch library, which houses Karl's vast collection of books from his offices in Cambridge and Berlin, as well as his library from Lakeview Avenue. Far and away the most unusual and innovative event in connection with my engagement with Karl's work was when the three editors of a volume called *The Return of the Theorists: Dialogues with Great Thinkers in International Relations* asked me in 2015, 23 years after Karl's death, to conduct an imaginary interview with Karl Deutsch. Some of the other greats interviewed in this volume are Thucydides, Plato, Aristotle, Machiavelli, Hobbes, Locke, Hume, Rousseau, Kant, Hegel, Marx, Weber, Nietzsche, Durkheim, Mumford, and Arendt.

My posthumous interview with Karl—which took place in his office on Lakeview Avenue—focuses on something he would have given everything to experience: the iPhone, a device held in human hands that revolutionized the reach of knowledge, of which Karl always dreamt. After discussing some of the adverse effects of new technologies, he ends our interview with the following optimistic thought: "But precisely in the aforementioned *longue durée* of things, human decency will always vanquish human turpitude."[10]

After Karl's death, Ruth remained a dear friend whom I would see whenever I happened to be in Cambridge. She got to know and adore Kiki, with whom she would talk at length about Austrian literature and Viennese theater. Ruth was our guest of honor at both our weddings, the official one on November 7, 1997, and the Jewish one on May 24, 1998.

Like Karl, Ruth had grown up in a family of the German-speaking *Bildungsbürgertum* in Prague. Her father was a civil engineer, her mother a homemaker. Ruth also had a sister, Edith. All three of her family members were murdered in Auschwitz, together with Edith's husband and their young son. In an email sent to me by the Deutsches' older daughter, Mary, responding to my request for some family information, she wrote: "My mother and father never once mentioned this. Unspeakable!" Indeed, in my lengthy association with Karl, during which we discussed virtually every nook and cranny of German politics and history, we never once discussed or even mentioned the Holocaust!

Ruth had studied German and comparative literature in Prague. She resumed this at Radcliffe, from which she was graduated in 1941. From 1944 until 1977, she taught German language and literature at Wellesley College. Between 1958 and 1967, while Karl held his professorship at Yale, Ruth taught German at the University of Bridgeport and at Southern Connecticut State College. In 1994, the Wellesley German Department named its new departmental library for Ruth Deutsch, in appreciation for her years of service and the donation of large portions of her personal library to the department and the college.

Ruth and Karl appeared to be inseparable. Their love was evident in every instance of their interaction. When I moved into their house in May 1976 to be the housesitter for the summer, I found a postcard on the

---

10 Andrei S. Markovits, "Karl W. Deutsch (1912–1992) Interviewed" in Richard Ned Lebow, Peer Schouten, Hidemi Suganami, eds., *The Return of the Theorists: Dialogues with Great Thinkers in International Relations* (New York: Palgrave Macmillan, 2016), 284.

kitchen table that Karl, who had left for Berlin before Ruth, had written to her. The card started with the obligatory "Ruth, my darling" and then went on to say how he missed her terribly even though he had been gone only a week or two. It ended saying this: "Hurry over here to brighten my life." Impressive after 39 years of marriage!

For the academic year 2002–2003, the Committee on Degrees in Social Studies at Harvard invited me to be a visiting professor. The University of Michigan kindly granted me leave to do this, even though I had only started teaching there in the fall of 1999. During our stay, Kiki and I made a point of visiting Ruth at her Brookhaven retirement home in Lexington every two weeks. Kiki and I were about to leave our Somerville apartment on a rainy afternoon to visit Ruth for dinner when the phone rang. The dean's office at the University of Michigan was calling to inform me that I was about to get an official email announcing that my college had awarded me a collegiate professorship. I accepted most gratefully, knowing this to be a great distinction. The person on the other end then told me this honor entailed my naming my own chair after a University of Michigan faculty member, current or past, to be followed by an inaugural public lecture.

On our drive to Lexington, Kiki asked me whom I would name this professorship after, and I told her that I had no idea. But once we were back in Ann Arbor in late May, I would scour the premises and find somebody who had some connection to Judaism as well as ties to Eastern Europe. Then, as we were pulling into the parking lot of the retirement home, it suddenly dawned on me that I had driven Karl to Logan Airport for his many trips to Ann Arbor, where he was working on research projects with Michigan professors. Might he have been on that university's faculty at some point? I told Ruth the good news and asked whether she remembered what Karl's affiliations were with the University of Michigan in the mid to late 1970s. Like me, she remembered the names of Karl's collaborators but not his status with the university. Later, I called my dean's office and asked whether somebody could check as to Karl W. Deutsch's affiliations with the University of Michigan in the 1970s. I also wondered what constituted Michigan faculty for this award's purpose. Reply: full faculty for at least one semester.

Three days later, I received a joyous email stating that a Karl W. Deutsch was indeed a full faculty member as a visiting professor during the fall semester of 1977. Thus, I could name my collegiate professorship after Karl W. Deutsch! Later that day, when I shared this information with folks at the Center for European Studies, all of them said my naming my chair after Karl Deutsch was fated. I called Ruth in Brookhaven. She was over the moon. Upon my return to Ann Arbor, I went to the person in the dean's office who was in charge of setting up the inaugural lecture and asked whether I might be permitted to jump the queue because I wanted a special guest, who was 91 years old, to attend this lecture. Gladly, this person replied, especially since the organizers always face the opposite problem: awardees of such professorships take their sweet time—often months and years—to give their inaugural lecture. I informed Ruth and her younger daughter, Margaret, that I would purchase first-class roundtrip tickets from Boston to Detroit for both of them and put them up at one of Ann Arbor's finest hotels because Ruth had to be here and I knew she was not going to come on her own.

And so it happened. Margaret's daughter Sophia, then living in Chicago, drove to Ann Arbor to spend the day with her mother and grandmother. All three of them had special seats in the Michigan League's Hussey Room, where this event occurred. Since then, September 2003, I have been the Karl W. Deutsch Collegiate Professor of Comparative Politics and German Studies, and with every email I send, I am reminded of Karl since his name appears in my signature. I also received the good news from our current dean that as per recent university regulations, the collegiate professor titles do not expire upon retirement, meaning I will be able to retain Karl's name attached to mine as professor emeritus thus until I die.

In March 2004, I lectured at Harvard and made sure to meet Ruth for lunch. A driver from Brookhaven dropped her off at her favorite restaurant in Harvard Square at noon sharp. I spent a delightful two hours with her, and she had a nice portion of the *cervelles* she always ate with such gusto at Sandrin's Bistro. I walked her to a cab at the taxi stand at the Kiosk in Harvard Square, paid the driver the fare, and sent her off with a big hug and a kiss to Brookhaven.

Ruth Deutsch died on September 20, 2004. On Saturday, October 2, we held a wonderful ceremony in Harvard's Memorial Church celebrating her life. Mary and Margaret asked me to be the main eulogist since, according to Mary, I had become the son Ruth never had. After the ceremony, Sam Carroll, Margaret's son, drove me from Harvard Square to Logan Airport, playing divine music he had prepared for the occasion: one of the legendary shows that the Grateful Dead played at the Music Hall in Boston in June of 1976. He had heard from his mother and aunt that I was a Deadhead, and so, to soothe my soul after his grandmother's funeral, Sam thought it appropriate to play some music that was dear to me. What a sweet gesture that was!

Thus ended my life at Harvard, which had begun on a bright September morning in 1975 with my chutzpah in thinking I could just show up on campus and work with Marty Lipset. Unlike all the other institutions with which I have been affiliated where negatives often outweighed the positives, I have never felt anything the least bit negative about my time at Harvard. No slights, no envy, no jealousies, no competition— just bliss! Marginalized in my beloved bunker in the Vanserg Building, I commenced all my future academic endeavors, be they about labor unions, social democracy, new social movements, global modeling, anti-Americanism, antisemitism, sports, and even dog rescue. The friendships, the camaraderies, the co-authorships that these years at Harvard bequeathed me will forever fill me with pride and joy.

What was the basis for this fortuitous association? Harvard became my spiritual and soulful home precisely because I had nothing to do with this institution in any formal manner. I was completely marginal to it. I was an interloper, an imposter, pure and simple, never a real member of this august university. In fact, the only time I was on its faculty was when I was visiting there from the faculty at Michigan. Nothing could have been more pronounced in its rootlessness than my association with Harvard University. Yet, precisely in this rootlessness did the place offer me a home the likes of which I will never find anywhere else in the world of the academy.

Dogs:
The Rescuer Rescues Himself

᪣

My love of animals reaches all the way back to my childhood in Timișoara, where, as will be recalled, I had a particular connection to bears. First, I had my favorite teddy bear, whom we named Dovi, which means "little bear" in Hebrew. This was the poor being that was ripped to shreds in the train at the Hungarian border when my father and I emigrated from Romania in 1958. Then there were the *Medved* chocolate bars that Josif brought me. And third, I fell in love with these animals out of my compassion and horror at their being tormented to dance and do all kinds of absurd tricks in public squares while chained through their noses—a bear's most sensitive part—to make money for their owners.

Despite this early love for animals, I can never recall asking my parents for a dog. I felt instinctively that this was out of the question because of the crowded conditions in which we lived. But I also got the sense my parents cared little for animals in general, or dogs in particular, beyond the few coloring books they had given me as a toddler. I never discussed this with my mother who died when I was not quite ten and whose illness surely would have precluded the presence of any pet. With my father, too, the topic of animals never arose, even when, a few weeks before his death in 1990, he met my dog Dovi in Cambridge. He was kind to Dovi and gentle; he tolerated Dovi; he even hugged him briefly before he departed. But I could tell he had no connection to dogs. I'm not sure he even realized the dog's name was identical to the name of the teddy bear whose historic destruction he had witnessed on the train as we left Romania. But I am fairly certain this indifference to dogs and other animals resulted from my father being Jewish and urban, two conditions which, in the history of European Jewry, have usually gone together.

While I have never come across any studies of Jews and pet guardianship (a term I much prefer to the outdated "ownership"), Orthodox Jews typically have fewer pets, dogs in particular, than do secular Jews and the general population. While certain passages in the Talmud refer to dogs as evil and others mandate that dogs be chained, a requirement confirmed by the great twelfth-century Jewish scholar Maimonides, I think the main reasons so few Jews kept animals solely for the sake of loving them are historical rather than religious. In ancient times, Jews were farmers and shepherds. In this agricultural world, all animals had a clear function, mainly transportation, protection, or nutrition. However, in Christian Europe, where Jews usually could not own land and therefore tended to live in cities, often becoming even more urbanized by being compressed into a ghetto, space was at a premium, with little room for extra living creatures beyond animals that were a source of food. Historians have demonstrated that possessing a pet solely for affective purposes presupposes a level of material comfort and social station most Jews did not attain in Europe until the late nineteenth century, if then.

Some people believe Jews came to dislike dogs by virtue of their association with their Nazi tormentors, who used these animals prolifically in the brutal treatment of their victims. Personally, I see the lack of space and material comfort as providing a much better explanation for the Jews' uneasiness with pets. Even though my secular Jewish world had little in common with that of my Orthodox coreligionists, certain strains remained common to the two communities, relations to pets being one of them.

During my Vienna years, I had two very positive encounters with dogs. The first was with Bill Gillespie's poodle, Schmutzi, who always cuddled up to me on Saturday nights when I stayed with Bill, making the evening and night there all the more special and cozy. And then there was Kiki's Mischu, who proved to be a special link in our relationship, mainly because I saw for the first time what pain the loss of such a being can inflict on a family. I encountered both Schmutzi and Mischu in my teens; my university years at Columbia and my post-doctoral years at Harvard featured no dogs whatsoever. Somehow, dogs played virtually no role in the lives of my friends, professors, or colleagues from that time.

Then, in the middle of the 1980s, I fell in love with a spunky golden retriever called Sascha who belonged to one of my colleagues at the Center for European Studies. I just loved this animal. Funny, cuddly, sweet, loyal! Every day when I saw him at the office, I laughed and delighted in petting him. I came to spend more and more time with him, walking him around the sprawling Harvard campus, often across the Charles River to the Business School. When his guardian was out of town, I took care of Sascha and occasionally kept him overnight at my place. I even harbored thoughts of stealing Sascha from his guardian, who, I came to feel more strongly every day, did not treat him with the care and love this wonderful creature deserved.

Before Sascha, it had never crossed my mind that I wanted a dog. My life was much too peripatetic and unstable to allow me to be a proper guardian to such a being. When I broached this topic with friends who were dog guardians, and who knew me and my lifestyle well, all of them dissuaded me from having a dog and said I would be downright irresponsible to get one. And yet, I could not dismiss my feelings for Sascha. By 1987, this desire became an obsession, and I was determined to prove I could be the responsible and loving guardian of a dog.

After constant nagging and nudging, I finally convinced my partner at the time, Miriam Shuchman, who loved dogs and had many of them while growing up in an enlightened American family, to get us a dog. Without any research or real preparation, we purchased a puppy from someone who had placed an ad in *The Boston Globe*. On a Saturday afternoon in the middle of December, we drove to a supermarket parking lot on Beacon Street in Somerville, paid fifty dollars in cash to some total stranger, and received a golden retriever puppy in return. Our plan was to drop off the puppy at Miriam's place and head to a movie, leaving him all by himself in a new environment. Outrageous and irresponsible, to say the least. But we simply did not know better. We had no knowledge of puppy mills, breeders, or anything relating to dogs beyond the child-like wish to "own" a golden retriever puppy. We named him Jascha—the closest we could come to Sascha and a tribute to the virtuoso Jascha Heifetz, who had died earlier that month and whose divine sounds on the violin we both adored. Thankfully, on the way home to Miriam's place, we decided to forgo the movie, which, in retrospect, was my first vaguely responsible act in this sorry affair.

Contrast this to two years later, when my relationship with Miriam ended, she departed for her position as an assistant professor of psychiatry at Dartmouth's medical school, and Jascha exited from my life. Upon hearing I wanted an adult dog, Jascha's veterinarian mentioned something called Yankee Golden Retriever Rescue. He knew little about this organization, but referred me to one of the fliers he had hanging in his clinic's waiting room. I read it and could not believe my eyes. One needed to fill out a lengthy application, then wait to be approved based on the content of this application—not to receive a dog, but to be accorded a home visit to ascertain whether the premises were to the group's liking. If approved—and approval was by no means certain—one then had to travel to a kennel in New Hampshire to meet the dog that the organization believed to be the best fit for the applicant. Even stranger, one could visit this kennel—a two-hour drive from Boston—only on Saturday mornings, since the breeder, who, solely by the grace of her heart, fostered these rescue dogs, could accommodate potential adopters only on that day.

But I persevered and eventually passed the arduous audition. The length of time involved and the obvious seriousness of the application process not only helped the organization get a good idea of who I was but also forced me to engage with the changes this new relationship would bring to my life. I purchased the best leash, the snazziest bowls, the most expensive food the local convenience store carried. (Years would pass before Kiki insisted I replace this low-grade fare with the healthy, home-cooked diet our dogs now receive. But I did not know any better then.) I read about dogs, golden retrievers in particular. I even hired a canine specialist to advise me as to what I should and should not do with an adult dog who was going to share its life with me.

At last, I met Brandi, an eight-year-old "owner turn-in" from Connecticut who had been spending his days alone because his owner had gotten divorced and needed to travel for his new job. He was Yankee Golden Retriever Rescue's 548th rescue (the organization is up to 6,000-plus rescues by now). I renamed Brandi in honor of my beloved teddy bear, and Dovi became my constant companion until December 1996, when he died at the ripe old age of nearly 16 in Santa Cruz, California. He traveled with me everywhere, from coast to coast, repeatedly, to Vienna via the Concorde, and I never left his side. Until Harvard banned dogs from its premises, Dovi was the Center for European Studies' mascot. When Kiki and I reconnected after 23 years apart, I am convinced she took to me once again because she fell in love with Dovi the instant she entered my condominium in Cambridge.

In barely two years, my relationship to animals had changed completely. Miriam and I had acquired Jascha to be our dog; I adopted Dovi to become my family member. This difference in mindset formed the core of what 25 years later became my award-winning book *From Property to Family: American Dog Rescue and the Discourse of Compassion*. In the wake of the considerable cultural and social shifts the United States and all advanced industrial democracies have experienced since the late 1960s and early 1970s, discourse around the disempowered has changed demonstrably. In *From Property to Family,* which I co-authored with my former undergraduate student Katherine Crosby, we describe a "discourse of compassion" that alters the way we treat persons and ideas once scorned by the social mainstream. This cultural turn also has affected our treatment of animals; in the case of dogs, this shift has increasingly transformed the discursive category of the animal from human companion to family member. One of the new institutions created by this attitudinal and behavioral change has been the breed-specific canine rescue organization, examples of which have arisen all over the United States, beginning in the early 1980s and proliferating throughout the 1990s and subsequent years.

The breed-specific rescue world is almost completely run by women. I did not encounter one man in the lengthy process of adopting Dovi or any of his successors, whether in Massachusetts, California, or Michigan.

Whereas veterinary medicine was heavily male until the middle 1970s, the field has become heavily female since then. The linkage between women and animals reaches deep into history with both groups often abused by the dominant patriarchy. The book highlights how women who do not perceive themselves as politically active or radical in any way have embraced the advocacy and protection of needy animals, in this case homeless breed-specific dogs, for whom they work tirelessly, performing amazing feats for no remuneration. Breed-specific rescue represents a tiny segment of the discourse of compassion and inclusion that became so salient with the movements of the late 1960s and early 1970s in all advanced industrial societies featuring liberal democratic polities.

The link between my interest in global politics and my involvement in the world of dog rescue is not an accident. The most salient factors in my life-long quest to find a home for myself have been my search for people and places who embody the qualities of compassion, generosity, and open-heartedness. These, more than erudition, intelligence, education, or accomplishments, have been the defining characteristics of the folks who became my favorite friends, colleagues, mentors, students, musicians, and trade union leaders.

Dogs in need—as all rescue dogs are—require compassion, generosity, and open-heartedness on the part of their rescuers if they are to have any chance of survival. The rescuer's motives are purely compassionate, since he or she derives no material gain from rescuing such a needy being and incurs lots of monetary costs and anxiety. But in the giving one also receives. And the love that I have received from these blessed souls has been immeasurable. Without Dovi, my relationship with Kiki would not have blossomed into the blissful marriage we have enjoyed for nearly 25 years.

Dovi transformed my elegant but cold condominium in Cambridge into a warm home that welcomed Kiki. I was a restless being before Dovi entered my life, professionally successful but unmoored. His presence gave me a home even in Santa Cruz, where I rented furniture and cutlery as a clear sign of not wanting to be there. But Dovi's constant presence in Cambridge, in Santa Cruz, in Vienna calmed me and gave me a serenity I had never before experienced. Without this serenity, I am sure I would not have been able to enter into a committed relationship with Kiki, which would have meant I was going to lose yet another wonderful woman as a partner and a spouse.

Animal welfare and dog rescue form a core identity Kiki and I share deeply and that is central to our love for each other. Since Dovi's death, we have adopted six other goldens, all from rescue organizations, with one exception: our current golden, Emma, having been a service dog in Alabama, hails—incredibly—from a breeder in Timişoara! What are the odds of that? But that is a whole other story!

Kiki and I are aware that our love for these divine beings would have been different had we been parents of human children, but surely that love would not have been less. Our dogs' well-being forms a central part of our daily lives. More important, our love for these goldens has enhanced our love for each other and created a common understanding we otherwise would not have enjoyed. We make serious donations to animal shelters and canine rescue groups across the country and have arranged vacations to visit these organizations, none more enthusiastically than Best Friends Animal Sanctuary in Kanab, Utah. Our shared affection for animals is every bit as salient and defining of our relationship as being Jewish and sharing Vienna in our past. However, while the latter are sources not only of mutual understanding and comfort, but also tension and disagreement, our shared love for goldens is a source of pure bliss—no tension, no second thoughts, no questioning, no regrets!

I would take this a step further. I am convinced I owe the proliferation of my professional output to Dovi and his successors, which is why I have thanked my golden retrievers in every one of my books and even some articles. Every idea for every new project—and every intellectual step necessary to implementing every project—has happened on my lengthy walks with my goldens, whether on a beach, in a forest, or on a city's streets. Since Dovi arrived in my life, I have never felt alone or lonely, which I clearly was before. So even though I have been the one who has given many dogs a loving "forever home," they were the ones who gave me a home with their love, their kindness, their compassion.

I always tell Kiki that, if there is an afterlife, I would love to meet all of my departed goldens and run around with them in some beautiful meadow. While this may be wishful thinking, I am convinced Bodhisattvas, such as these creatures were, have reached Nirvana and frolic in it. Then again, don't Bodhisattvas forego this bliss precisely to deploy their boundless compassion to lessen the pain of the needy? The goldens who have enriched my life very much fit this mold, which has always saddened me because at least once in their existence I want them to get more from me than I have gained from them.

Germany:
Admiration for the *Bundesrepublik*,
Discomfort with *Deutschland*

German was my second mother-tongue, next to Hungarian. The latter disappeared from my life with the death of my father in 1990, most certainly since the passing of my aunt Manci in 1994; the former continues its powerful daily presence by virtue of my speaking it with my wife, Kiki. I am fine with the German language but for one crucial drawback: its inevitable connection to Germany. Why can't the Greeks speak German? Or the Swedes? Or the Canadians? Or—the Jews?

Wait a minute. The Central European Jewish bourgeoisie did, in fact, make German its language of choice, beginning in the late eighteenth century, with the Jewish masses farther to the east speaking a German-related language called Yiddish. The point is that German, the language, had absolutely nothing to do with Germany the country for me in my years growing up in Timişoara and becoming schooled in the beauty of this language, its poetry, and its literature.

I might be forgiven as a professor of German politics if I claim that Germany has been Europe's most important country all through the continent's past one thousand years and remains so to this day, even if many of its elites—particularly of the left-liberal variety—do not admit to this and find the truth troubling. That reality makes the current incarnation of Germany—the *Bundesrepublik Deutschland*—exceptional in that its discomfort with power hails from Germany's troubled history, which arises from its position as Europe's most important country—a country that always envied the power of others and believed the power it had was not commensurate with its importance. In a way, Germany's problem with power continues. If, in the course of the nineteenth and the first half of the twentieth centuries, Germany's power-envy brought Europe two world wars, its current possession of power leaves German elites unable and unwilling to handle that power properly and with confidence, precisely because the country's former reach for power had such dire consequences, not only for Europe as a whole but for Germany itself.

Most political scientists believe their country of expertise to be more important than it actually is. But I can't help thinking my claim about Germany's position in Europe is correct. After all, the other major players—Britain, France, Spain, the Ottoman Empire, Russia, Italy—are either too peripheral geographically or, because of that physical distance, engaged in matters much less relevant to Europe's development. Britain, as evidenced by Brexit, does not see itself as part of Europe. (I have always been startled to realize that when Brits talk about Europe, they mean the Continent, never Britain. As my dear friend, the venerable don Peter Pulzer, told me as we dined at a nice Oxford restaurant, where I had taken him to celebrate his ninetieth birthday in May 2019: "Only the waiters and waitresses from Poland and Romania feel European here, none of the English patrons do!")

France most certainly does see itself as part of Europe, but its location on the Atlantic and its active colonial past have rendered its actions less salient to Europe's overall development, even if the French might not like to hear this. Ditto Spain, which became a European player only by reason of the German house of Habsburg ruling it while reigning over German lands. The Ottoman Empire played a crucial role in the heart of Europe, but only by dint of its showdowns and clashes with those German lands that had become defenders of European Christendom against the Muslim challengers from the east.

Twice—in 1529 and 1683—the Turks were rebuffed at the gates of Vienna, dashing their ambitions to rule Europe. Russia played an important role in Europe on a number of occasions in the nineteenth century and, as the Soviet Union, in the twentieth, but on the whole it remained peripheral to the European continent's development. Italy, via the Catholic Church, housed the most significant European player next to Germany, with the two parties often engaged in bitter conflict. (The Protestant Reformation, anyone? And the ensuing Counterreformation, mostly fought on German lands?) But Italy, apart from its culture and history, had no political impact on Europe.

Europe's unsettled history cannot be separated from Germany's thousand-year struggle to make its state and nation-building less fraught than it actually became. This struggle was at the heart of the "German Question": Germany's restlessness in its failure to create a potent state that also might accord the German nation a unified home. Germany was a kaleidoscope of independent states vaguely held together by a crazy entity called the "Holy Roman Empire of the German Nation," which actually torpedoed the goal of creating a viable central polity and instead specialized in exporting its aristocracies to become kings and queens of other European countries.

The search for unity—that is, the full congruency between state and nation—did not come about until October 3, 1990, when the former German Democratic Republic ceased to exist and the Federal Republic of Germany became the sole political entity to govern the German people. Until then, it was never clear what state one had in mind when one said "Germany." East Germany? West Germany? Habsburg Germany? Hohenzollern Germany? Nazi Germany? What on earth was Germany? Where was Germany? Who was Germany? Not until thirty years ago did this question receive a final answer. In terms of world history, 1990 was two seconds ago! No more irredentism, no more "*heim ins Reich*" for Austrians wanting to join Germany, no more Germans living all over Europe with ambiguous feelings for their home state and Germany. The German Question met its definitive answer on October 3, 1990! No more uncertainty, no more restlessness! End of story!

This relentless restlessness, this inability to make state and nation-building coincide, lay at the heart of Hitler's rise to power and the creation of the Third Reich. Remember that immensely appealing slogan to a frustrated nation after the Paris Peace conferences: "*Ein Volk, ein Reich, ein Führer!*" Hitler promised to achieve what a thousand years of German history could not. In so doing, he ruined Europe and killed millions upon millions of people including six million Jews.

I will never forget a meeting at the Center for European Studies at Harvard sometime in the 1980s, when a bunch of us started telling each other why we had decided to study the country we had. The answers for France, Italy, Sweden, and Spain included a wonderful high school teacher instilling a love of the language, a trip abroad one summer, an enthrallment with a nation's magnificent scenery, its fantastic wines, its stunning cities, its poetry, its opera. In the case of the Germanists among us, we revealed that a variation of the "German Question" had led us to study this land, its history, and its politics. We all had chosen Germany as an object of study, not for its beauty and serenity, nor its music, nor its poetry—all of which it possesses in abundance—but for its deep troubles, which had caused so much pain for its European neighbors, not to mention the sorrows that Germany had imposed on some of the families among us. Whenever I ponder why I became a German specialist, I remember Karl Deutsch's dictum about the tasks of political and social science: "Andy, remember that we social scientists ought to be like pathologists, always studying illness and disease, never beauty and harmony." For an American Jewish professor with my European roots, Germany's troubled past, which manifested itself so lethally in the Shoah, was a natural choice for a career.

In calculating Germany's importance to the rest of Europe, we must also take into account the exculpating construct of the *Bundesrepublik*, that bastion of liberal democratic virtue that finally arrived on the scene in 1949 to defang the horrible history of *Deutschland's* quest for power and glory, its domination of all Germans within the borders of one state, and that state's subsequent hegemony over the rest of Europe. Though imposed by the Western victors over the Nazis and initially perceived by most Germans as a foreign occupation, the *Bundesrepublik* eventually became the hallmark of a new Germany by delivering economic successes of unparalleled dimensions and a lasting peace to an integrated Europe. Above all, this new state offered stability and a rule of law within a liberal democratic order the likes of which Germany had never seen.

It was this Federal Republic of Germany—this Western, moderate, and in some ways quite modest, even boring, incarnation of Germany—that came to play such a profoundly beneficial role on the European continent. Far from its former disruptive and intimidating tendencies, the new Germany exuded an aura of comfort rather than threat, of ordinariness rather than ecstasy.

And yet, as important as Germany has long been to Europe, Germany as a country did not become real for me until 1966, at the earliest. Of course, plenty of Germans populated my life in Timişoara. I was surrounded by human beings who spoke German and were of German descent. However, virtually nobody called them Germans, but rather Swabians, an erroneous assignation, as this group of German settlers hailed from every part of the German empire *except* Swabia. And lurking in the shadows were the Germans I never saw, the phantom Germans, the Germans who had done horrible things to my family before I was born, the Germans who made my aunt Manci scream for her mother when I spent the night there, the Germans about whom my mother and father told me virtually nothing.

But "Germany" as a country didn't appear in my life until the German soccer team confronted the sensational Hungarian "golden team" in the World Cup final on July 4, 1954, at the Wankdorf Stadium in Berne, Switzerland. As discussed in the introductory chapter, this match became a crucial marker in my life by dint of my father making clear that he hated both countries these teams represented. All that mattered to us, my father stated clearly, was that this match occurred on the Fourth of July, the birthday of the United States of America. Here was a young father and his little boy rooting against the two teams whose native tongues were the same two languages the father and son constantly spoke and lovingly shared! What a telling picture of post-Shoah Jewry in Central Europe!

Germany then disappeared from my life for a dozen years both in Romania and in Vienna. Now and then, my father and aunt would erroneously call the Austrians "Germans," especially during sporting competitions when my father cheered for Austria's opponents to defeat the home team. Once, in the early 1960s, my father and I went to see the

Austrian national soccer team play the Soviet Union in Vienna's famed Prater Stadium. We were sitting so close together in this crowded arena that our bodies touched. When the Soviet team scored a goal, I could feel my father's body tense up, ready to jump for joy, a move he wisely aborted. Wow, I thought, this man's hatred for Austrians and Germans must run deep if he is secretly rooting for the Soviet Union, a place he detests by virtue of its communism, its Stalinism, its illiberal traditions, its gulag, and its historic pogroms against the Jews.

My Encounters with the Bundesrepublik: From College Entrance Exams in 1966 to Academic Researcher in the Late 1970s

In Vienna, I also encountered the *Bundesrepublik* side of Germany in the form of the monthly checks my aunt and uncle received from the Federal Republic of Germany's government as reparations for the horrors the Germans had inflicted on them during the Shoah. Lest I paint too rosy a picture, my aunt and uncle had an extremely difficult time convincing the German authorities that the two of them were legitimate recipients of these payments. They faced obstacle upon obstacle, mostly in the form of endless documents they were required to muster, many of which they did not possess because they needed to flee Romania with two suitcases per person, a journey which did not allow them to transport obscure documents to an uncertain future. Then they needed to fill out all these documents and have them notarized by the only notary in Vienna accredited to do so for this particular purpose by the consulate general of the Federal Republic. Then came the final interview, which, especially for my uncle, was deeply humiliating, since the German official all but accused him of extorting the German taxpayer with the guilt my uncle's alleged suffering had unjustly caused the German people.

The sums my aunt and uncle received were woefully inadequate restitution for their brutalization. Still, here was a regime ruling the western part of Germany that wanted to atone for the crimes committed in Germany's name by the preceding generation. I found this commendable on many levels, even though no form of atonement, no sum of money, was close to appropriate, given the crimes the Nazis committed in Germany's name against many peoples, first and foremost the Jews.

The *Bundesrepublik's* attempts deserved praise, especially in light of the passivity of the other two successor states to the Nazi regime, the Republic of Austria and the German Democratic Republic (East Germany), who did nothing of the sort. In fact, the GDR vigorously participated in the communist world's openly antisemitic propaganda which appeared with alarming regularity. East Germany also engaged in diplomatic endeavors designed to weaken, perhaps even eliminate, the state of Israel. Austria used the cover of having been the first victim of Nazi Germany's expansion in 1938 to good use not to confront its own complicity with the Third Reich until the 1980s. And consider Japan, the country that truly started the Second World War with its attack on China on July 7, 1937 (the conventionally accepted date of September 1, 1939—Nazi Germany's attack on Poland—has always struck me as Eurocentric).

Despite its brutal occupations of many East Asian countries and its enslavement of thousands of young Koreans—the so-called "comfort women"—for the sexual pleasure of the Japanese army, Japan did not engage in any restitutive measures until recently. Of course, unlike Germany, Japan was also a victim of the nuclear devastation of its people, which no other nation on earth has endured. But a German counterpart to the Japanese leadership's formerly regular visits to the Yasukuni Shrine, which honors some of Japan's most brutal war criminals, would be unthinkable in the Federal Republic of Germany, not least because no equivalent shrine was ever built in Germany, precisely lest such pilgrimages occur.

Finally, let us not forget that Willy Brandt spontaneously dropping to his knees on December 7, 1970, before the monument of the Warsaw Ghetto Uprising of 1943 still represents the only such act of contrition expressed by a head of government for the wrongs committed in her or his country's name. Yes, certain meek apologies have since been uttered by Jacques Chirac, Bill Clinton, Barack Obama, and Shinzo Abe to various victims of their countries' wrongs. But none have come close to Brandt's gesture, which, though extreme, was very much in line with the *Bundesrepublik's* policy of contrition, and had as its precursor the Adenauer governments' reparation to the Jews in the 1950s.

And yet, even with my aunt and uncle receiving reparations for what they had suffered in the Holocaust, I did not encounter the concrete entity of Germany until the fall of 1966, when I needed to take the Scholastic Aptitude Test and three advanced achievement tests in order to apply to universities in the United States. At the time, the SAT was not available anywhere in Austria. But my father and I unearthed the possibility of taking these tests on a United States army base near Munich, the closest location to Vienna we could find. Unlike Austrian citizens, who could travel unencumbered to Germany, my father and I had to obtain German entry visas since we were both stateless, a status manifestly featured in our passports labeled "Fremdenpass" (alien passport) instead of being real passports denoting full membership called "citizenship" in an actual country. Acquiring these two travel documents took effort and time, but eventually we traveled to Munich, arriving on a Friday evening so we could get to the army base first thing Saturday morning for the exams.

It was raining terribly when the taxi pulled up at our small hotel, which was not far from the base, but outside Munich proper. The next morning, we arrived at the base, produced the documents that indicated the reason we were there, and were directed to a large hall full of desks. An official detained my father from entering, but my father gave me some German marks in notes and coins, which he had converted from our Austrian schillings the previous night at the hotel. Much more importantly, my father also gave me a bunch of Dixon Number 2 yellow pencils that he exerted much energy to obtain for me in Vienna, where such items were not readily available, so that I could take the SAT. I then entered this large hall full of scared youngsters ready to tackle the test that was to influence, if not determine, their future lives.

When lunchtime arrived, I proceeded to the mess hall to get some food. "Sorry," I was told, "we don't take German money, only United States currency." My father had forgotten that this was de facto United States territory! I ran to the vending machines I saw in the distance, but only US coins were operational. Needless to say, by the time the third achievement test rolled around in the late afternoon—the exam on world history—I was famished. My scores were passable—good enough so that Columbia accepted me—but I will always wonder how I would have performed had I been properly fed that day.

My father and I returned to Vienna that night, and Germany once again disappeared from my world. To my Jewish circle in Vienna, Germany simply did not exist. Folks vacationed in Italy, in Greece, in Spain, at camps in England or in France, never in Germany. I spent summers with my uncle in New York City. True, all boys—Jewish ones included—read Karl May books, which came from Germany, and many of the popular TV series we watched were produced in Germany. But Germany did not register in our consciousness as an actual place, inhabited by people who might have done serious harm to our parents, grandparents, and other relatives.

Kiki was typical of this milieu's relation to Germany in that she did not visit that country until January 1992, when she was 42 years old, and I invited her to join me at a conference in Hamburg. That a Jewish person had to live in Austria was bad enough—one could not help being born there because one's parents had gotten stuck on their way to someplace else. But why purposely go to Germany, which was neither sunnier, prettier, nor more exotic than Austria—and an equal perpetrator of the Holocaust? To Viennese Jews of my generation, Germany was like Austria, except with a harsher accent in its spoken German that grated on Jewish ears just like on Gentile ones in Austria. Germany had only downsides, no upsides whatsoever.

In the spring of 1974, I attended a lecture or two on German social theory delivered by Wolf-Dieter Narr, a young political science professor visiting Columbia from his permanent position at the Free University in Berlin. Though far too abstract, his lecture on Weber was sufficiently intriguing that I paid Narr a visit during his office hours. He was happy to see me, and happier still when I switched from English to German because, as he correctly said, his English was not up to the level of discussing the complexities of Weber in a proper manner. But his greatest satisfaction came from hearing my perfect German delivered with the profound lilt of a Viennese intonation (though not the patois of Viennese German).

We met a number of times in New York that spring, and Wolf-Dieter became the first German I actually got to know (he was not only my first German, but my first bona fide Swabian, since Wolf-Dieter hailed from the state of Baden-Wuerttemberg near Stuttgart, Swabia's heartland, and spoke German with a heavy Swabian accent). At dinner at—where else?—Tom's Restaurant, I was introduced to the immensely complex emotional issues and contradictory sensibilities I later came to recognize among Germans of my age and social standing, the so-called *Achtundsechziger*, or "Sixty-Eighters." Many of these Germans exhibited the sensibilities of the *Bundesrepublik*, a categorization most of them would disdain since, unlike me, none of them would differentiate so cavalierly between the virtuous *Bundesrepublik* and the evil *Deutschland*, seeing the latter as still dominating the former with the *Bundesrepublik* undeserving of any praise whatsoever.

Never having met a Jew, Wolf-Dieter became very moved when I told him that I was Jewish and recounted the bare contours of my history and my parents' losses in the Holocaust. Until that evening, I was simply some American kid who happened to have learned perfect German in Vienna, which explained the much-admired Viennese-accented German. I sensed that Wolf-Dieter's empathetic reaction originated in something deeply personal, because it went way beyond the usual soothing words one utters upon hearing a friend describe his difficult childhood or his family's suffering. He hinted at something in his own family history that he dreaded, something that made him unbearably ashamed.

Only in the late 1980s, or even the 1990s, did I find out through friends in Berlin that Wolf-Dieter's father was a sufficiently high functionary in the Third Reich and a sufficiently committed Nazi that he needed to go into hiding for several years after the war to escape prosecution. Wolf-Dieter, who had been eight when the war ended, must have experienced his father's attempt to evade punishment for his crimes. I never researched the veracity of this story, because his father's behavior was completely irrelevant to my high regard for Wolf-Dieter's integrity and his deep anti-Nazi positions. But it was through Wolf-Dieter Narr that I came to observe firsthand the immense torment and division between Germans of my generation and their parents, fathers in particular. Not by chance would I argue in some of my scholarly work on the German Left that the Sixty-Eighters created a generation gap within the liberal democratic left in every country of the advanced capitalist world, a gap that, in its German manifestation, was much more profound than anywhere else. I called it the "Holocaust effect."

Gratefully, Wolf-Dieter and I also bonded over soccer. With the World Cup to be played in Germany in June, Wolf-Dieter invited me to visit him in Berlin, visit his institute at the Free University, and possibly attend a game or two at the stadium where Adolf Hitler watched Jesse Owens's victories with fury and disgust during the 1936 Olympics documented by Leni Riefenstahl. I accepted Wolf-Dieter's offer and spent one week in his spacious apartment full of books. I slept in his study, which was adorned with three huge posters: one of Karl Marx and two of Bobby Orr, the great Boston Bruins defenseman who helped his team win the Stanley Cup in 1970 after a long drought. One of Wolf-Dieter's posters showed Bobby Orr scoring his Stanley Cup-winning goal while flying through the air, completely horizontal, perhaps the best-known photograph in NHL history. Wolf-Dieter had fallen in love with the Bruins, Orr in particular, during his year at Harvard as a John F. Kennedy Fellow—a program whose recipients, thanks to Guido Goldman, I was to chaperone for two decades, beginning two years later.

I went to World Cup games in the evening, but during the day I took in the sights of Berlin, which included a visit to the wall separating the city into East and West. I found the wall—and the idea behind it—horrendous, and was surprised how many left-leaning intellectuals had come to accept this shameful edifice as part of West Berlin's daily life in the 13 years since its erection. I was particularly astonished that neither Wolf-Dieter nor any of his friends, colleagues, or doctoral students seemed the least bit bothered by the wall. Moreover, they seemed to know next to nothing, and cared even less, about the people on the eastern side of the wall or the regime that built it. This willful silence, this studied ignorance about the German Democratic Republic and its dictatorial ways, was a key part of the *Bundesrepublikan* discourse and mindset that I came to observe in subsequent years.

Through Wolf-Dieter, I met Volker Bahl and his wife, Angelika Bahl-Benker, both graduate students at the Free University's Department of Political Science, with Volker about to complete his dissertation under Wolf-Dieter's supervision. Volker and Angelika became dear friends and have stayed so until today. Alas, my relationship with Wolf-Dieter disintegrated in the 1980s. My work on German trade unions and my moderate political stance on various issues central to the left came to bother him. He saw the unions as much too meek and compliant concerning capitalism and viewed them as eager partners in a corporatist relationship with capital. This construct was to form the famed *Modell Deutschland* of the Social Democrats whom Wolf-Dieter hated even more.

Above all, I did not oppose and criticize the *Bundesrepublik* to his sufficient liking and resisted any attempts to call it fascist and a continuation of Nazi rule. For Wolf-Dieter Narr, Andy Markovits was not sufficiently radical. Later, when I got to know Joschka Fischer, the leader of the Green Party and subsequent foreign minister of the Federal Republic, Wolf-Dieter's enmity toward me was complete. He hated Fischer, whom he insisted on calling the formal "Josef" instead of the Hungarian diminutive "Joschka," lest Fischer be accorded a pass of cuteness and endearment for policies Wolf-Dieter deemed traitorous to the Left.

I must say I always will hold it to Wolf-Dieter's credit that I never saw his name on any of the lists that attacked Israel or me, or in any of the numerous public controversies that involved what I came to call "the thing," a noxious and indeterminate but clearly discernable amalgam of antisemitism, anti-Israelism, anti-Americanism, German nationalism, Nazism, and anti-Westernism, to name only its main ingredients. Jews in some fashion were at its core. "The thing" never disappeared from my involvement with anything related to Germany—so much so that by the early 2000s, I refused to enter these never-ending debates and withdrew from my role as a public intellectual. *No mas*, as Roberto Duran so memorably stated in Round Eight of his bout with Sugar Ray Leonard as he exited the ring in the midst of a fight.

Enough for me with these endless debates. My exit annoyed many of my German friends and allies who valued my voice and commitment to their battles. Some have never forgiven me for abandoning my commitment to the fights involving "the thing" and replacing it with research on topics which my erstwhile German friends and allies found meaningless and frivolous, such as women in sports, Jewish students at the University of Michigan in the first half of the twentieth century, and—worst of all—dog rescue. How could these compare to controversies about renewed German antisemitism or debates about how deep the *Bundesrepublik*'s acceptance of Western values has reached, or what the relationship between leftwing radicalism and German nationalism might be?

In these battles, they thought, Andy Markovits was one of our most important allies and strongest voices. Now he is messing about with dog rescue and women's soccer? Very sad! Kiki forbade me to engage in these continued controversies because, as she insisted, "the thing" was unresolvable and not good for my health. And she had it right on both counts!

At the end of my stay in Berlin, I traveled with my father to Munich to attend the World Cup final between host Germany and neighboring Holland. My father and I desperately wanted Germany to lose, as we had in 1954, the last time the team was in a World Cup final, when we were glued to our Blaupunkt radio in Timişoara. But unlike the finals in 1954, when we did not want the Hungarians to prevail, this time we adored the Dutch, not least because of the sensational display of their offensive soccer skills, honed by their ingenious coach, Rinus Michels. For me, there was an additional reason to love the Dutch team. Its players, with their long hair, the relaxed manner in which they stood for the national anthems, and their habit of smoking marijuana, embodied the counterculture, all in contrast to the utterly disciplined German team.

The Dutch also featured the one and only Johan Cruyff, superstar of Ajax Amsterdam and an avowed friend of the Jews and other minorities, even back then, when soccer was so *völkisch* and racist—characteristics, alas, that it has yet to shed in full on the fans' side half a century later. The Dutch embodied this liberal spirit to such a degree that I learned from a number of my German *bundesrepublikan* friends that they, too, were rooting for the Dutch against their own national team because the Dutch were so cool and such pronounced exponents of the counterculture. This admiration for the Dutch team and its players by German countercultural intellectuals also manifested itself in a rejection of any hint of nationalism, German nationalism in particular. Sadly, the Germans won the match and attained their second world title, with the Dutch yet to win one to this day.

The Dutch team's loss to Germany added to my already negative associations with Munich, rendering this otherwise beautiful city so deeply fraught for me. Munich was the hub of the *Bewegung* immediately after World War I—the city in whose beerhalls Hitler and his SA thugs made their first public appearance. Munich was the city in which, on November 9, 1923, Hitler and his cronies, aided by reactionary military leaders such as Erich Ludendorff, tried to topple the Weimar Republic in a coup that has come to be known as the Beer Hall Putsch. Their putsch failed, but Hitler soon emerged strengthened and more determined than ever to attain power using legitimate institutional means, such as electoral victories, rather than putsches that were doomed to fail. Hitler turned the courtroom where he was convicted into a powerful pulpit from which he could delegitimize the institutions of the Weimar Republic. He went to jail in Landsberg a hero and used his incarceration there to write his infamous *Mein Kampf.*

Munich also became the location where France and Britain caved in to Hitler at a time when resisting his expansions could, and would, have succeeded due to their military superiority over Germany at the time. But Hitler's coaxing and bullying in Munich prevailed, leading to the destruction of Czechoslovakia, Central Europe's only functioning liberal democracy. This historical event has edged "Munich" into the lexicon of global politics, where it stands for the phenomenon of acceding to a dictator's bluster and bullying in lieu of standing up to and fighting him if necessary.

At a more personal level, Munich is the location where a soccer team that had caught my imagination in far-away Timişoara was all but destroyed in a terrible plane crash. On February 6, 1958, the so-called "Busby Babes"—the fabulous Manchester United team full of very young players (hence the name) coached by Sir Matt Busby—crashed on a snowy runway in Munich-Riem airport while carrying the team home to Manchester after a game in Belgrade. Twenty-three of the forty-four passengers died, some of the team's star players among them. I heard about the crash on Radio Budapest back in Timișoara, and immediately cemented my emotional bond with this team. This relationship constitutes the deepest love affair among all my sports affinities, preceding and superseding my affection for the New York Yankees and New York Knicks. I have paid my respects to the monument commemorating this tragedy both in Munich and at Old Trafford, United's legendary home field, where the loss is beautifully memorialized. Once in my life I hope to be present at Old Trafford on a February 6, when, at 3:04 p.m. Greenwich Mean Time, the time of the crash in Munich, fans gather to remember the team and share their grief. Finally, Munich remains infamous for me as the location where the actions by Palestinian terrorists led to the murder of 11 Israeli athletes during the Olympics of 1972.

During this first stay in Germany in the summer of 1974, I came to notice something that would forever play a role in my relationship with Germans. Everyone, particularly in Berlin, went gaga over my Viennese-inflected German. (This was not the case in Munich, where Bavarian-accented German sounds similar to Austrian-accented German, rendering a Viennese pronunciation less exotic.) But the same folks in Berlin (and everywhere in Germany north of the Main River) who adore Viennese-accented German (please note: I mean high German spoken by a Viennese, not Viennese dialect or patois, which is perceived as low class and would not be understood in the first place) completely disdain Bavarian-accented German, even though the phonetic difference between Bavarian-accented and Viennese-accented German is marginal. But we all know that margins count, especially as regards cultural markers that signify social standing, geographic origin, and other key ingredients by which people gauge others. The vast majority of Germans perceive Bavarian German as uncouth and provincial, whereas they experience Viennese-accented German as elegant, old-worldish, romantic, sophisticated, and utterly charming.

Germans react to Viennese-inflected German the way Americans react to British-accented English: with awe, viewing it as superior to their own diction and far more sophisticated. I have always found it fascinating that the obverse does not pertain. Brits find American accents inferior and never worthy of imitation, with the exception of the world of rock and country music, which actually reinforces American English's lack of sophistication in British eyes. And Austrians disdain the Germans' diction as harsh, mechanical, not mellifluous, inelegant, and lacking in any charm. They call it derisively *piefkisch*, which is the adjectival word for *Piefke*, a slightly pejorative Austrian term for Germans. The word's origins say it all: Johann Gottfried Piefke was a Prussian bandleader and composer of military music who composed, among other martial hymns, the *Königgrätzer Marsch*, glorifying the Prussians' decisive defeat over the Austrians in the Battle of Königgrätz in 1866. This led to the expulsion of Austria from the German Federation and Germany's unification under Prussia in 1871, constituting the so-called Second Reich. Piefke apparently not only sounded the part, he even looked like the prototypical Prussian officer.

In the late 1990s, during our stay in Berlin, Kiki came home from the market with some extra tomatoes. "I got these because I said *Paradeiser* [the Viennese word for tomatoes] instead of *Tomaten* [the German word for tomatoes], and the salespeople went nuts." Another time, she arrived with an extra container of cottage cheese because she said *Topfen* instead of *Quark*; free rolls appeared with some frequency because she said *Semmeln* instead of *Brötchen*. Kiki received these extra goodies solely because she spoke with an accent the clerks at the market found classy, cultured, charming, and cute.

The good-natured but insidious and deeply *völkisch* dimension of this phenomenon also manifested itself when Kiki went to get her hair done in Berlin. Kiki is of dark complexion and had jet-black hair at the time. When she began to tell the stylist what she wanted done, the stylist exclaimed: "Oh goodness, I love your accent! And thank God you are Viennese! I already feared that you were a foreigner." When Kiki replied that last time she looked, Vienna was not in Germany, which, in fact, did make her a foreigner, the stylist said: "No, I mean a real foreigner. As a Viennese, you are one of us, except cuter and much more charming." In a similar vein, a world-famous German physicist and his wife often made it a point to sit next to Kiki and me on Thursday evenings—family night—at the *Wissenschaftskolleg* just so they could delight in hearing Kiki and me speak. And right on cue, as I was proofreading this manuscript, I received an email from a German friend, eminent professor of philosophy, who—in a context totally unrelated to me—extolled the virtues of what to him constitute the two most beautiful languages in the world: French and Viennese-accented German.

Rendering my Viennese-inflected German even more potent was the fact that it emerged as a complete surprise to my interlocutors: "Hold it, I thought you were an American, but you are not. You are a charming Viennese. What is going on here?" When I responded that I was indeed an American who happened to learn his German in Vienna, invariably the response was: "You might be carrying an American passport, but that does not make you American. You are a Viennese. End of story!"

This response will forever send my blood boiling, but nowhere more acutely than in Germany and—worst of all—among German leftists. Hello? How deeply does your *völkisch* definition of citizenship and belonging go? Accent over passport? This essentialist, rather than civic, categorization of belonging remained paramount and virtually unchallenged in Germany, even among the country's leftists, until the advent of the Greens in the Bundestag in the late 1990s and Jürgen Habermas's crucial exhortation in favor of what he so rightly called "*Verfassungspatriotismus*," or constitution patriotism.

Whether *Verfassungspatriotismus* really exists in today's Germany beyond certain seminar rooms at universities is doubtful. Indeed, the essentialist and *völkisch* attitude towards categorizing people's real identity is still dominant in Germany, as well as elsewhere in Europe. I often encounter the following conversation in reference to a colleague or a friend: Question to Andy: "What is so and so really?" Andy's response: "He or she is American." Response to Andy: "No, I know that, and that is not what I mean because we all know that being American is not a real identity. What is he (she) *really*, not as regards his (or her) citizenship papers or passport, but in real life, which goes deeper than passports and papers?" The emphasis always is on the word "really," and that identity always excludes passports and implies some deeper existence, some essentialized identity that citizenship papers can never convey. My Viennese-accented German became, and continues to be, one of my three irresistible magic wands with which to woo Germans of all classes, ages, and genders.

Permit me to turn to a brief description of my second magic wand. After July 1974, with Germany in my rear-view mirror, I gave that country no further thought until I joined the Center for European Studies when, in 1977, a group of us commenced work on European labor's response to the crises of capitalism in France, Italy, Sweden, Britain, and Germany. In Harvard's Manpower and Industrial Relations Library in the basement of Littauer Hall, I immersed myself in the history of German trade unions and labor, and soon came to love my work on this topic. I found a complete reading of *Gewerkschaftliche Monatshefte*, the German trade union federation's most intellectual and scholarly periodical, of particular value. In an issue from 1977, I perused the inside cover to find out who the editors of this fine publication really were, and lo and behold, I saw the name Dr. Volker Bahl, *stellvertretender Chefredakteur*, assistant or associate editor-in-chief. Hey, I knew that name. Wasn't this Wolf-Dieter Narr's doctoral student, whom I had met with his wife in Berlin in the summer of 1974? Even though I seemed to recall that Volker's dissertation topic was not directly related to labor, I thought the coincidence was simply too great.

I ran to my office in Vanserg, composed a letter to Volker, and mailed it that evening. Two weeks later, a wonderful reply arrived, brimming with pleasure that I had contacted him, asking me to stay in touch, and commenting with reverence on the letterhead on which I had written my note: "Harvard University!" he exulted. (Though I signed the letter as Assistant Professor, Department of Government, Wesleyan University, the project for which I contacted Volker emanated from the Center for European Studies at Harvard.)

In the fall of 1978, when I knew I would soon need to start my eight months of field work on German trade unions, I turned to concrete matters such as where to begin, how to proceed, and where to travel. Reflecting Germany's historical decentralization, union headquarters were situated all over the country, which meant I would need to travel extensively during my stay there. Whereas my Center colleagues on the trade-union project needed only to travel to and stay in their country's capital to get their work done, I would need to spend time in Frankfurt, Hanover, Stuttgart, and Düsseldorf to do my research properly.

Where to begin? Well, how about at the top, meaning the *Deutscher Gewerkschaftsbund* (German Trade Union Federation) in Düsseldorf, umbrella organization for all 17 of the Federal Republic's main trade unions. But how to do this? Just arrive at this massive office building and crash the place? Volker Bahl to the rescue. This time, since the day of my departure was getting close, I telephoned him at his office at *Gewerkschaftliche Monatshefte*.

"Oh, we are so sorry," a female voice said, "but Dr. Bahl left us one month ago and is now assisting the chairman of *IG Bau Steine Erden*— the construction workers' union—in Frankfurt. Who may I tell him is trying to reach him?"

"Andy Markovits, Assistant Professor of Government at Wesleyan University currently at the Center for European Studies at Harvard University."

A pregnant pause. "From Harvard University? Really? But you sound so Viennese! I love that accent! I have never met anybody from Harvard University, but I will be sure to mention your call to Dr. Bahl when I next talk to him."

Ten days later, a letter arrived from Volker on *IG Bau Steine Erden* letterhead telling me of his move to Frankfurt to work with the chairman of the construction workers union as his *chef de cabinet*. He sensed something urgent was happening on my end, so he gave me permission to call him at his new office. When we connected, I told him that I was about to embark on a major research project on German trade unions, and I would very much appreciate any and all assistance he could give me.

The Alien but also Familiar World of the German Trade Unions

"Well," he said, "start in Düsseldorf and get to know people at the Federation there for about four months before you then spend the rest of your time researching the individual unions in Frankfurt, Stuttgart, and Hanover. And since you will have two really major unions in Frankfurt— *IG Metall* [the metal workers' union] and my union [construction workers]—please stay with Angelika and me while you will be in town. We have an extra room and would love to have you for however long you will need to be here. In the meantime, I will alert Gerhard Leminsky, my old boss and editor-in-chief of *Gewerkschaftliche Monatshefte*, of your impending appearance there on the first Monday in January. He will have at least a desk for you where you can work and leave your stuff, perhaps even an office. And he will introduce you to all the important folks at the DGB, whom you will need to interview for your project."

And so it went. I arrived early on that Monday morning in early January 1979 at the DGB Haus and took the elevator to its seventh floor, where the rooms for *Gewerkschaftliche Monatshefte* resided. A smiling man with a kind demeanor, white hair, and a professorial look welcomed me and introduced himself as Gerhard Leminsky. I barely had time to reply with my name when he blurted out: "I love this Viennese accent. Where on earth did you pick this up? I love it! But I cannot imagine that they teach German like that at Harvard."

Leminsky took me to the building's ground floor where we walked to an adjacent building with only two floors. "This is the *Wirtschafts und Sozialwissenschaftliches Institut* of the DGB. This is where all our social scientists work—nearly forty of them. I got you an office here all to yourself that you can keep until the last day of August. We even arranged to have your name on the door. Of course, you will have lunch with us in our cafeteria. I paid for the first full week for you, but thereafter you will need to buy your own lunch tickets. Lunch is subsidized. Two marks per meal, not a bad deal. All drinks, including wine and beer, are included. You will meet many of these researchers at lunch, but I also told them of your presence so do not be surprised if one or the other pops by to introduce themselves. After all, everybody wants to meet a Harvard professor!"

"Dr. Leminsky," I interjected, "I am not a Harvard professor. I am a researcher on a project funded by the Ford Foundation and anchored at the Center for European Studies at Harvard University. My professorship is at Wesleyan University in Middletown, Connecticut."

Somehow this was completely lost on Leminsky, as it would be lost on everyone else to whom I repeated this dozens and dozens of times in my eight months in Germany. They had heard or seen the magic word

"Harvard" in connection with me and that was it. "Harvard" crowded out all other information and details as useless chatter. Harvard prevailed! Open sesame! Roll out the red carpet! Give this man all he wants and then some!

I must say I have never seen anything like Harvard's reputation in Germany. Harvard, of course, has a lustrous glow of recognition everywhere in the world, but the singularity I encountered in Germany then, and ever since, is astonishing. In other places, Harvard is on top but palpably followed by Yale and then some combination of Princeton, Stanford, and maybe Berkeley. I am here talking about the broad-based knowledge of the educated public, not professors and academics, who know many other American universities, having had colleagues and collaborators at many of them, and having attended conferences or lectured at this or that institution of higher learning. Harvard's singular presence in the German public's awareness, with no Yale or Princeton on the horizon (perhaps Stanford is a distant second, these last two decades), has always baffled me. The diction is telling. It is always "Harvard Professor so-and-so" as opposed to "Professor so-and-so *an der Yale Universität*."

By the end of that first week, during which I did indeed meet many of the WSI researchers, it was clear to me that I had two magic wands in my possession: Viennese-inflected German and Harvard! I have never stopped wondering what would have happened had our project been anchored at Berkeley, Yale, Columbia, or Michigan, all world-class universities as well, never mind at a lesser-known institution with little pedigree. Would doors have opened so widely and so readily had I been associated with X State University? I doubt it! And what would have happened had I spoken German with an American accent, as everyone expected to hear even before I opened my mouth since to all my interlocutors I was an American before they then robbed me of this identity precisely based on my accent? Or even a standard German accent, without the charm that made most Germans smile upon unexpectedly hearing my first few words of Viennese-inflected German? Who knows? But I am sure I would have had a much harder row to hoe.

To be sure, this Harvarditis infected the German intelligentsia and learned classes such as my new pals at WSI since they all were holders of advanced degrees in economics, political science, sociology, organizational behavior, and law. With this crowd, the disease ran rampant. In contrast, the actual trade union functionaries and elites remained immune to the illness and could not have cared less about Harvard because they were all members of the working class, and therefore suffered none of the pretention or envy that afflicted the university-educated staff and experts. In fact, virtually none of them spoke any English, which was quite revealing in a country where many regular folks spoke at least some English by the late 1970s.

I have always argued that as a latecomer to colonialism and the loser of two world wars, Germany constitutes the only large country where people speak a second language reasonably well. This is certainly not the case in Britain, France, Italy, Spain, or, least of all, Russia and the United States. That the Dutch, the Danes, and the Israelis read and speak oodles of languages is due to their small size and the exotic nature of their mother tongues, which no one else speaks, forcing them to learn other people's languages if they wish to join the global conversation. So in a certain way I have always been more impressed by "normal" Germans' command of English than that of their Dutch or Danish counterparts.

Then there was the third magic wand that helped Andy Markovits ingratiate himself to his German hosts: being Jewish! The efficacy of these three magic powers and their odd interconnection catapulted me onto a platform in Germany that I could never attain anywhere else, least of all the United States, where none of these abilities renders me even vaguely exotic, charming, or exceptional. In Germany, I became an insider-outsider: one of them, but not quite; someone who knew their language and culture inside and out, but who was not really German; an American who in their eyes was not a real American—not the yahoo, the peasant, the parvenu, the uncouth, arrogant being they associated with Americanness, not the usual "ugly American," but an "attractive American," if such a term were not an oxymoron for Germans, indeed most Europeans.

As I wrote later in a number of scholarly articles published in German, Italian, and English, these were the same reasons Barack Obama became so wildly popular in Europe, particularly in Germany, where thousands cheered him fanatically at the Victory Column in West Berlin well before he was elected president. He was cultured; he was sophisticated; he was *almost like us*, though, thankfully, not quite, because he was much more exotic than a boring German. *"Il parle comme nous,"* as the Swiss foreign minister Micheline Calmy-Rey exclaimed the night of Obama's first victory in 2008. "He speaks like we do," in contrast to that uncultured dolt George W. Bush, the cowboy and thus true American; even in contrast to that rascal Bill Clinton, whose philandering behavior we found appealing and attractive and, truth-be-told, so European, especially in view of the wretched puritanism ruling America, which we now see among its feminists as well.

To all this, add the Jew, the son of the Holocaust-ravaged generation! Deeply Jewish, but not threateningly so. Not an Orthodox Jew, not a Jew who spoke—horror of horrors—a Jewish-accented German. Rather, a Jew whom we Germans can tolerate, a Jew whom we let chastise us from time to time, a Jew who may even offer us a sense of expiation for our singularly horrible past by virtue of our good deeds toward him, and even towards less appealing Jews, which we accomplish with our voices, our publications, our repentant lives. To my great horror, I sometimes felt that some of my German friends looked to me quietly but no less hopefully to offer them absolution for the sins of their parents as rewards for their righteous deeds in our contemporary world. I never knew how to handle this in all my decades of involvement with Germans and Germany!

I am not saying that any of my German interlocutors of the past fifty years consciously thought any of what I just described or acted toward me with an instrumentality that consciously valorized any of these deeply felt emotions for their own ends. Far from it. I am describing a situation that provided me with a position in Germany that was *sui generis,* and which I could never have attained anywhere else. By January 1979, at the very beginning of my stay in Düsseldorf and my involvement with Germany, which was to last for over forty years, I understood that, for these Germans, who Andy Markovits was and what he represented for them was more important than what Andy Markovits actually did or produced. Clearly, what I wrote and taught mattered greatly; my publications and lectures were the basis of all that followed. But my becoming a public intellectual in Germany had everything to do with the three magic wands that opened doors for me in those early days and whose power were never to wane in the ensuing decades.

Let me be more precise: I became a public intellectual not in *Deutschland*, but in the *Bundesrepublik*; not in the current Berlin Republic, but in its Bonn predecessor. On thinking back to that fateful day when the *Bundestag* voted to depart from Bonn as the newly unified country's capital and make Berlin its seat of governmental power, I find good reason for being so sentimental about this transition. An era of a construct that gave rise to social forces that rendered Germany for the first time in its recent history not only palatable to its neighbors, but downright attractive to many in the world, was about to end. The *Bundesrepublik*, in its Bonn guise, rendered Germany's power civil instead of military, consoling rather than threatening, liberal rather than authoritarian or even fascist. The *Bundesrepublik* gave birth to a generation that created the Green Party—imperfect, but still a fine voice for compassion and inclusion, and for an exemplary humaneness.

The *Bundesrepublik* became a liberal leader of a European Union that, with all its shortcomings, has rendered war among its 27 members unthinkable and, at least to my knowledge, emanated from the only state-building process that occurred without one shot being fired, its members joining voluntarily, rather than by dint of being conquered. Lastly, the *Bundesrepublik* allowed me to gain friends and colleagues I could not have found anywhere else, precisely because the three wands I wielded to grant me access to their lives would have worked their magic nowhere else.

Homage to Heinz Kluncker: Stout Friend in Complex Circumstances

Strangely, my three powers even helped me connect with Heinz Kluncker, the 300-pound leader of the public employees' union, the *Gewerkschaft Öffentliche Dienste, Transport und Verkehr*, or ÖTV. When I first saw this man on the evening news in early January and heard his booming baritone voice, I thought: *This* is what a union boss ought to look like, and this is how he ought to sound! The man exuded such presence and charisma on my television screen that even though my research did not include public employee unions and concentrated solely on workers organized in industries of the private sector, I decided I had to meet this Kluncker and interview him for my project.

I was familiar with the name Kluncker—how onomatopoetic for a union boss!—as belonging to the person who allegedly brought down the popular Brandt government in 1974 by receiving an 11-percent raise for his union's members, an inordinately generous increase at a time when the German state was experiencing shortfalls due to the oil crisis of 1973. Getting to meet and spend time with a busy union boss of such importance was well-nigh impossible, but then again, I am nothing if not persistent in pursuing material for my work.

I telephoned Kluncker's office at ÖTV headquarters in Stuttgart and got connected with his *chef de cabinet*, who, being a university graduate and holder of a doctorate, as staff members of union leaders often are, was duly impressed by Harvard. He took my coordinates and told me that he might arrange for my meeting Kluncker, but this could happen on short notice and under odd circumstances, such as riding in Kluncker's limousine as he was being driven from one meeting to the next. I had to stand by and be ready at a moment's notice.

Two weeks later, at 4 p.m., the phone rang in my WSI office. The ÖTV man asked whether I was ready to meet Kluncker in two hours when he—and all the other 16 heads of the DGB unions—would be departing from the DGB building, getting into their cars, and, in Kluncker's case, heading to Hamburg. Was I ready to ride with Kluncker to Hamburg, where we would arrive late in the evening, but, this being Germany, there would always be a fine train back to Düsseldorf at all hours of the night? Naturally, I agreed.

At 6 p.m., I was waiting by the building's entrance when one Mercedes limo after another arrived to pick up the union bosses, some of whom I would meet later in the year for interviews in Frankfurt, Hanover, and Stuttgart. Out came this huge man with an outstretched arm and a broad smile who said to me in English: "Hello, I am Heinz Kluncker! Welcome to Germany. There is my car, let's get in and go!"

Many Germans speak English, but, as mentioned above, union leaders are usually not among them since, at least in the old days, they all hailed from the working class and attended neither *Gymnasium* nor university. But here was this bear of a man who spoke English to me with a slight American accent. As we sat in the back of the car, I heard on the stereo: "Always late with your kisses! Won't you come to my arms, sweet darling, and stay?" What? Lefty Frizzell playing in a German union leader's car? I asked Kluncker in German about his taste in music, and he responded that he absolutely loved American country music and was especially taken by Frizzell, Waylon Jennings, Merle Haggard, Loretta Lynn, and Tammy Wynette. I had to pinch myself. How was this possible?

Well, it turned out Kluncker had been incarcerated in an American prisoner-of-war camp in Alabama during the war, as many German soldiers were. But there was also a twist to Kluncker's story: he had to be protected by the US authorities day and night because otherwise the rest of the German POWs would have killed him out of hatred for his having deserted the Wehrmacht in France in 1944 and sought refuge with the advancing Americans. Kluncker was born in 1925, the only son of a locksmith in the city of Wuppertal, which was also Friedrich Engels's birthplace. He was training to become a commercial expert in the textile industry when he joined the Hitler Youth, a move he would regret for the rest of his life and something he mentioned to me constantly, almost seeking my absolution for this *Jugendsünde*, this sin of his youth, as the Germans so aptly call such trespasses. Drafted into the Wehrmacht, he deserted to the Americans and became a life-long fan of America, the liberal democratic West, and Germany's close attachment to the United States.

Having returned from Alabama with his love of country music and American-accented English, Kluncker joined the Social Democratic Party and rose through the party's ranks. More rapidly still, he rose through the public employees' union, becoming chairman in 1964 at the age of 39, making him the youngest union leader in the Federal Republic of Germany. His love of the United States and American culture made Kluncker a rare exception among Social Democrats and unionists.

Kluncker also was the first West German trade union leader to reach out to the communist unions of the Eastern European countries, as well as to *Solidarność*, the Polish union of the late 1970s and early 1980s that initiated the collapse of the Soviet empire. Again, neither of these positions were common among run-of-the-mill German unionists or Social Democrats who had disdain for East Europeans and were deeply suspicious of any positions that they regarded as deviating from their orthodox position of non-revolutionary, non-Leninist Marxism.

My ride with Kluncker to Hamburg in his limo formed the foundation of my entry into the world of the Federal Republic's social democracy, which I maintained for over forty years, and solidified my burgeoning presence in the Federal Republic's union milieu, in which I flourished for twenty years. My many publications on topics related to German social democracy and organized labor had their origins in the January days of 1979 when, in addition to taking this ride in Kluncker's limo, I became ensconced in the research and policy sector of organized labor in Germany.

On a personal level, I remained close to Kluncker for many years after his retirement as leader of ÖTV in 1982. I invited him to Cambridge, where he delivered a fine lecture on wage bargaining in the public sector at the Center for European Studies sometime in the early 1990s. Heinz Kluncker died in 2005, after years of illness. For me, he embodied the best of the *Bundesrepublik*: emanating from the working class; succeeding on his own to become the leader of a mighty organization that improved the lives of a large number of diversified workers, from civil servants to garbage collectors, from nurses and doctors to pilots and flight attendants; joining the Nazis but then renouncing his Nazi affiliation; always remaining cognizant of the singularity of the Nazis' crimes committed in Germany's name; fostering close ties to the United States, its culture and Western liberal democracy; reaching out to groups all over Europe that were opposed to each other in a quest to create a lasting peace on this war-torn continent; and remaining a Social Democrat to the core, always concerned about the well-being of working people. I actually perceived many parallels between Heinz Kluncker and Willy Brandt, whom Kluncker's roughhouse bargaining tactics allegedly compelled to resign as chancellor of the Federal Republic (both denied this vehemently, but the perception of Kluncker as "the Brandt killer" remained alive for many years).

In addition to establishing my presence within the Social Democratic/labor venue of the Federal Republic's public discourse, an event in February 1979 propelled me to participate in the much murkier, tension-filled world of Jews and related topics—an arena of discussion, debate, and controversy I came to call "the thing" as already mentioned. NBC's television series *Holocaust*, starring Meryl Streep, aired in the United States in 1978 and was to be shown in Germany on four nights in February 1979. I had watched one or two episodes back home in Cambridge, largely to see whether I agreed with the devastatingly bad reviews of the series, or whether my pet peeve that critics disdain even good movies, books, and television shows if they appear to be entertainment rather than art would again be confirmed. Both predictions proved true: I thought the episodes I watched were well acted, but that Meryl Streep keeping her flowing hair in Auschwitz was seriously off the mark. Above all, the series did not reveal one fact or insight about the camps I had not already known, rendering the episodes uninteresting, rather than inferior in quality. Still, I found one aspect of the series quite powerful: the highlighting of all of history's horrors, not with numbers and mounds of dead bodies, but via the fate of two German families, one Jewish, the other Gentile.

This series was to be shown on Germany's third channel, the regional network on which each of the ten federal states aired their own programs. Tellingly, it was not aired on Germany's first or second channels, which were national in reach and the venues where blockbuster series appeared. Channel 3 had the air of public television or C-SPAN in the United States—solid, informative stuff that was often boring. Never had anything on Channel 3 come close to dominating the ratings. The German public authorities who owned and operated all television channels at the time, with no private networks yet present in the German market, were clearly torn about showing this series. They could not suppress a show about the Holocaust, but they could consign it to the backwaters of Channel 3. Yet even in those backwaters, something special happened: all ten of the independent stations decided to air the series, with no single state opting out.

I remember mentioning this series during lunch at WSI and telling my colleagues I was going to watch it on the small black-and-white television in my sublet. I was surprised most of them had never heard about the series and certainly had no idea of its impending airing on Channel 3. At lunch on the day after the first episode, one or two of my colleagues asked me sheepishly and *sotto voce* whether I had watched the episode the night before. When I replied that I had, their reactions were priceless: one exclaimed that the rise of Nazism affected the working class a lot more than the Jews; the other asked whether I would mind having tea with him later that afternoon, which I did.

At that stage, nobody at the WSI or the DGB or any of these institutions knew I was Jewish. Some, I am sure, surmised as much because an American who spoke Viennese-accented German naturally fell prey to suspicions of rootless cosmopolitanism. But most of my colleagues weren't able to classify me because none of them had ever seen or met a Jew. And even though some people say one would need to be deaf and blind not to perceive me as Jewish, I disagree because I do not look particularly Jewish, so my Jewish mannerisms and diction only become evident to someone deeply attuned to Jews and Jewish ways, which my German hosts clearly were not. And I sure as heck did not pepper any of my diction with my usual Yiddishisms that, in any case, I only use in English never in German.

After the second episode, the newspapers began reporting on this series. More important than the episodes themselves were the open-ended panel discussions Channel 3 aired after each installment, lasting deep into the night. What began to emerge was a kind of a national dialogue, a reckoning and recognition of the fact that the Germans had committed an unspeakable atrocity. Even though none of this was new, and even though—at least since the Auschwitz trial in Frankfurt in 1963—most of the details about the Holocaust had often been reported in the German media, and even though many documentaries already had aired revealing the horrors of the concentration camps, all this remained in the realm of elite culture. Only Hollywood produced entertainment could create such a high level of consciousness, such a broad-based soul searching, such a mass reckoning with the nation's history.

In one episode, we see Jews being herded into a synagogue in Poland or Belarus or Russia that the Wehrmacht then sets aflame, burning everyone inside. A huge debate developed in the discussion portion of the telecast as to whether this could have been true, or whether this was merely a Hollywood gimmick to create empathy or malign the Germans. These post-film panels and discussions also accepted telephone calls from viewers across Germany. The panel leader took one such call, paused for a long time, then informed the audience that someone had just called to say he had been in charge of precisely such an act of burning Jewish civilians somewhere in Russia.

By the end of the series, the increased awareness of the Holocaust generated by the series had transformed the Federal Republic and the WSI cafeteria. Lengthy debates sprouted in all the major newspapers and on all the major radio stations. I was asked, totally impromptu, by my colleagues at the WSI whether I would be interested in talking about my own experiences of being Jewish at a gathering they were going to organize privately on a Saturday evening, along with snacks and refreshments. To this day, I have no idea how my colleagues in the cafeteria figured out I was Jewish, but by series' end, this had become clear to everyone. What I found even more interesting was the way they assumed something bad had happened to my family during the Shoah, even though I had never said a word about what my relatives suffered.

This meeting did, in fact, occur and turned out to be intense. For starters, I thought it appropriate to give a brief overview of the extant scholarship on the Holocaust, even though the audience was comprised almost entirely of what the Germans aptly call *Akademiker*, meaning people with university diplomas. Then I spoke about the TV series, what I had found helpful and what I viewed as less so. I delineated the singularity of Nazism and the Holocaust but situated both within the larger context of fascism. I made sure to clarify that not all fascist regimes are inherently antisemitic, let alone commit crimes even vaguely similar to the Shoah; this did not make fascism less heinous than Nazism, only different. I ended with a long discourse on antisemitism, its history and manifestations.

I talked for well over an hour, and the audience listened to every word I said with complete attention. After I finished speaking, audience members asked me many questions. Clearly, some felt ill at ease, but no one dared leave. Finally, at the very end of the evening, the hostess, a labor economist, timidly but with acute empathy, asked: "Could you share a few words about how the Holocaust affected your family? Please forgive me if my question is not appropriate in any way. You obviously know a great deal about all the causes and developments and history of this horrible event. But I would like you to say something about your own involvement, which I think is not minimal. Only if you want to, please."

After I had recounted a bit about my family's experience in the Holocaust, the room fell silent. Then a woman I did not know asked very quietly: "How can you stand to come to this country? What on earth are you doing here?" I answered by saying that she and her group were different Germans from the Nazis, that they were citizens of the *Bundesrepublik*, that I didn't believe in collective guilt and found such a concept truly objectionable, but that yes, on occasion, I did find it difficult to separate the past from the present, particularly when I sat on the bus and saw an elderly man who clearly must have served the Nazis in some capacity.

Already that evening I noticed an interesting divide within my left-liberal milieu that was to accompany me to this day. Those who welcomed and appreciated the Federal Republic's *freiheitlich-demokratische Grundordung*, or FDGO, as it came to be called—that is, the republic's liberal democratic order—and who appreciated that republic's ties to the West and feted its Western values of liberal democracy showed much more compassion for, and interest in, me, my story, and the Jews than did their counterparts who disdained the *Bundesrepublik* as basically a continuation of fascism, as they called it (never "national socialism" or "Nazism," which is telling in and of itself), by dint of its Western values and defense of capitalism.

To the latter group, the main issue centered on capitalism with the Holocaust being a sad and tragic side-effect. Not surprising to me, a number of those who disdained the *Bundesrepublik* later drifted right, with some becoming outright German nationalists, even Nazis. The former group developed antibodies to any ideology that was even vaguely antisemitic, thanks to the *Bundesrepublik's* powerful culture and institutions, which were anchored in liberal democracy; the latter group developed no such immunity, because its members believed that liberal democracy was a system that had to be opposed, indeed destroyed, by dint of its association with capitalism.

As I began speaking and publishing on German attitudes toward Jews, antisemitism on the left, and other topics related to German-Jewish relations, I entered the world that was to rule much of my intellectual life until the 2000s. One of my publications, which appeared in 1980 in the well-known American journal *New German Critique*, compared the reaction to *Holocaust* in Germany to the reaction in Austria, where the series aired in March 1979. The comparison could not have been more pronounced. Whereas in Germany the show caused a national debate and unearthed major forces in the collective psyche, virtually nothing of the sort happened in Austria and the series passed without commotion. As I had experienced in my years in Vienna in the 1960s and my subsequent visits and scholarly involvements in the 1970s, Austrians continued their happy existence on the island of the blessed, refusing to confront their ugly Nazi past by leaving those atrocities to the Germans to confront. After all, the Germans had raped Austria in 1938, so all this turmoil served them right. Not until the beginnings of the infamous Waldheim Affair, in 1985, did Austria awaken from its lies and obfuscations to confront its own crimes committed under the Nazis' aegis.

A few days before my departure from the WSI in late August to return to the United States and commence my fall semester's teaching at Wesleyan University, my hosts and colleagues threw me a lovely farewell party in the cafeteria. There, Gerhard Leminsky asked me to write a piece for *Gewerkschaftliche Monatshefte*, not so much about the main issues confronting the German trade unions, but about the impressions I had gained in my eight months immersed in the life and daily existence of German unions. The journal had never published anything like this in its thirty-year existence, and Leminsky thought I would be the ideal author of such a piece by virtue of my position as an insider-outsider, as he aptly labeled my relationship to the unions. Moreover, I was to appropriate and expand upon Leminsky's characterization of my status to include not only the unions, but all of the Federal Republic of Germany.

Back home at my office in Vanserg, I sat down one evening and wrote the whole piece in one sitting. Off it went to Leminsky. Entitled "Daily Life in German Trade Union Headquarters: Impressions of an American Social Scientist," the article was full of praise but included some criticisms, among them my observation of how deeply sexist all these institutions were. This, I argued, mattered a great deal in a structure whose very purpose was to help the disadvantaged. I would not have raised the issue of this sexism had I been researching top-level German multinational corporations, because I would have expected nothing else. But unions? The only women I had met in my eight months—with the exception of a few social scientists at WSI—were secretaries serving me tea and cookies while I waited to interview their bosses, all of whom were men!

When the piece appeared in the December 1979 issue of the journal, the reactions were incredible. Germany's two alternative newspapers had become part of the burgeoning scene of the new social movements and the counterculture that had come to dominate major sections of the Federal Republic's urban landscape, and these papers amply reported my observation of sexism in German unions. No one had ever raised anything of the sort, making me a hero to Germany's nascent feminists, who were still much less present in the country's mainstream conversation than was true in the United States. My name entered the subculture of the new social movements from which it never receded. When I introduced myself to folks four years later at the Green Party's raucous celebration in a huge warehouse on the outskirts of Bonn feting the party's entry into the German Bundestag in March 1983, most of the women knew my name. "Oh, you are the guy who called the trade unions sexist. Good for you! I loved that! Long overdue to call out those machos hiding behind their social democratic screens!"

I also received blow-back from some trade unionists, notably some of my few female colleagues at the WSI, one of whom never spoke to me again since I had broken the code of class solidarity in favor of some new-fangled, American-influenced countercultural gimmick called women's liberation. One person whom I feared to have offended with my piece reacted only with praise and thanks: Big Heinz Kluncker! He had his secretary—female, of course—call me and read into my answering machine a glowing message he dictated, informing me that he even had brought up my article at one of the regular meetings convened by the DGB for the heads of its constituent unions, asking all those assembled to think of ways one could repudiate the sexism in the unions Markovits mentioned in his article.

All told, this publication and its reception well beyond the world of the trade unions opened all the doors for me in what one could call the Federal Republic's "Green" venue—that is, the world of the Left, apart from and in opposition to the established "Red" venue of the social democrats and organized labor. With the publication of a monograph on the West German trade unions by Cambridge University Press in 1986, I now shifted my German research into this separate but related sphere.

Sadly, in my repeated battles with representatives of the German Left, Red and Green, Deutschland's ugly head reared itself again. Invariably, the controversies entailed some strain of what I took to calling "the thing." Making matters worse was that these resentments were never confessed to, which rendered those who voiced such views not only wrong and dangerous but also woefully hypocritical. In some cases, the enmity became so stark that I encountered open antisemitism directed at me.

These encounters made me fear that the immense progress created by the *Bundesrepublik* may not have eradicated some of the darker sides of *Deutschland*. I expected nothing else on the country's political right since *Deutschland* and its tropes constituted, almost by definition, what it meant to be on the right. But on the left? It took quite a while for me to accept this reality, and, truth be told, it became the main reason I abandoned this world and concentrated instead on sports and dogs, passions I can explore without the pain, disappointment, and resentment that became constant as a result of those earlier intellectual pursuits.

I should note I never fought these battles on my own. I had wonderful German allies who rallied to my aid and supported me with their own publications and public voices. I will never forget Kluncker's booming baritone on my answering machine—this time calling by himself, since by 1991 he no longer had a secretary—as he expressed his total solidarity with my position in a bitter controversy over the Gulf War of 1990–91, I conducted with Jürgen Hoffmann, in full-length pages in one of Germany's leading newspapers. I fully reconciled with my opponent in this battle. But tellingly, it was the music of the Grateful Dead and Dire Straits that brought us back together, and not our differences about the West, America, and Israel. By sheer chance, I found myself in Hamburg in September 2009 and made it a point to visit Jürgen in his home. His partner led me to his bed where Jürgen lay in excruciating pain. We held hands for quite some time. We talked and cried! I was present when the ambulance picked him up from his apartment to take him to the hospital, from which he was never to return, losing his final battle with cancer the following day.

Still, all the friction took its toll, and I turned from studying German labor unions to studying sports. The German version of my article "The Other 'American Exceptionalism': Why Is There No Soccer in the United States?" became a hit not only among German academics but also in broader intellectual circles, and its publication in 1987 opened all kinds of doors for me. The *Studienstiftung des deutschen Volkes* (Educational Foundation of the German People), the country's most prestigious institution bestowing academic prestige and financial assistance on the best students at German universities—something akin to our National Merit Scholars program—invited me to offer a course on sports, politics, and culture at one of its numerous summer schools. The organization held these programs all over the country so its awardees could broaden their intellectual horizons with topics that were unusual for a regular university curriculum. In August 1995, I spent almost three weeks at Schloss Salem, near Lake Constance, where I made lifelong friends among my students and fellow faculty members. (This is also where I experienced Jerry Garcia's death.)

The invitation to the august *Wissenschaftskolleg zu Berlin* for the academic year 1998–1999 was in part due to my work on sports, though also my cumulative output on various topics relating to German politics and society. It was at the Kolleg that I wrote my book *Offside: Soccer and*

American Exceptionalism, which Princeton University Press published in 2001. One year later, the book appeared in German translation from a fine German publishing house.

My other preoccupation during that exceptional year in Berlin was to travel all over the country giving lectures about my book *Das deutsche Dilemma*, which was published in September 1998, a few days before the new Red-Green coalition of the Social Democrats and Greens was to take power. This switch was crucial for a number of reasons. First, it ended the 16-year reign of Helmut Kohl and his center-right CDU/CSU and FDP coalition, also ending the political career of one of Germany's and Europe's most important statesmen. Second, it feted the arrival at the country's political summit of a Social Democratic/Green coalition. While such had existed in various municipalities and also on the state level, those coalitions remained minor league compared to playing in the majors of the country's overall leadership. And third, it signified the arrival of a former streetfighter, vehement protester, and radical leftwing activist at the center of established German and European power: Joschka Fischer became the Federal Republic's foreign minister. As unlikely a candidate as one can imagine, Fischer, a brilliant autodidact, rose to the leadership of the Green Party, which then catapulted him into becoming Germany's second-most powerful politician.

As noted earlier, I had met Fischer through my work on the Green party, and we became ideological soulmates, though not quite friends. He wrote the preface to *Das deutsche Dilemma*, having read and liked its English original, *The German Predicament: Memory and Power in the New Europe*, published by Cornell University Press in 1997. The preface turned out to be a dry run for the brilliant speech Fischer delivered to the *Bundestag* upon becoming foreign minister. Fischer and I have remained in touch over the years, and I was pleased that I was able to facilitate his traveling to Ann Arbor to receive an honorary doctorate from the University of Michigan in 2012.

In *The German Predicament—Das Deutsche Dilemma*, my co-author, Simon Reich, and I grappled with the theme of *Bundesrepublik* vs. *Deutschland*. In 2003, Simon and I (along with Michael Huelshoff) co-edited a collection of essays on German politics and society that we titled *From Bundesrepublik to Deutschland: German Politics after Unification.* That we were preoccupied with this topic barely two years after Germany's unification can best be demonstrated by the title of one of our articles, "Should Europe Fear the Germans?," published in *German Politics and Society*'s summer 1991 issue. The topic's relevance and urgency were evident from the many citations and media appearances the piece garnered. This question epitomizes my ambivalence about Germany which never seems to abate.

In the views of Barrington Moore and Ralf Dahrendorf (a German politician who belonged to the liberal FDP—liberal in the classical European manner, not its social democratic American version—and later became director of the London School of Economics and warden of St. Antony's College, Oxford), Germany never achieved a successful bourgeois revolution the way Britain, France, and the United States did. This meant the country continued to be ruled by autocratic, illiberal forces, rather than a liberal democratic order, well into the twentieth century. Dahrendorf argues—brilliantly, in my view—that it was Hitler, rather than the German bourgeoisie, who eliminated the German landowning aristocracy—the Junkers—after the failed attempt on his life, which, perversely, brought about the same political outcome that the victorious bourgeoisies of the three aforementioned countries achieved.

As Moore succinctly stated: No bourgeoisie (by which he meant bourgeois rule), no democracy. With no successful bourgeois revolution in German history, liberal democracy had to be imposed on Germany from the outside. That is exactly what the *Bundesrepublik* is: a successful imposition from the outside of a whole new political order with an accompanying culture that has yielded one of the most stable and wealthy liberal democracies in the world. Lest there be any misunderstanding: if we are to exclude the transformation of East Germany in 1989, the Germans never established democracy by themselves, but rather had it thrust upon them.

The transformation of Germany and its values from the Nazis to the citizens of the Federal Republic has been among the starkest in human history. This is a key example of the absurdity of the idea that national characteristics are innate and immutable. All such characteristics are learned traits that originate in the particular institutions and mores of a given time, all of which are mutable.

When the *Bundesrepublik* was first imposed on the western part of the divided country, it was anything but popular. Most Germans resented losing the war, and saw the Allies as the occupiers they were. But some occupiers became more legitimate than others, with the Americans and their Western allies France and Britain becoming more accepted by the Germans who were occupied by those forces than the Soviets were accepted by the Germans whom they occupied. The *Bundesrepublik's* growth in legitimacy and acceptance in the west of Germany derived from the constant comparison to the Soviet-ruled situation in the east, which was deficient in every measurable respect, economic comfort and personal liberty most potent among them. The British, the French, and most particularly the Americans mutated from resented occupiers of the West to welcome liberators from Nazism and—most significantly—cherished protectors from the Soviets, who never advanced from occupiers to liberators in the East. The former occupiers created the respected and appreciated—if not beloved—institution of the *Bundesrepublik*; the latter reaffirmed the profound illegitimacy of the German Democratic Republic, leading to its collapse like a house of cards in the fall of 1989.

The question then becomes: How deep has the institutional and cultural transformation that created the *Bundesrepublik* been? Should one trust this shining example of liberal democracy's triumph over evil? How stable is that transformation? Or is it the case, as one of my Green friends told me after a vigorous public debate in which I argued we ought to trust German power and he argued that we should shun it, that one never gives even a drop of alcohol to a former alcoholic? To this day, the Federal Republic has not learned to wield its power. As I always tell my German left-liberal friends: "You want to be Switzerland or Austria, but you can't be passive and detached, as they can and must be because they are small. You are big, you are powerful. Take responsibility! Switzerland and Austria can opt out. In fact, that is their mantra. You Germans, however, cannot opt out!"

Many an American president from Kennedy to Obama has tried to convince the Germans of this, but the Germans have always recoiled. They have never quite trusted themselves to handle such power; and the rest of Europe would never let them try because deep down the rest of Europe still fears Germany, especially a powerful Germany. To many in Europe, German power remains uncanny and strongly associated with mighty *Deutschland* rather than cuddly *Bundesrepublik*.

In some ways, that is true for me, too. On an intellectual level, the *Bundesrepublik*'s institutions have been an unmitigated success, for which I have nothing but respect and admiration. But this trust does not smoothly carry into the realm of emotions. There, the dangerous and ugly tentacles of *Deutschland* loom large—and increasingly larger, with disturbing events reaching all the way back to the 1990s and intensifying in the course of the ensuing two decades.

Respect and admiration are not love and devotion. I regret I have grave emotional reservations towards a country that hosts a university whose faculty and administration thought me worthy of an honorary doctorate. I feel uneasy that a country where colleagues compiled a beautiful *Festschrift* for me in which they feted all six areas of my academic career—trade unions, new social movements, anti-Americanism, antisemitism, sports, and animal rescue—does not receive more of my emotional gratitude. Even though I am deeply honored and forever grateful that the Federal Republic of Germany awarded me one of its highest civilian distinctions granted to Germans or foreigners—the *Verdienstkreuz erster Klasse*, the Cross of the Order of Merit, First Class, an award established by the Bundesrepublik's first president, Theodor Heuss, in 1951—I will never root for its national soccer team. This remains true even though the Mannschaft's players increasingly boast first names like Mesut, Jerôme, Marc-André, Serge, Ilkay, Emre, Leroy, and David in lieu of traditional German names like Heinz, Hans, Karl, Helmut, Wolfgang, Sepp, Fritz and Franz.

Making matters worse is that Germany has bestowed all these honors on me in return for my berating it, in return for my constantly reminding it that its sins run so deep that, regardless of how many honors it may bestow upon me, I will never be assuaged. This is unfair on my part, and I am ashamed of my irrationality. The Federal Republic of

Germany has awarded me many more kudos than the United States ever could or will. In the former, I became a public intellectual whose words counted, whereas, in the latter, I am a run-of-the-mill professor with few, if any, distinctions—certainly with no voice outside the walls of the academy and often not even within them.

But I cannot quite escape that Fourth of July in 1954 when my father and I listened to Radio Budapest broadcasting the Hungary–Germany World Cup final and my father expressed his hatred of both teams and told me that the only good part of the day was its being the birthday of the United States of America. No matter how unfair that judgment might be, and no matter how wonderful the *Bundesrepublik* has been in trying to confront and overcome *Deutschland*'s past, Germany simply never had a chance to win my heart.

EPILOGUE

At the end of this book, Lou Gehrig's legendary farewell speech that he delivered on the Fourth of July 1939 at a packed Yankee Stadium comes to mind. Arguably one of the most celebrated speeches in American sports history—possibly in American history itself—my fellow Columbia University alumnus' words of "today, I consider myself the luckiest man on the face of the earth" resonate with me as I conclude the writing of this memoir. Not because I dare even for a second compare my accomplishments to the Iron Horse's singularly illustrious career as the New York Yankees' first baseman. Nor because of any comparisons in my life to the horror that Gehrig must have gone through being inflicted by the lethal disease (amyotrophic lateral sclerosis) that was the reason for the speech, and that to this day remains incurable and bears his name. But because I, too, have nothing but thanks and gratitude for how my life has unfolded.

Of course, I have also experienced setbacks and disappointments. The sole real tragedy that befell me was losing my mother, just shy of turning ten. The ensuing departure from my home in Timișoara with my father, first to Vienna and then to New York, was no cakewalk. Still, on the grand scale of things, I have led a blessed and charmed existence. For comparison's sake just recall my parents' lives: brutalized by National Socialism and Stalinism, two of the worst evils in human history. (Yes, I am aware of their historical differences and no, I am not equating them under the common denominator of totalitarianism). My father being bullied and beaten repeatedly as a child and as a young man simply for being

Jewish, then losing his parents and siblings to the inferno of Auschwitz. My mother having had the comfort of avoiding many of these horrors by virtue of being privately tutored and sheltered by her elderly parents. But she, too, had to endure many negative experiences simply because she was Jewish. She, too, lost her mother to Auschwitz. I could continue.

All of this remains unimaginable and unthinkable to me! Of course, I also experienced the tail end of Stalinism during my early years in Timișoara, but they were actually fun-filled days for me, cushioned by my parents' unconditional love and a wonderful apartment building whose multicultural, multilingual, and multi-religious inhabitants all got along in a supportive manner. Even Stalinism's immediate tentacles, in the form of the Red Army officers that lived with us in the early 1950s, had nothing but positive connotations for me. I devoured the Medved chocolates that Josif brought home for me in the evenings, I loved riding on his lap on the passenger seat of the Veelees that picked him up every day, and I benefitted throughout my life from the chess prowess that Josif so lovingly shared with me when I was a young boy.

Yes, Josif's successor beat his little girl virtually every evening, which frightened me terribly, but here, too, I was sheltered by the glorious sounds of Beethoven's and Verdi's music that my mother turned on full blast while holding me tightly to her body. Significantly, I experienced absolutely no antisemitism growing up in the Timișoara of the 1950s, even though I came to realize as an adult how profoundly this perennial scourge had been ensconced in Timișoara as well. To be fair, it was not present there one iota more than just about everywhere else in Europe of the time—but still present. I had always sensed from my parents that deep down they felt both insecure as Jews and untethered. Clearly not Romanian by dint of speaking Hungarian, we, however, were also not Hungarian by virtue of something that remained unspoken, but that clearly was due to our being Jewish. We certainly were not Germans, even though that high culture permeated pretty much everything my parents, my mother in particular, valued. But from early childhood onwards, I experienced this rootlessness, this un-belonging, this multi-culturalism, as something enriching, even liberating, never as being anchorless and forlorn.

This changed somewhat in Vienna, where—especially during my middle to late teens—I did encounter antisemitism. But here, too, it was never vicious nor particularly overt towards me, though most assuredly to many others whom I knew well. I disliked Vienna so much that I never even attempted to fit in and become part of it, even though I surely could have tried. I am quite sure that all my efforts would not have sufficed to making me a genuine Austrian and Viennese, despite my accent-free, Austrian-inflected German diction. Jews simply could not become unquestioned and unqualified Austrians. There always remained some unspoken qualifier, a *"but,"* a *"really?"*, something that rendered Jews sometimes subtly, but nonetheless solidly, a clear "other." This even pertained to who was arguably postwar Austria's most successful chancellor and politician, the venerable Bruno Kreisky.

As to my life in the United States over the past 50-plus years: I personally have never experienced any antisemitism directed at me or anybody close to me, neither in my private nor my public life. I was never beaten or insulted for being Jewish anywhere or anytime in my life. Moreover, I was never beaten or insulted for anything in my life shy of being the supporter of a sports team whom its opposing fans hated. But that is not serious stuff, certainly in American sports as opposed to European soccer where antisemitism and racism are deeply ensconced and remain troubling. I was never humiliated, I was never belittled, I was never vilified. I was never unemployed, I was never hungry, I was never sick. I never had surgery other than having my tonsils extracted as a child in Romania. In my nearly 73 years, I only spent one night in a hospital for precautionary observations. I have traveled widely, I have enjoyed the company of wonderful friends and, most important of all, I have a wife with whom sharing my life for nearly thirty years has been a blessing. I also have had the amazing fortune of having lived most of my life in a very rare historical epoch in which—due to the Shoah's singular enormity—antisemitism was by and large unacceptable, if not an iron-clad taboo, in the public discourse of most liberal democracies. Alas, this is diminishing by the day.

In short, it would be sinful for me to complain about any aspect of my life, including my academic existence. I became a reasonably successful academic with an internationally recognized profile. But it was the less prestigious and weighty side of this professional engagement—its teaching component—that truly delighted me and made me love every second of my professorial existence. Remember that at a first-class research university where I mostly spent my professional life, being a good teacher is tantamount to being a fine chef or an accomplished birdwatcher: nice and accepted but always humored and rarely respected. Perhaps because I never had children of my own, I came to view my students as people whom I loved to engage intellectually but with many of whom I also forged emotional bonds and friendships. Above all, I went the extra mile to help them in every way I could. Among my achievements, I will forever remain proudest of my teaching and mentoring. Nothing fills me with greater satisfaction and pride than maintaining close relations with hundreds of accomplished people all over the world who at one time or another, between 1974 and today, were my students at some university where I taught. Many of these people became successful doctors, lawyers, and professionals of all kind. Some attained prominent professorships at prestigious universities in the United States, Germany, Holland, Israel, Australia, and Turkey among other places. Most succeeded in creating happy lives for themselves and their families and became proud parents whose children, in many cases, are now also my friends.

The nearly 2,000 letters of recommendation that I have penned in my academic career—approximately 40 a year—remain by far the most important products of my writing. Some articles I published garnered some attention, some books I wrote and edited received a few good reviews and were translated into various languages, but their actual effect on helping people, on creating ideas that led to tangibly relevant outcomes in someone else's life, have been—truth be told—next to naught. I understand that in Germany, as I discussed in the chapter of this book featuring my relations to that country, I had a voice that counted to some by dint of who I was more than what I said. Of course, my ideas and published work have mattered, but at the end of the day, their effect remains elusive and intangible. Not so with my letters of recommendation. I know that I helped nearly 2,000 people get into law school, enter a doctoral program, attain a desired fellowship, join a medical school or secure a coveted job. Indeed, I am proud to say that every single one of my letters eventually proved successful, maybe not by getting the candidate into her most preferred institution, but at least the fourth or fifth on her list. I have successfully written letters of recommendation for students and colleagues applying for support from the most illustrious foundations and wishing to receive the most prestigious fellowships in Europe and North America. Every one of my attempts led to a positive result eventually. Only one prize has eluded me but I still harbor hopes that before I retire from academic life I will succeed in helping one of my students receive this honor: The Rhodes Scholarship at Oxford!

My life has been both successful and rewarding. But things might have gone in completely different directions. At many junctures in my life, my good fortune became reality solely by virtue of another individual's good will, a person who, most of the time, had no idea how her or his good deed shaped my life in the most fortuitous manner. I want to end this book by offering a shout out to a few individuals—strangers, really—who do not appear prominently in my text but whose seemingly minor acts of kindness influenced my life immeasurably:

– The kind soldier/border guard who talked to me about soccer in the railroad car of our detained train at the Romanian-Hungarian border when my father left me to tend to weighty matters regarding our exit papers.

– Mr. M, the Bazooka-gum-chewing-pink-bubbles-blowing Immigration and Naturalization Service officer at Idlewild Airport in New York City who welcomed me to the United States and made me feel at home from the get-go.

– The young admissions officer at Columbia College with whom I discussed the movie *Blow-Up*, a conversation which set me at ease and paved the way for my being admitted to Columbia University.

– Seymour Martin "Marty" Lipset, on whom I barged in unannounced on a September day in 1975 and who—literally minutes before his final departure from Harvard on his way to Stanford—proceeded to write a note to Guido Goldman that commenced my more than 25-year blissful association with the Center for European Studies at Harvard.

"In My Life, I've Loved Them All"
John Lennon and Paul McCartney